Wisdom as It Relates to the Holy Quran

Wisdom as It Relates to the Holy Quran

Omar Njie

MONCKS CORNER, SOUTH CAROLINA, USA
JUNE 21, 2017

Library of Congress Control Number:		2018900034
ISBN:	Hardcover	978-1-5434-7462-6
	Softcover	978-1-5434-7461-9
	eBook	978-1-5434-7625-5

Print information available on the last page.

Rev. date: 01/03/2018

To order additional copies of this book, contact:
Xlibris
1-888-795-4274
www.Xlibris.com
Orders@Xlibris.com
769302

CONTENTS

ACRONYMS

ALA	The Most High
ABC News	American Broadcasting Company (ABC) News
AD	After the Death of Christ or Anno Domini
CE	Common Era and is also used in place of AD
DNA	Deoxy Ribonucleic Acid, sometimes called the molecule of life
GPS	Global Positioning System is a constellation of approximately thirty well-spaced satellites that orbit the earth to enable ground receivers to pinpoint their geographic location (from 100 to 10 meters).
ORG	A generic top-level domain used on the Internet truncated from *organization*
SAW	Sallallahu Alayhi Wasallam
Ta Ha	Mystic letters in the Quran
Viz-a-Viz	Used as an abbreviation for *namely*
UNHCR	United Nations High Commission for Refugees
6C's	(These are the 6C's of Character: Conscience, Compassion, Consideration, Courage, Control, and Confidence)

ACKNOWLEDGMENTS

I N THE NAME of Allah, Most Gracious, and Most Merciful, I wish to take this opportunity to express my utmost appreciation and gratitude to Allah whose infinite wisdom, mercy, and guidance led my son Mohammed Omar Njie to inspire me to embark on devoting more of my time on reading the Quran. It occurred at a time when both my wife Mariama Njie, commonly known as Mamie Omar Njie, and I resigned from our jobs in Maryland to relocate to Moncks Corner, South Carolina, in the United States of America. Our decision to relocate was also inspired and facilitated by Mohammed after he got us a house next to his residence in Moncks Corner, less than fifty meters apart. As his parents, we also thank Allah for using him as an agent of change for this remarkable decision to relocate to an environment where we can worship God much better.

Mohammed and his wife Asatou Thilo Ba were blessed with a baby girl, whom they named after my wife Mariama, just few weeks before we resigned from our jobs in Maryland. May Allah give baby Mariam long life, good health, and prosperity, and make her to be among the best of Muslims. We were all elated about the birth of baby Mariam, which we saw as a noble gift and blessing from Allah. We pray for Allah to immensely reward Mohammed and Asatou both for their hospitality and generosity which facilitated our stay with them in Moncks Corner, South Carolina. My wife and I would also wish to extend our immense love and gratitude to our able teacher, mentor, and brother Sheikh Harun-Al Faqir Faye for his spiritual guidance and Islamic teachings which in earnest increased our affinity and love of Allah. The same goes to the Mustafawiyya Fuqara of Moncks Corner, South Carolina, for their invaluable support and unconditional love that they showed us at all times.

Last, but not the least, my sincere and profound thanks go to my wife Mamie Omar Njie for her relentless efforts, sacrifices, countless support, and devotion that she rendered to me, my family, including the extended family, throughout our marriage of almost fifty years now. May Allah, with His infinite grace and mercy, bless and reward her in abundance throughout her life's endeavors.

ABSTRACT

THE MAIN PURPOSE of this book is to serve as a source of spiritual information, enlightenment, wisdom, and guidance to those believing servants, Muslims as well as non-Muslims, to come to terms in reaffirming the fact that there is a creator (Allah). It is He who is responsible for the creation of the heavens, the earth, mankind, the angels, *jinns*, and all that is known and unknown in this universe. His creations include both the hidden and the unseen world of which very little is known to man. This is due to the fact that all sources of knowledge, power, and wisdom belong to Allah, and He giveth or withdraweth any of these gifts to whom He wills. The book looks at the wisdom in the Quran and its related guidance to purify the souls of man. We have also drawn references from a wide range of Islamic literature reviews, including Hadith narrations, and correlated them to enrich our discussions of various topics in the book. These include but are not necessarily restricted to man's weakness to falter sin and/or transgress, which could be avoided by having a strong faith in Allah, fearing Him and staying righteous so as to control his *nafs* (soul). This control is to battle (*jihad*) with his *nafs*, which yearns for evil, and to restrain it in order to purify it to that of a spiritual state of perfection so as to maintain righteousness and attain the love of Allah in order to attain bliss.

In chapter 5 we explainthe three basic requirements of *Tawbah* (repentance) after the Muslim commits a sin or has transgressed by acts of wrongdoing, after which he should vow sincerely not to repeat the same again; for Allah loves those who ask for His forgiveness by performing *Tawbah*. The book also deals with how Allah created man in various forms, such as the case of Adam, Eve (Hawa), and Jesus (Esa). He has also showed man the two ways (right and wrong) accompanied with his freewill to choose. But this freewill must not be misconstrued with that of the divine guidance believers receive as a gift from Allah.

This divine guidance renders man's freewill limited, because God's will and plan predominates our actions. The book also reminds Muslims to frequently renew their *Sahada* (to testify that there is only one true God and that the Prophet is His servant and messenger) in fear of Allah, and to constantly say His praises. We have explained how Allah has inspired some individuals such as Mariam (Jesus's mother), Luckman the wise, and Al-Khidr (the guide sent to Prophet Moses by Allah), who received divine inspiration and knowledge, respectively, in order to accomplish their individual missions as ordained by Him. Similarly, but at a more sophisticated spiritual and divine manner Allah inspired prophets such as Moses, Jesus, and Muhammad with both spiritual hidden knowledge and wisdom beyond man's imagination. Finally, the book explains the last sermons of Prophet Muhammad (saw) during *Hajj* in Mecca when Allah's revelation came down to him to perfect Islam as a religion of guidance and truth for all of mankind. In that same speech the Prophet warned mankind that "whosoever follows the two things (the Quran and his Sunnah) that he left behind will not go wrong."

CHAPTER 1.0

Introduction

AS MENTIONED IN the above abstract, I wish to reiterate the fact that my quest to write this book, *Wisdom as It Relates to the Quran,* came from my son Mohammed Omar Njie, who inspired me to read the Quran on a more frequent basis. As I embarked on this noble task of reading the Quran, I began to fully appreciate and comprehend some of the messages contained therein, which now made me see the world differently from a dual perspective, one material and the other spiritual. Pursuant of the former by man, this path of life is consumed by the temptations of this world, which are deceptive and elusive by nature. Furthermore, it is a tedious journey that is enduring, and in reality is tantamount to a futile endeavor, especially when the time comes for man to depart this world and account for his deeds. As regards to the latter (the spiritual journey to purify the soul), it is more realistic and beneficial because of the fact that it has the capacity and tenacity to induce moral and ethical values which shape the character of the individual to fear and believe in Allah. The belief in Allah does facilitate a believing Muslim to yearn to perform good deeds and nurture a positive spiritual desire to establish a close affinity with his creator. The nature of such an affinity purifies the soul of a believer, makes him righteous in order to reap the benefits of those who are successful in this world (i.e., the *Muttaqoon*) as the inheritors of paradise. The testimony regarding this statement is revealed in the Quran when it states: "O you who believe: be careful of your duty to Allah and seek means of nearness to Him and strive hard in His Way that you may be successful" (Sura al-Maidah 5:35).

Furthermore, we discuss in this book that it is those believers who purify their souls that will be prosperous both in this life and that of the hereafter. Relative to this statement, the Quran reminds us that "those will prosper who purify themselves, and glorify the name of their Guardian-Lord, and (lift their hearts) in prayer" (Surah Al-Alaq 85: 14-15).

In view of the foregoing discussion, we can acknowledge the fact that the path to Islam is easy only for those servants who have faith in Allah, fear Him, stay righteous and truthful, and perform regular prayers and charity. The reason being that Islam is based on the Quran and Sunnah of the Prophet (saw), which lead to the straight path for those who want to elevate themselves spiritually and attain bliss or salvation. In order to attain this salvation as Muslims, it is imperative that we cleanse ourselves in body, mind, and soul, which will then put us in a conducive state to worship and to proclaim Allah's praises. While the former (salvation) is derived from the mercy and guidance of Allah to benefit his believing servants, the latter will require the constant reinforcement of faith, consistency, adherence to the practices of Islam based on the Quran and to follow the Sunnah of the Prophet's noble character and way of life. Muslims who embrace these two noble practices should find it easy to maintain the straight path that leads to righteousness and good deeds in order to purify their souls.

Moreover, when we exalt Allah and request for the forgiveness of our sins, this removes arrogance from our hearts and makes us humble. Similarly, when we reflect on the elusive and deceptive nature of this world, and at the same time reflect and remember the hereafter and the Day of Judgment, it should make us less attached to the world and inclined to help others for the sake of Allah. To this end, it is these salient issues that are discussed in this book as matters of importance for the Muslim, and for it to serve as a spiritual and moral guide and to inspire those who are willing to turn to a new direction to change their past lives of living in ignorance, deceit, wrong deeds, and lack of solid faith in God.

The book is also quite befitting to cater to and assist those who are new to Islam, as well as those whose hearts and intentions are contemplating to know the fundamentals of Islam as a religion. To these categories of people and others who are interested in the spiritual and moral development of the individual to peruse through this book, ponder and reflect on its contents with sincerity of heart, mind, and soul. Once this task is complete, it should facilitate readers to rejuvenate and inculcate in their minds the spirit of truth, righteousness, humility mercy to serve their families, friends, communities, Islam, and mankind in general just for the sake and love of God in order to enable man to adhere to these noble and moral virtues of Islam, the book reminds its readers to adhere to the five fundamental pillars of Islam so that they will not only be Muslims by name, inheritance, or tradition but will strive to live by the guidance of both the Quran and that of the Sunnah of the Prophet Muhammad (saw). In fact, this is the way the Prophet led his life, and the fact of the matter is that if we want to be true and devoted Muslims then we have to sincerely succumb to the dictates of the Quran and that of the way of life of the Prophet, of which he reminded us in his last sermon during *Hajj* in Mecca. Actually, as a reminder to our readers, we have discussed about the prophet's last sermon in which he emphasized both the significance of the Quran and the Sunnah, during which he received a revelation from God to perfect the establishment of Islam as a religion. We have also discussed in detail how Islam could swiftly reform the lives of the individual from being neglectful of his spiritual duties to Allah, to becoming someone who is ready to seek knowledge through the guidance of a sheikh and/or a spiritual teacher and join the ranks of the knowledgeable, truthful, and righteous believers who will turn in true penitence to Him again and again, both in adversity and prosperity.

What is implied here regarding the motive to turn to Allah in true penitence is referring to the heart and its hidden and secret motives, by which man is judged: for God is aware of all of them. Furthermore, it is a fact that Allah does reward those who use the Quran, follow the Sunnah of the Prophet, do good deeds, and stay righteous. To this end, the Quran reminds us that "verily this Quran doth guide to that which is most right (or stable) and giveth the glad tidings to the believers who work deeds of righteousness, that they shall have a magnificent reward" (Sura Bani Israil 17: 9).

The book has also drawn references from both the Quran, the Sunnah of the Prophet, and varieties of Islamic literature and Hadith materials to enable the reader to derive pleasure, knowledge, and guidance to gradually learn about Allah, his creations both in the heavens and on earth. In this way, the reader will eventually begin to grasp and acknowledge both spiritually and morally through discovery mode of learning about the immense infinite power, grace, mercy, and wisdom which are attributed to Allah. Among His attributes is His majestic throne and kingdom from which He created both the heavens and the earth, including the solar system and the galaxies. The divine complexities and mysteries of the creation of the heavens and the earth are mentioned in various parts of the Quran, such as in Sura Al-Baqarah 2:29 and Sura al-Araf 7:54. We have also acknowledged the fact that the Quran mentioned in detail the nature of these sophisticated types of creations almost fourteen hundred years ago, way before modern science. For example, as regards the sophistication of the solar system, we knew through the revelations of the Quran that the earth and planets rotating around the sun constitute an organized world of dimensions, which to our human scale appear quite colossal. We now know through modern science that the earth is approximately ninety-three million miles from the sun, and the furthermost planet from it in the solar system (Pluto) is about forty times the distance from the earth to the sun; i.e., approximately 3,672 million miles away.

Furthermore, if we take a snapshot of the galaxies, the sun of which we are a satellite like the other planets surrounding it, is itself an infinite tiny and/or a small element among a hundred billion stars that form a whole called a galaxy. On a typical clear summer night, when the sky is visibly filled with stars, one can easily discern the formation of sporadic stars known as the "Milky Way." According to modern science, it would require an estimated ninety *thousand* years to go from one extreme to the other of the most compact group of stars that make up the galaxy. Now we can actually have a notion of some of the magnitude of Allah's creation when we talk of the earth and the heavens, including the solar system and the galaxies. We know that the stars are heavenly bodies like the sun. They are the scene of various physical phenomena, of which the easiest to observe is their illumination of light. All of these explanations are necessary in order to highlight the Quranic expression of the lowest heavens denoting the "solar system." Moreover, it is an apparent phenomenon that among the celestial elements nearest to us there are no other permanent elements apart from the heavenly bodies mentioned in the Quran some fourteen hundred years ago, which modern science now refer to as the planets.

As far as the sun is concerned, it is a star that generates intense heat which is also emitted to earth in the form of light rays by its internal combustion. Unlike the moon, which does not give off light itself and is an inert body (on its external layers at least), which is known to merely reflect the light received from the sun. Apart from issues discussed in the preceding paragraphs that specifically gave emphasis to the fact that God is the sole creator of the earth, the heavens, the solar system, and the galaxies among other aspects of His enormous creations discussed in this book, the Quran also provides information on astronomy and the universe some fourteen hundred years ago.

Notwithstanding the sophistication of Allah's creation of the earth, remains the fact that the knowledge of the heavens is hidden, of which man only has very little knowledge about. In this regard, we have made efforts in some parts of the book to facilitate readers to understand, acknowledge, and appreciate some of the hidden powers and knowledge of Allah which is manifested in his creation of the heavens and the earth, including man, to whom he gave a special place in his creation. The infinite knowledge of Allah is traceable in the Quran, for example in Sura Saba 34.3; Sura Al-An'am 6.59; Sura al-Mulk 67.14; Sura Ali Imram 3.5; Sura Qaf 50.16, to name a few.

Allah honored man to be His agent, and to that end endowed him with understanding. Upon all these glorious gifts, He purified man's affections and gave him spiritual insight so that He can understand both nature and himself through various mediums such as learning, reflection, spiritual, and divine inspiration and by cognitive and deductive reasoning in line with the "Right Path." The book also lays adequate emphasis on learning the Quran, which will give pleasure, and to complement it by seeking knowledge of the Sunnah of the

Prophet (saw). The fact of the matter is that both (the Quran and the Sunnah) are divine spiritually active material and/or mediums of learning, education, observation, and their inferences to wisdom and positive reasoning based on truth and righteousness.

As regards man's pursuit of knowledge and wisdom, he should strive to acquire useful knowledge that will be beneficial to him, his community, and society in general. What is implied here is the fact that apart from the commitment of the individual to strive for the acquisition of Quran knowledge, he needs to uphold certain moral principles and values which are inherent in Islam, such as the belief in one God, truthfulness, honesty, and righteousness, among other factors, for the building of his character. Having attained these moral virtues, he should then be committed to transferring his knowledge and skills to positively benefit his community, the greater good of society, so that it will have a multiplier effect to benefit his era and future generations. The need and justification to nurture and promote good communities is based on the premise that good communities are a model of unity, care, and love, for which Allah's hand and blessings will always be with them. On the contrary, bad communities are evil, treacherous, violent, and not trustworthy to be around, and they coexist with *Shaytan* or the devil, depicting the absence of God's hand in such a community.

Relative to the above salient points regarding knowledge and wisdom, we have ventured in this book to explain some of their fundamental factors and gave an example that the very first verse of the Quran revealed by God through Angel Gabriel to Prophet Muhammad (saw) on the twenty-seventh night of Ramadan in 611 AD reads:

> *Proclaim! (or read) In the name of your Lord and Cherisher, who created man, out of a (mere) cloth of congealed blood: Proclaim! And your Lord is Most Bountiful, He Who taught (the use of) the pen, Taught man that which he knew not. (Sura al-Alaq 96:1-5).*

Allah also created man out of the best of molds and showed him the two ways (the right way and the wrong way). As Muslims we need to take heed of the honor that Allah gave to mankind coupled with the fact that He has allowed and guided mankind to choose one of the two ways; i.e., Allah's way or the way of Shaytan. He has clearly shown man the two ways, and guided mankind by appointing messengers and sending the Book of Guidance (the Quran). Added to these factors, Allah has given mankind the intelligence and the freewill to choose between the right way and the wrong way without any force or pressure. Therefore, it is a fact that whatever good we do is complemented by Allah's will, and whatever evil we do is from our own lust and desires of our *Nafs*. And that is precisely the test Allah has mandated for mankind for a period of one short transitory life on this earth. The reality of this transition, which is short-lived, should serve as a reminder to the reader that God has created man to toil and struggle, but he also gave the soul the power of choice and the sense of right and wrong. Therefore, let man strive to keep it pure in order to attain salvation. We are reminded of this fact when the Quran states: "Verily we have certainly created man into toil and struggle. Does he think that no one has power over him? He may say (boastfully): wealth I have squandered in abundance! Does he think that no one has seen him? Have we not made for him two eyes and a tongue, and a pair of lips? And have showed him the two ways? But he has not broken through the difficult pass" (Sura Al-Balad90:4-11).

The book will also throw some spiritual insight to the reader that God also gave man the gift of wisdom so that he will know Him through His wondrous signs, which will be discussed later in some chapters of this book. Furthermore, God taught man how to glorify Him using His many names and to do it in truth, reverence, and unity. The reader will also come to terms gradually that the effort that he will take to read this book could mark the beginning of a positive transformation of his life to fear Allah and do things that will benefit others and Islam just for the sake and love of Allah. Based on my experience, it is also this kind of inspiration and quest which drove me to have that affinity to try and read and comprehend some of the divine messages in the Quran which eventually became a divine force which consumed me into a state of strong conviction to venture more and learn more about its divine messages and the wisdom it embodied. In fact, this experience was like being caught up in the spiral of a quicksand, where the more you wriggle, the deeper you sink. Having gone deep into my reading, I then pondered for a while and asked myself *what is wisdom, and how does it relate to the Quran?* It is in this regard that I discovered the very theme of this topic that I will venture to discuss in this book, *Inshallah* (God willing)!

What Is Wisdom?

WISDOM AS DEFINED by the *School and Office Dictionary* (Random House Webster's, 2000) is related to the following three statements; namely (1) the quality of state of being wise, (2) scholarly knowledge or learning, and (3) a wise act.

Before we proceed to find out what wisdom is all about, it is imperative that we briefly elaborate on each of the three statements from a dual perspective. *Firstly,* we will venture from a literal point of view to analyze each of them. *Secondly,* efforts will be made to embark on their analysis from a religious perspective based on the Quran. The reason for using the Holy Quran is due to its authenticity as a revelation from God to Prophet Muhammad (saw) through Angel Gabriel. In addition, it is a book of wisdom which covers all of the domains of religious and social domains of life to guide man to adopt the straight path and purify his soul. It is also a book in which God vowed to guard it so that its contents will not be tampered. This evidence is manifested in the Quran when it contends that "We have without doubt, sent down the message and will assuredly guard it (from corruption)" (Sura Al-Hijr15:9).

Moreover, it is the book perfected by Allah and revealed to Prophet Muhammad through Angel Gabriel, and embedded in it are the elements of spiritual, moral, divine, and hidden knowledge; wisdom and guidance, and the manifestation of the might of the creator through which Islam (the religion of peace and truth) was pronounced by his messenger through Allah's revelation on the day of his last *Hajj* pilgrimage in Mecca. A testimony regarding the abovementioned statements is in the Quran when it states: "The revelation of this book is from Allah, the Exalted in power, full of wisdom" (Sura az- Zumar 39:1).

2.1

The first statement refers to the quality or state of being wise. The analysis of this statement has an inference of an act of a condition and/or conditions which could display a measurable degree of either cognitive or psychomotor skills of an individual. The three main words in the first statement—i.e., quality, state, and wise—are all measurable terms, because they each have conditional parameters and an assessment function with differing variables such as environment and time. For instance:

> "*According to the Random House Webster's Dictionary (2001), the word* quality *could be ascribed to differing measurable functions as follows:(a) an essential characteristic, property, or attribute;(b) character or nature belonging to or distinguishing a thing; (c) degree of excellence or fineness (d) superiority; excellence; (e) a personality or character trait; (f) of or having superior quality.*"

The mere fact that the statement emphasizes *quality* makes it vital that we consider it as a pivotal aspect of the consideration of being wise. For example, in order to assess or ascertain the quality of things, we are keen to use words like *good, bad, fair, poor, worse, high, low, negative, positive, best, exceptional,* and so forth to qualify the nature of our statement. Using this example, we can now put quality in a continuum ranging from poor on one end of it and exceptional at the other end. It will then subjugate this measurable criterion to base the assessment of quality on the level of cognitive and/or psychomotor skills that are manifested for the required task at hand. In this regard, it is noticeable under normal general discussion for one to make statements like "that was a positive thought or argument." Similarly, if the points of the arguments are not coherent and convincing, then one could claim that the arguments made were negative. Therefore, it is imperative to note that the measure of a gist in an argument would generally aim to look for the assessment of the quality of knowledge of the subject matter, mode of argument, experience, facts, questions posed, and nature of analytical skills presented among other factors. All of these factors, when assessed to a pinnacle of positive ratings, could lead to the individual recognition of wisdom by those whom he interacts with daily.

In view of the foregoing analysis, it is worthy to note that although emphasis is based on the assessment of the quality of knowledge, and it must not be misconstrued with wisdom. From an Islamic perspective, man's search for spiritual knowledge is a vital prerequisite to raise his awareness and discover the signs of God in the universe. As for the Muslim, this spiritual search must therefore be regarded as an obligation and/or duty first for him to submit to the will of Allah. This obligation is backed by the fact that a Muslim is one who submits to the will of God, and as such, his prime duty in life is to venture to pursue knowledge so long as he lives. Furthermore, God, through his infinite mercy and wisdom, has raised the status of those who have knowledge, and described them as fearing him. This elevation of the Muslim should be a driving factor to encourage him to consistently strive in the pursuit of knowledge, while striving hard at the same time to fulfill his moral obligations and duties as ordained by Allah in Islam. In this regard, therefore, the Muslim quest for knowledge needs to be reinforced by rehearsing the Quran, seeking its understanding, establishing regular prayers to improve his spiritual affinity with his Lord, spending in the way of charity to assist the poor and the needy, and as a loan to his Creator. Similarly, God said: "Those who rehearse the book of Allah, establish regular prayer and spend (in charity) out of what we have provided for them, secretly and openly, hope for a commerce that will never fail" (Sura Fatir 35:29).

In fact, what could be derived from the abovementioned verse of the Quran is giving an assurance that those who devote their time to read the Book of Allah, perform regular prayers, and give out charity from the provisions that they have are actually engaged in a business where they are guaranteed to reap the rewards and benefits. This mode of business between the believing servant and Allah is like a trade where he invests his money and labor and capabilities with the belief that he will not only get back the capital that he invested but will surpass the break-even point and make his profit in return. It is like a never-failing business with enormous gains and profits at the end of an individual investment. In a nutshell, it is like a believer who invests his wealth and his time and money and labor and capabilities in carrying out Allah's commands and his service and worship and in the struggle to promote the cause of his religion with both the intention and hope that he will not only get his full rewards for it, but having the faith and commitment that Allah will bless him with much more from his bounty as well. However, it is imperative for Muslims to come to terms and distinguish the fact that there is a difference between engaging in a conventional worldly trade and/or business where the aim is to control labor input and maximize profits. In this kind of worldly business, there is the risk of loss along with the hope of profits. However, contrary to this is the guaranteed bargain that a sincere Muslim servant devotedly undertakes with his God, knowing fully well that there is no risk of any loss whatsoever.

We can derive from the above stated discussion that it is vital for the Muslim to have at least a basic knowledge and understanding of both the Quran and the Sunnah (the teachings and way of life of the Prophet). The essence for the Muslim to be equipped with such fundamental knowledge and understanding about his *Deen* (Islam) will put him in a better stead to serve and worship God than the ordinary Muslim who is ignorant of the divine messages in the Quran and the Sunnah. Evidently, there is a clear distinction between a servant who has knowledge and fear of Allah as against a mere Muslim without these two types of knowledge. My argument relating to these two types of Muslims is also questioned in the Quran when it contends that "is one who worships devoutly during the hours of the night prostrating himself or standing (in adoration), who takes heed of the hereafter, and who places his hope in the mercy of his Lord like one who does not? Say: 'Are those equal, those who know and those who do not know?' It is those who are endowed with understanding that receive admonition" (Sura az-Zumar 39:9).

Relative to the abovementioned verse, we need to be mindful of such qualifying words like "worships devoutly," "takes heed of the hereafter," followed by the question "are those equal, those who know and those who do not know?" It is along these similar lines of explanation that we have similarly pointed out in subsection 2.1, with emphasis on the attainment of excellence, as one of the vital elements ascribed to the measurable criteria of knowledge. Notwithstanding this fact, unless excellence is in itself understood and its meaning determined, it will not be possible to acknowledge it as an attribute to knowledge or any other trait associated with it. Complementary with this line of discernment, it is imperative to note, therefore, the following:

> *Excellence is derived from the infinitive to excel, which is excrescence. When, therefore, of two objects which are similar, one has an extra characteristic, that object is described as excelling the other, no matter what its excellence may be. For instance, while swiftness is an excellent (future) in the horse, in itself it has no excellence. Also, by saying that the horse is more excellent than the donkey means that the horse shares with the donkey the capacity for carrying burdens, but excels it in charging, wheeling, swiftness, and beauty. (Imam Al-Gazzali (Ra) 2008).*

In view of the abovementioned analysis, we can derive the fact that knowledge, however, is in itself an absolute excellence apart from any attribution. To this end, therefore, knowledge which reinforces absolute excellence emanating from the infinite powers and mercy of God to mankind, one of which is to provide him with his daily sustenance. For example, Allah gave man the brain to think of and invent various items, objects, and machineries to aid food production, health improvement, housing and infrastructural developments, all of which are tied to the socioeconomic development of man in general. The central focus of this mode of development is driven and/or manipulated by the evil temptation of money as an object valued by man to an extent that in some cases it precedes or overrides his moral and religious obligations with God. Part of the reason for this neglect of man's religious and moral obligations with God is propelled by his lust for the precious cosmetic values attached to money and the material things associated with it. In this regard, Imam Al-Gazzali (Ra), 2008, explained the point:

> *A precious and a desired object may be of any of three categories: (a) what is sought as a means to an end, (b) what is sought for its own (intrinsic) value, and (c) what is sought for both. What is sought for its own (intrinsic) value is nobler and more excellent than that which is sought as a means to an end.*

In view of the foregoing discussions, we will now discuss the impact of scholarly knowledge and its relationship with learning and wisdom. In order to do this, we will now focus our discussion on issues relating to the second statement (scholarly knowledge of learning) which is mentioned in chapter 2.0 above.

2:2

The second statement refers to scholarly knowledge or learning. As human beings, there are instances when we may find ourselves in a situation which reflects any one of the three statements stipulated in chapter 2.0 above. These three statements, though listed separately, could be performed by the individual at the same time. Scholarly knowledge, preferably, requires both a sheikh, or a Mullah (teacher) and a student, thereby enabling the former to guide, instruct, and impart knowledge to the latter. In other words, in an educational setting, be it formal or informal, the sheikh is responsible for the transfer of knowledge while the student receives the imparted information. Nowadays, scholarly knowledge could also be attained through distance learning techniques, such as the Internet, video and audio-visual aids, among other methods. Be it a formal, informal, or distance learning, the use of a sheikh is much preferred over engaging oneself in self-study. The reason being that the sheikh, apart from inculcating the appropriate knowledge to his student, will also guide the student on know how to arrive at a spiritual climate close to Allah. In this regard, the sheikh, as part of his obligation, will venture to show the student how to put what he taught him into practice. The essence of linking theoretical knowledge with practice is due to the fact that the former is beneficial when applied and/or tested through experience. However, in line with this statement, Mirza Ghulam Ahmad of Qadian (1996) also states the fact that

> *knowledge that is merely academic and has not been the subject of experience is without beneficence.*

The perfecting of knowledge is linked to the excellence of teaching as mentioned in the Quran relating to teaching, guidance, and to refrain from the concealment of knowledge. To this end, it is incumbent for the Muslim to *adab* (path to courtesy) to himself in a manner that will enable him to submit to what Allah has intended for him, not what is dictated by the habits of the self and its inclination to follow the whisperings of Shaytan. In this regard, Hajj Mustafa A. Shawqi (1998) explained that

> *the best way to accomplish this task is to take the company of a living sheikh. He can help you discriminate between what is from Allah and what is from your lower self, reacting to the impulses of Shaytan.*

It does imply that Shawqi's explanation above establishes a learning environment between the Muslim who met a living sheikh as his inner reality, manifested in experience, as a mirror reflecting his heart as his own true nature. He further argues that as wealth is multiplied by commerce, in the same way knowledge arrives at its spiritual climax through practical experience. This practical experience is the principal means of perfecting knowledge and bestows a light upon knowledge. The sheikh, therefore, is the one who appears with an outward light and an inward secret. It is through the sheikh's guidance and the company of a practicing community that you are saved from languishing in self-involvement. Understanding and submitting to this is the *adab* to self. His teaching and inculcation of the requisite knowledge and skills to his student (*murid*) will take place, for which love is required on either side. In order to clarify what is meant by *murid*, we will refer to Hajj

Mustafa A. Shawqi (1998) when he contends that "the word 'murid' is derived from 'irada' (will) and it depends on sincerity ('ikhlas'). The true meaning of 'murid' is one who has stripped himself of his own will and accepted what Allah wills for him."

Actually, love is the connective tissue or medium that permits the transmission of the necessary knowledge and skills by the sheikh to the *murid* to be successfully implemented. A testimony to this kind of teacher-student relationship cemented by love is expressed by Hajj Mustafa A. Shawqi (1998) when he states:

> *Love transcends the intellect, yet does not discount it. It breaks all barriers so that the divine light can flow.*

It is incumbent upon the sheikh who is in possession of knowledge to continue to nurture this healthy dual relationship so that he doesn't conceal that knowledge and/or the truth he is acquainted with. Complementary to this fact, it is love of the sheikh that transports the *murid* to love of the Prophet, and finally annihilates the *murid* in the ultimate divine love. The completion of this unveiling of love is called *marifat* or illumination of the heart of its divine nature.

In view of the foregoing discussion, it is vital to note that once the learned believer has acquired scholarly knowledge he must now venture to transfer that knowledge appropriately to others. Knowledge from another perspective, when compared to worship, has a more rewarding benefit. Imam Al-Gazzali (Ra), 2008, elaborated on this point when he contends that "the Prophet said, 'The superior rank the learned man holds over the worshipper is similar to the superiority of the moon when it is full over the other stars.' And again, 'They will, on the day of resurrection, intercede {before God} the prophets, then the learned, then the martyrs.'"

In view of the above, one can distinctly see how the importance of knowledge is valued and rewarded by God, both in this world and the hereafter. We will now proceed to discuss issues relating to the third statement stipulated in chapter 2.0 above.

2.3

The Third Statement refers to a wise act.

Before we embark on the analysis of the third statement, it is important to briefly explain what is meant by the word *wise*. According to the School and Office Dictionary (2008), the word *wise* exhibits three meanings as follows: (1) having or showing discernment and good judgment, (2) having or showing scholarly knowledge or learning, (3) knowing or informed.

However, we will try and conduct a brief analysis of how these three conditions may influence and/or impact the Muslim from an Islamic point of view. A fundamental criterion for a good Muslim is to submit to the will of God. By submitting to the will of Allah he is acknowledging the fact that there is a creator and he is ready to serve him according to the principles, guidelines, and moral ethics of Islam. This submission should also serve as a constant reminder which should facilitate the noble act of taking and/or renewing the *Shahadah*. This performance of taking the *Shahadah* may apply to Muslims who have already embraced Islam, and to newcomers enlisting in the religion. Under normal circumstances, there is no harm for a Muslim who has already embraced Islam to occasionally renew his *Shahadah* in order to reaffirm his allegiance to Islam and faith in Allah. The reaffirmation of the renewal of faith by the Muslim goes with a spiritual dimension which differs from the physical and psychological elements that go with its affinity to worship and propagating Islam. However, one of the fundamental values of the word *Islam* connotes both to "surrender" and is linked to the Arabic word *salam,* or peace. As far as worship is concerned, Allah reminds us in the Quran when he says:

> I have only created Jinns and men that they may serve Me.
> (Sura Adh-Dhariyat 51:56)

Relative to the abovementioned verse, this, literally from a religious point of view, is in conjunction with worship. However, from an Islamic perspective, how do we interpret the word *worship*?

According to Mufti Muhammad Taqi Usmani (2007) the word used by the Holy Quran for the worship is "ibadah" which has a much wider sense than worship. In English, the word "worship" normally indicates some specific acts or rituals meant exclusively to show one's reverence to his Creator. But the word 'ibadah' is not restricted to such acts or rituals; rather, it embodies any act done in submission to Allah's commands and to seek His pleasures.

In order to elaborate on the word *ibadah* as an act of worship to God, we therefore need to relate it to the fact that there are various acts which are common and/or mundane in their nature, such as earning a living in a *halal* (permissible) manner to sustain the welfare of one's family and related dependents. These acts of *ibadah* are twofold: the former relates to those acts that are solely meant to worship God such as prayer, fasting, and their like that are not attached to worldly objectives. These are referred to as direct acts of *ibadah*. As regards the latter, they are associated with those fundamentally mundane, which are translated into *ibadah* when they are performed in conformity with Shariah law (Islamic law) with an intention commensurate to one's religious obligational duties that are treated as acts of indirect *ibadah*. The bone of contention here is for the Muslim to be mindful that the direct acts of worship (*ibadah*) are of paramount importance and hence are regarded to be superior to the indirect ones.

In view of the foregoing discussion, it is important for the Muslim to note that on the one hand he should give priority to the direct *ibadah* that impinges on his daily life pursuits like *salah* (prayer), which is performed five times a day. On the other hand, he should also be mindful of those indirect *ibadah* such as eating, drinking, work activities to generate income associated with one's livelihood, family, parents, relatives, friends, and other people in society such as the poor and the needy. Due to the fact that the nature of these indirect acts is mundane, it becomes apparent that man is easily swayed and tempted by his desires and lust of this *Dunyah* which makes him succumb to the worldly pleasures that he craves and yearns for on a daily basis. Because of his cravings for such worldly pleasures, man becomes so absorbed in pursuit of these worldly things that can easily influence him to succumb to their material temptations and overrides his spirituality. In this regard, these acts have less spiritual strength than the direct acts of worship. The reason for this less spiritual strength associated with the indirect *ibadah* is due to the fact that the direct acts of *ibadah* (worship, service, or servitude) are very few in one's daily life as compared to the indirect ones. Moreover, the dominance of the indirect acts of *ibadah* has the tenacity to slow down one's spiritual progress vis-à-vis his material progress. The crux of the matter, therefore, is to ask the question as to how one can seek a balance between the material and spiritual in one's life yet try to maximize the direct acts of *ibadah*, as well as minimize those pure mundane activities in order to improve one's spiritual attainment and mend its loss during the course of the year. In order to answer this question, we will refer to Mufti Muhammad Taqi Usmani (2007) when he states the following:

> *The month of Ramadan has been designed to maintain a balance between material and spiritual aspects of the human life.*

Muslim fasting during the month of Ramadan is an act of *ibadah* for each designated day, observed by depriving oneself of eating and drinking for the prescribed number of hours, which has the reward of lessening the bad spiritual effects, if any, of the material pleasures. The month is also meant to maximize the direct acts of *ibadah* and to minimize the pure mundane activities so that one may accelerate his spiritual progress to make up the distance and to repair the spiritual progress loss one may have suffered through his deep involvement in the mundane activities during the year.

Complementary to the observation of this act of *ibadah* during the day, the nights of Ramadan also tend to keep the individual active in offering *Tawhid* (oneness of God) and waking up for *tahajjud* (the voluntary night prayer) and *suhur* (predawn meal before fasting), thereby depriving him of his regular pattern of daily sleeping hours. In addition to these acts of worship, the individual is supposed to render as much optional *nafil* (optional prayer) *ibadah* as he could on a voluntary basis. By adhering to this pattern and acts of *ibadah*, it will have the propensity to elevate the level of one's spiritual activities during the month of Ramadan more than the remainder of the months in the year.

The importance of this reminder of the difference between direct and indirect acts of *ibadah* as discussed in the preceding paragraphs is to renew our will in adhering to the spiritual and moral principles of Islam as a religion of truth and righteousness. Notwithstanding, if we transgress against Allah's warnings and/or guidelines, then it is vital that we seek his repentance. To this end, the Quran reminds us of the significance of seeking forgiveness from God when it contends: "Be quick in the race for forgiveness from your Lord, and for a garden whose width is that (of the whole) of the heavens and of the earth, prepared for the righteous" (Sura AliImran 3:133).

As Muslims, the Quran teaches us to be wise and always act justly, enjoined to respect Jews and Christians, the "people" of the Book who believe in God, including our neighbors. An example of this kind of social integration, respect, and understanding prevailed even during the time of Umar ibn Al-Khattab as *khaleefah*; he protected the properties of the Jews and the Christians and allowed them to practice their Faith. Dr. Ali Mohammed M. As-Sallaabee (2010) states:

> In a letter Umar ibn Al-Khattab sent to the people of Eeliyaa, he made the following guarantees to them: he guaranteed that they would not be harmed; that their wealth was safe, and would not be wrongly taken or seized; and that their crosses and churches would not be destroyed or harmed.

The significance of the foregoing discussion is to enable the Muslim to nurture both spiritual and moral guidelines in order to propagate peace, righteousness, and understanding with all believers and other people among their neighbors and communities. It also shows how Umar ibn Al-Khattab laid emphasis on the nature of this guarantee to ensure that in Muslim lands the people of the Book (i.e., Jews and

Christians) freely practiced the tenets of their faith in their homes and in their places of worship. The significance of this kind of commandment to Muslims is mentioned in the Quran Sura Hujurat, (49):13. In this particular verse God did not address either the Muslims, Christians, Jews, or the disbelievers but rather the whole of mankind. He invoked all of mankind by reminding us of our creation from a single (pair) consisting of a male and female. After which, "He then made us into nations and tribes so that we may know each other and not despise one another. He further reminded us that the most honored among mankind in the sight of God are those that are most righteous, and that He has full knowledge and is well acquainted with all things." As human beings occupying planet Earth, it is important to note that since the creation of man until at present we are still unable to adhere to the proclamation of God, who instructed us to nurture an understanding so that globally we may coexist as children of Adam in peace and harmony.

The importance of the above commandment from God is still befitting to mankind all across the globe. The reason being that mankind in general has failed to take heed of this commandment in order to enable him to nurture those spiritual and moral values of love, tolerance, respect, patience, righteousness, and understanding among other factors. In actual fact, in order to enable the Muslim to stay truthful and righteous, and to be mindful as to whom he associates himself with so that his spirituality will not be corrupted or influenced by his friends and/or associates. For instance, mingling with friends and/or associates who could easily sway you to the habit of alcohol consumption, illegal sexual relationship before marriage, stealing, vandalism, and similar acts that go against the moral principles of both Islam and society could be devastating and counterproductive to a believing servant.

However, it is quite explicit that the abovementioned statement reminds us of Allah's warning for the believing Muslim not to take the character of the hypocrite or the disbeliever. Relative to this vital reminder, we will venture to see what kind of relationship is expected between the Muslim and other believers of the Abrahamic faiths such as the Jews and the Christians. In this regard, the Quran states that "your (real) friends are (no less than) Allah, His Apostle, and the (fellowship of) Believers, those who establish regular prayers and regular charity, and they bow down humbly (in worship)" (Suraal-Maidah 5:55).

Today, we are continuing to witness a world perpetuated by eroding spirituality and lack of moral values at an unprecedented level, which in a way does subject man not to discern, rationalize, and evaluate his thoughts before acting against his fellow human beings. Part of the reason for this irrationality, lack of spiritual and moral values is tantamount to a host of factors such as the senseless hatred associated with race, nationality, religious intolerance, tribalism, greed, politics, and jealousy to name a few. For example, Dr. Ali Muhammad M. As-Sallaabee (2010) gave an example of how Umar ibn Al-Khattab purified his heart to an extent that he was devoid of jealousy against his fellow believers. In this regard, he states that "Umar's heart was pure and free of jealousy. He shared in the joy of his fellow believers, never begrudging them for any successes they enjoyed."

All of the above negative tendencies are gross manifestation of the fact that man has not yet reached a high level of maturity and understanding in order to enable him to act rationally and wisely. In this regard, man has still not learned how to guide his thoughts and intentions in a rational manner that will facilitate him to make wise decisions and take desirable actions for the promotion of a peaceful and harmonious relationship with his fellow human beings.

In order for man to nurture and maintain a home, community, and society where moral and spiritual values dictate the order of the day, first he needs to be in possession of a noble character such as that of a believer. For instance, someone who fears God and will venture to do good deeds, has good manners, be righteous, impartial, truthful, and be generous, among other factors. He will also acknowledge the fact that life in this world is ephemeral, illusive, deceiving, and above all else, temporal. Therefore, it is vital for man to quickly learn that his good deeds are best and pleasing in the sight of God the Almighty.

In addition to these noble virtues, man needs to take stock of his deeds, acknowledge his sins and transgressions against both his creator and his fellow human beings. Secondly, he needs to repent and seek forgiveness from God and those people he might have offended. Thirdly, he needs to be sincere to himself and from a moral and spiritual perspective submit to the Will of God in order not to return to his old habits as a sinner or a transgressor. Finally, he needs to acknowledge the fact that God is merciful, His decisions in some instances are strict but in favor of mankind, for He is oft forgiving and knows best. For example, there are instances when man is faced with hardships, trials, and tribulations, and we sometimes feel so disgruntled and helpless about our prevailing situation without much understanding that it could be the best for us at that particular moment. For there cannot be ease without suffering; likewise, after every suffering or hardship comes ease.

An example of a Muslim's dealings with a person of different faith such as a Christian happened between Umar ibn Al-Khattab and a slave he had named Ashaqq. In this regard, Dr. Ali Muhammed M. As-Khattaab (2010) explained the following:

> After "Umar" died, Ashaqq told others the following story: "I was a Christian slave, and my master was Umar. One day, Umar said to me, 'Embrace Islam,' so that we can use you to take care of certain matters that pertain to Muslims. For indeed in taking care of their religious affairs it wasn't appropriate for them to rely on the help of non-Muslims. I refused, upon which he said: 'There is no compulsion in religion' (a reference to the following verse of the Noble (Sura Al-Baqarah2:256). And later, when death was about to overtake Umar, he freed me {from the bonds of slavery} and said to me, 'Go wherever you want.'"

Indeed, the Muslim should take heed of Umar's example of compassion and hospitality that he established between himself and his slave Ashaqq, who was a Christian. The crucial factor to note here is the fact that God is he who created mankind with freewill, showed him both ways (right and wrong) for man to understand that his good deeds are rewarded and his bad and/or evil deeds punishable both in this world and the hereafter.

Another example of man's performance of a wise act is for him to rise up as a Muslim and denounce and enjoin what is right and strive relentlessly to prevent what is wrong. For example, a *hadith* based on the authority of Abu Sa'eed al Khudree (may Allah be pleased with him) contended how he heard the Messenger of Allah (peace and blessings of Allah be upon him) say, "Whoever of you sees an evil, let him change it with his hand, and if he is not able to do so, then let him change it with his tongue, and if he is not able to do so, then with his heart—and that is the weakest of faith" (Muslim). The main factor to note from this *hadith* is the point that a Muslim should be proactive in serving and helping positively on matters pertaining to his community. For instance, he shouldn't play the passive role of innocent bystander; he is obliged to act wisely and justly to stop wrongdoing.

But as human beings with a free will to apply this fundamental principle and right to shape the moral and divine character of who we are as believers is restricted by our passive role of being afraid to speak the truth and to stand out for justice that will free mankind from such bondage of mental slavery. In this regard, man's failure to stand up for the truth and to pursue justice and reconciliation of our differences at the individual, community, national, and international levels are worrisome for the peace and prosperity of mankind.

Today, we are witnessing the character deterioration of man, because some societies still haven't realized the positive role and transformation that religious tolerance and its positive participation at all levels of the community could effectively promote peace and unity among the entire spectrum of society. The role of networking to enhance peace, dialogue, and understanding for the promotion of ethical, moral, and other social values could be established among the various religious groups for the prosperity of their communities. The use of debate forums, conferences, and other voluntary social programs to assist the elderly, poor, and the needy could be done collectively to break the social and religious barriers that exist in our societies. Societies need to work closer together at the home level, school level, community level, national and international levels before the impact of a peaceful coexistence among mankind is realized. The crux of the matter is that a positive and progressive change of this nature could not be implemented without having leaders who are righteous and fear God. Today, we are witnessing the fact that there are some people who call themselves Jews, Christians, and Muslims outwardly but inwardly do not fear their Creator deep in their hearts and souls. A crucial factor to note here is the fact that spiritually there is a relationship between what we do in terms of deeds that will establish a relationship between the individual and God, and in particular the show of good deeds.

The nature of what drives us then to engage in good or bad deeds could vary depending on time, place, fear of Allah, intention, and a good heart, among other factors. The Muslim must always strive to be righteous, fear Allah, and do good deeds knowing that He rewards good deeds and punishes evil doers. Therefore, it is crucial to note that the condition of the heart and mind of the individual will propel his intentions and motives, which are later manifested as actions. In other words, the intention of the individual is a direct reflection of his action. In this regard, it is vital to note that the condition of the state of mind coupled with his action is a crucial part of his spirituality and morality. It is apparent, therefore, for the believing servant when he intends to act, especially in relation with his fellow human beings, including Allah's creations, to imagine as if he is in front of him. Adopting this approach and way of thinking will guide him to do good deeds. This guide in trying to do good deeds is fundamental, and efforts for the believing Muslim to be constant and foremost in good deeds could be guaranteed by Allah's guidance on the straight path (i.e., adherence to both the Quran and the Sunnah). Complementary to this statement, the Quran also draws our attention to the fact that

> Allah does not change the condition of people until they change what is within themselves. (Sura ar-Ra'd 13:11)

Apart from the fact that people are a product and/or reflection of their society or prevailing environment. Added to this factor is the reality that our leaders are also a product of the society or community they belong to. For instance, if the community is evil and corrupt, it is most likely that they will produce a leader like them. When a society is faced with a leader as described above, they often tend to put all of the blame on him, forgetting that there always prevails a social relationship between the community and their leader. The nature of this relationship is even more pronounced between the leader and his followers because of the environment that they share, including their affinity to each other. However, the degree of evil and corrupt practices could be exacerbated if the leadership style is authoritative and believes in the power coercive nature of managing things. Too often, based on the experience of the writer, leaders of this caliber are resentful of their position not to be challenged by his subordinates and the greater good of society, thereby opening the door for him to turn into a dictator. Ironically, the leader-follower trait coupled with his relationship with society could be seriously jeopardized if he is the kind of leader who doesn't fear God but cherishes the temptations of this material world where deceit, lies, nepotism, corruption are part of the order of the day.

However, it is sad to see that mankind is perpetually witnessing the decay and degeneration of societies, both in developed and developing countries, due to man's lust, greed, and desires to downplay the spiritual and moral obligation of man at the cost of bureaucratic and political interest of their leaders. For instance, the notion of the populace in a democratic society is to choose and elect leaders who will serve their interest with honesty, sincerity, impartiality, dignity, and justice at all cost. Generally, in some societies today, these moral and ethical norms and values that the populace envisage for their leaders are gradually being eroded due to untruthfulness, dishonesty, nepotism, racism, tribal, ethnic and religious discrimination, among other factors. The mere fact that politics and religion have diverse values of interest doesn't imply that one shouldn't stand up for the truth when there is injustice which could lead to the decay of society in various spheres of life. Relative to man's intervention to condemn what is wrong in society and venture to propagate what is just and right, the Quran reminds us of this fact when it states:

Let there arise out of you a band of people inviting to all that is good; enjoining what is right, and forbidding what is wrong: They are the ones to attain felicity. (Sura AliImran 3:104)

It is important to acknowledge the fact that when man, with his inalienable civic rights and responsibilities, fails to commit to all that is good, enjoining what is right, and forbidding what is wrong, then there is no doubt that its resultant effect will bring about a downward spiral toward an immoral and decaying society. However, the symptoms of a decaying society are usually noticeable by its lack of spiritual and moral values, which in turn will have the dynamics of negative social norms with their affinity to sway and mislead man to transgress against their own souls and that of the laws of society in general. The nature of this lack of spiritual and moral values will become part of the norm of the day, where man's negative social actions will dominate. Notably, the manifestation of such negative social dominance that will sway man to evil deeds will be detrimental to society, and could eventually lead its victims to a helpless situation whereby they will no longer care to uplift and purify their souls. It is crucial, therefore, for the Muslim to be wary of factors of this nature in a society where evil deeds become the order of the day, which in turn is a reflection of lack of good leadership, including poor governance to promote spiritual and moral guidance among its citizens. The prevalence of a society of this nature is also a reflection of man's failure to act wisely in order to control the lust and desires of his soul and/or *nafs* which he adores.

In view of the foregoing analysis, we cannot avoid asking the question what could the Muslim do to avoid engaging in everyday social activities of life that will make him transgress and corrupt his soul? The answer to this question requires the frequent renewal of faith and cleansing of the soul and mind. Relating to this answer is the continuous struggle for the Muslim to frequently make all of the efforts necessary to combat the negative effects of his worldly lust and desires in order to purify his soul. A significant lesson that we have learned in relation to the cleansing of the soul was found in Dr. Muhammed Ali al-Hashimi (2005). In this lesson we captured how Umar ibn Al-Khattab (the rightly guided *khaleefah*), AKA Umar al Farooq, who was so righteous and performed so many acts of worship, felt the need to care and worry for life, to refresh his soul, and cleanse his heart.

Based on the abovementioned fact, it is imperative, therefore, that the Muslim also seek to strengthen his soul through various kinds of worship which he performs out of obedience and fear of God. Among these kinds of worship are the regular reading of the Quran carefully and with understanding. Furthermore, the Muslim should devote some of his time to practice the remembrance of God with humility. He has to train himself to perform regular prayers correctly and with ease of mind, engage in *tarbiyah* (education, development) of the individual, keep the company of learned people in order to seek and attain truth (*haqq*), and to exercise patience and constancy(*sabr*)among other factors.

In addition to the abovementioned discussion, it is important as a prerequisite guidance for the Muslim to *first* venture to know how to read the Quran properly (with *tajweed*) and to understand its meaning. Second, he should try to learn some of the sciences of *hadith*, the *seerah* of the Prophet, and the history of the *Sahaabah and Taab'ieen*, who are prominent figures of Islam. Third, he should acquire an adequate knowledge of *fiqh* in order to ensure that his worship and daily dealings are correct. Fourth, he needs to ensure that he has a sound grasp of the basic principles of Islam as his religion. Fifth, he should turn to his own specialty and strive hard with a great deal of vim and vigor to it. Moreover, it is of great essence for the Muslim to strive and do his best in all of these religious spiritual requirements. He should take these activities seriously, in a manner like he believes that it is a religious obligation to work in his field of specialization such as in *shari'ah* (a religious doctrine of Islamic study), medicine, science, engineering, mathematics, physics, chemistry, astronomy, industry, commerce, economics, and law, among other areas of study. He shouldn't stay aloof, but must rather venture to keep abreast of developments in his field of specialization through reading, research, and developments to attain success, recognition, and authority as a professional. Finally, the Muslim should perform *da'wah* (to invite people, both Muslims and non-Muslims to understand the worship of Allah and the Sunnah of the Prophet Mohammed) by ensuring that he presents it sincerely and earnestly, based on the spirit of Islam and its teachings and principles.

Another example of a religious wise act is based on the findings in Dr. Ali Mohammed al-Hashimi (2005). In it, it is revealed that Islam has made knowledge a duty, whereby the one who seeks it draws closer to Allah and adopts it as a means of earning his pleasure. So we see that the scholars of the early generations used to emphasize these sublime principles in their introductions to their books, because through the knowledge that they spent their lives spreading they were seeking to earn the pleasures of Allah, and they presented the results of their study purely for his sake.

It is also worthy of note that the foregoing analysis is presented as a guideline to assist the Muslim in his choices of selecting and performing wise acts that are intended to purify his soul and draw himself closer to Allah. However, as much as we acknowledge the fact that these guidelines are essential factors to assist the Muslim develop his mind and soul, he also needs to be able to discern those negative social factors in his environment and/or society and refrain from their temptations, and assist others in doing the same. The reason being that there are more underlying factors (as highlighted in earlier sections of this study) in today's world which could easily sway the minds of individuals to succumb to sinful and evil deeds which will haunt and erode their souls with mischief and legacy that they will transfer to future generations. The Quran has reminded us of this kind of legacy where mischief prevails as a normal way of life of a community and/or society when it explained:

> Mischief has appeared on the land and sea because of (the mead) that the hands of men have earned, that (Allah) may give them a taste of some of their deeds; in order that they may turn back (from evil). (Sura Ar-Rum 30: 41)

The lesson to be derived from this verse is the fact that in ancient Rome the Greeks used to make alcohol from fermented honey and water, which led them to enormous mischief in the land. However, experience has shown that following the footsteps of Satan and man's *nafs* (lusts and desires) is a contributing factor to the root causes of all human evils. To this end, we share the concerns of the Quran and its reminder that the results of man's evil deeds are contended in Sura Rum: Commentary #182, which emphasizes the fact that the result of evil is evil. So mischief spreads, but God will restore the balance in the end. He did create all things pure and will purge and purify, as He does the physical world with winds. Destruction awaits those that break His harmony and law: it will come when least expected. Let the righteous wait and endure with constancy, for evil is shaky, with no faith in itself and no roots, and is doomed to perish utterly.

The evil deeds of man are nothing new, for it dates back to the past till present times, and are ascribed to man's lack of retort to *figh* and have control over his lower soul or self *(nafs)*. The lust to follow one's own *nafs* will tempt man to be enslaved by the pleasures of this world. The Quran reminds us of the consequences of succumbing to the dictates of Satan and man's *nafs* when God says:

> *O you who believe: Follow not Satan's footsteps; if any will follow the footsteps of Satan, he will (but) command what is shameful and wrong: And were it not for the grace and mercy of Allah on you, not one of you would ever have been pure; but Allah doth purify when He pleases: and Allah is one who hears and knows (all things). (Sura An-Nur14.3–21)*

However, man should take heed of the fact that by following his lust and dictates of his *nafs*, including Satan, will also lead him to go astray and subsequently starve his moral depravity. In fact, among men who choose these negative ways of life are harming their own souls, tarnishing their personality and character, which in turn will distance them away from Allah. Today's world is dominated and influenced by the use of social media, which has both positive and negative gains on both the individual and society at large. Therefore, the onus is on man to discern and weigh both its advantages and disadvantages and utilize its functions in a beneficial manner, taking into consideration those moral and guiding principles of Islam that we discussed earlier. If we take, for example, how man has become a slave to this little electronic device that we so cherish called cellular and/or cell phones. Some people will spend a thousand plus dollars to catch up with its latest programs and functions. Others do so for show of prestige in order to use it as an exhibit of prestige or class.

Notwithstanding the irony in relation to its users remains the fact that it has turned families into unintended form of robots, making us forget those traditional values of how in the past families used to sit together and discuss everyday life. The nature of such family forums was beneficial to both parents and their children. It was a forum of joy, enabling the nurturing of family life where both parents and children will come to know each other better and to also establish a mutual and coherent family environment. It was also an atmosphere exhibiting love through promoting civic education, where children will ask questions about the harsh realities of the real world out there, thereby enabling parents to exploit the opportunity to teach them the do's and don'ts and the rights and wrongs of life, and the social norms of society that are beneficial, as well as those that are detrimental and could jeopardize their way of life.

Nowadays, the fact that this kind of family forum and way of life is gradually diminishing in our societies makes the necessary parental guidance lacking, thereby making our children vulnerable to the attractions and temptations of Satan, bad peer-group influence that could lead them to engage in smoking, the use of alcohol, drugs, crimes, and moreover crimes that may lead them to be incarcerated. The crux of the matter, as well as question to be asked, is are we trading the general excuse of lack of time usually expressed by parents as against lack of parenting that will eventually transform our children into a negative regrettable situation which will lead to the pointing of fingers at each other? Notably, if as parents we take the opportunity to switch our cell phones which are programmed to constantly serve as a tool of distraction to sway us from the more vital issues of the day apart from work, such as our spiritual relationship with God, and to inculcate such values to our family. Complementary to this fact, if the parents in each household were to endeavor to engage in this kind of practice and way of life, to engage, intervene, and discipline (EID) their children, then it is apparent that we will build much better homes, schools, communities, and societies both at community and national levels. The creation of such a healthy spiritual and moral environment will obviously generate a society where spiritual and moral values are nurtured and enhanced, thereby bonding us together to trust each other and be our brothers' keeper, irrespective of race, creed, religion, and ethnicity. In fact, the use of media by way of television or cellular phones can be addictive and time consuming for people who find it difficult to act wisely and control their lust and desires in this regard.

Nowadays, there is the tendency that the more man is consumed by the attraction and/or addiction of media, like sports, comedy, theaters, such as cultural and other entertaining television shows, the more likely it is for him to sway from fulfilling his spiritual and moral obligations with his creator. Furthermore, the more we are addicted to this kind of behavioral characteristics and tendencies, the more difficult and heedless it might be for man to engage in the remembrance of Allah. To this end, once man is inclined toward these kinds of habits that dictate his lust, it will lead him to a moral depravity and of ignorance of feeding his own desires, hence his lack of guidance and mercy from God.

So far, we have discussed some of the fundamental factors associated with wisdom, and we will now proceed to illustrate from the Quran how God's divine wisdom has impacted some of the prophets and wise men like Luqman.

CHAPTER 3.0

God's Divine Wisdom on His Prophets

ABSOLUTE WISDOM BELONGS to Allah, and it is He who guided and sent down the revelations of wisdom to man. Allah, with His infinite grace and mercy, taught Adam the names of things which even the angels and the *jinns* didn't know. Is this not divine wisdom as to why He chooses man above all of His creations? God later revealed the Holy Quran, full of wisdom, through Angel Gabriel to Prophet Muhammad (saw), a man who was unlettered in Arabic. The testimony of this wisdom is manifested in various parts of the Quran. We will not venture to explore it in details, but will proceed with the undermentioned example when God says: "By the Quran full of wisdom" (Sura Ya-Sin 36:1).

The concern in relation to the above stated verse is the fact that not all of mankind can be called believers. The fact of the matter is that even with the nonbeliever that's their choice of life, and for Muslims they have to acknowledge the fact that Islam forbids any compulsion in religion. This fact is revealed in the Quran when it contends:

> *Let there be no compulsion in religion: Truth stands out clear from error: whoever rejects evil and believes in Allah, hath grasped the most trustworthy handhold that never breaks. And Allah heareth and knoweth all things. (Sura Al-Baqarah 2:256)*

This verse, therefore, is decisive in establishing that every individual has the right to make his own choice about embracing any form of religion, including Islam. As for the spread of Islam through its teachings, this is supposed to take place peacefully by disseminating the message based on the Quran and the Sunnah. The nature of this dissemination, once explained to people (an audience or an individual) and heard without obstruction or hindrance, is all that is required as proof of deliberation. To this end, the Muslim who is committed to spreading the words of Islam should know that his job is done as a service to spread the message of God. Subsequently, then, those who want to believe are free to do so, and those who prefer to disbelieve are likewise free to do so.

> Actually, a case in point with reference to the foregoing discussion should also remind us of Umar ibn Al-Khattab, whose invitation to a Christian slave he called Ashaq to embrace Islam wasn't materialized. We have discussed in chapter 2.3 that when Ashaqq turned down his request Umar replied in short that "there is no compulsion in religion," and this reply, together with our citation of Sura Al-Baqarah verse 256 above, should serve as examples of how a Muslim should manifest good character and respect when inviting non-Muslims to embrace Islam.

However, it is imperative to note for Muslims who took covenant to submit to the will of God that they are duty bound to adhere to the five fundamental pillars of Islam consisting of *Shahadah, Salat, Zakat, fasting during Ramadan,* and *Hajj.* Muslims, Jews, and Christians do acknowledge the existence of God, but worshippers such as Freemasons don't believe that there is a creator. Irrespective of these different faiths and religions that prevail in the world, Muslims are taught to respect and not to criticize other faiths or religions. The Quran bears testimony to this kind of reasoning when it states:

> *Say O you that reject faith! I worship not that which you worship; nor will you worship that which I worship. And I will not worship that which you have been Wont to worship, nor will ye worship that which I worship. To you be your Way, and to me mine (Sura al-Kafirun109:1–6)*

The above-cited quotation is a typical example of the religious tolerance, peace, and wisdom in Islam. It is quite explicit that even those who reject faith are treated and addressed with some degree of respect and dignity and not with arrogance and harshness. In relation to these kinds of circumstances, Dr. Ali Muhammad M. As-Sallaabee (2010) explained the following:

> In Kitaab Al-Amwaal, Abu Ubaid related a story how one day Umar passed by the door of a house and saw an old beggar asking for monetary assistance so that he can pay the jizah tax . . .Umar took the old man to his home and treated him hospitably, then gave him a small gift. He then changed the tax law to exempt old people.

The attention, manner, and treatment that Umar gave to this old man attests to the peace in Islam, as well as his determination to ensure that justice and mercy prevail over the people he ruled, including non-Muslims. The reform Umar did pertaining to the tax law led him to then send the following message to the man who was in charge of the Muslim Treasury: he instructed him to keep in mind this man and others that are like him (i.e., do not make them pay the *jizah* tax). Umar further reiterated that his administration would not have been just with the non-Muslims if they eat from their youth (i.e., from what they earn during their youth) and then abandon them during their old age. Umar then made a new policy which exempted elderly men like the one described above, and then wrote to his governors, updating them on the new policy. Similarly, as regards those with faith and believe in God, such as the Jews and Christians, the Quran also addresses them in a similar fashion with respect, wisdom, and understanding. For example, the Quran contends, "Say you: 'We believe in Allah, and the revelation Given to us, and to Abraham, Ishmail, Isaac, Jacob, and the Tribes, and that given to Moses and Jesus and that given to (all) Prophets from their Lord: We make no difference between one and another of them; and we bow to Allah (in Islam)'" (Sura Al-Baqarah 2:136).

Again, the above cited quotation serves as evidence of the divine wisdom in the Quran which does not differentiate between one prophet of God and another. This kind of impartiality in dealing with believers of God in different faiths is unique and unprecedented in religious theology.

But let us not forget that not all men do have the wisdom to discern and acknowledge the fact that God is their creator who also made the heavens and the earth and all that is therein. These categories of men, therefore, need to be enlightened about God so that they will come to realize the fact that He is the source of all things, and that all power, wisdom, beauty, and truth flow from Him. God, in His wisdom, created man with the best of molds, but man transgressed, took the wrong path of discord, sorrow, pain, selfishness, and degradation. Men who failed to fear Allah and submit to His will, no matter what status they may attain in life, their failure to purify their souls spiritually could lead them to follow the path of Satan. The path of Satan will surely be guided by spiritual ignorance, hatred, despair, and unbelief in the signs of God, including the unseen world and the hereafter. This category of unbelievers is also poised to stain both their personality and character in this world and will be answerable for their lack of belief, disobedience, and their evil deeds due to lack of spiritual wisdom and guidance, which poisoned their lives and made them succumb to their lust and desire for wrongdoing.

In fact, when man is bent on doing evil his animal state dominates. It is this state of man which in recent times has caused a lot of global political and civil unrest at an unprecedented scale. Part of this evil is due to the fact that man's soul rises against himself, and his self-discord among his fellow human beings, either due to his race, tribe, ethnicity, religion, and culture, among other factors. We now are witnessing a world where man's lack of spiritual guidance has made man shift his fear of God to that of the strong in authority. This shift has also made those in authority in some circles to oppress the poor and the weak. The crux of the matter is how do we reconcile the lack of religious inclination for these two categories of men (leaders and their followers) who have shifted from the fear of God to the pursuit of their worldly desires. In fact, these two categories of men, although differing in social rank and status, share one thing in common in the eyes of God and society: they are unbelievers who are at a loss, lack spiritual guidance and acknowledgment of the truth. As Muslims, the Quran did send a clear message in this kind of situation, which says:

> Let there arise out of you a band of people inviting to all, that is good, enjoining what is right, and forbidding what is wrong; To attain felicity." (Sura AliImran 3:104)

The prevailing times have also led man to boast in prosperity and curse in adversity. The reason for this kind of arrogance from man is due to his insular nature of failing to have the wisdom that God is responsible for his sustenance rather than believing that it is due to his own efforts. Actually, the nature of man's arrogance, greed, lust to compete for material gains, power, and status are contributing factors for human beings to tear each other down at their own peril. Man is akin to pursuing phantoms, finds it difficult to acknowledge and render the truth, and his egocentric tendencies have undermined the old communal way of life in some traditions to that of a nuclear concept of living. This new social concept of promoting nuclear families has morally affected communities and societies immensely and greatly diminished and eroded the reality of human unity and the notion of sharing, all of which is gradually vanishing from the minds of men. This kind of social trend that is emerging in both developed and developing societies is contrary to Islamic social principles and practices among each other and in particular to extending kindness to one's parents. The notion of extending kindness to your parents might be seen as a cultural norm in believers who fear the instructions of God as revealed in the Quran, which states:

> Thy Lord hath decreed that ye worship none but him, and that ye be kind to parents. Whether one or both of them attain old age in thy life, say not to them a word of contempt, nor repel them, but address them in terms of honor. And out of kindness lower to them the wing of humility, and say: "My Lord! Bestow on them thy mercy even as they cherished me in childhood." (Sura Bani Israil17: 23–24)

In view of the above stipulated verse, we can accept the fact that Islam has clear directives to honor and respect both parents. However, based on the Sunnah, mothers are given particular gratitude and high degree of respect. This kind of preferential treatment to mothers is understandable if we acknowledge the hardship and suffering that they experience in their lives, and in particular, the tedious pain of pregnancy, labor, and delivery of a child, among other things. Therefore, it is imperative to dispel the novice, naive, and ignorant statement that Islam doesn't respect women; it only endorses the fact that they know nothing about the guiding principles of this religion.

Now that we have highlighted some of man's insular, insincere, and ungrateful nature toward his creator, his defiance to submit to God's will remains a big challenge for him. The fact of the matter is that without man submitting to the will of his creator he will find it difficult to purify his soul, both morally or spiritually, and to earn his reward both in this world and that of the hereafter. Muslims who desire to purify their souls should relentlessly make positive efforts and strides to struggle and control their *nafs* from the temptations of this world that will undermine their spirituality. Muslims of this caliber are among the true believers with guidance and wisdom from Allah.

Another characteristic of believing Muslims is linked to their ability to suppress their lust, desires, and any form of influences and/or temptations under the dictates of Satan. Relative to this statement, it is imperative to point out the fact that when man fails to submit to the will of God and follow his lust and desires, this is a path that is doomed to failure. The failure is exacerbated when man continues to operate from his lowest state of existence, known as the animal state of man, a legacy of defiance and insubordination to God that we inherited as the children of Adam. But this nature of insubordination, defiance, arrogance, and impatience remains a fundamental part of his inherent animal intrinsic behavior which permeates his evil tendencies if he fails to control and nurture his *nafs* (soul) to align with the moral or spiritual state of his being. These stages of the *nafs* (soul) and their relationship to shaping and influencing man's behavior and character are discussed briefly in chapter 5.0 and extensively in subsection 5.3.

In view of these ongoing discussions about the Quran and the wisdom it entails, the purpose of the following subsections is to give us an insight that will help us learn some of God's divine wisdom revealed in the Quran, including those he gave to the prophets. The essence for us to explore some of these examples is to give us a gist of their personal relationships and encounters with the people to whom they were sent. Moreover, we will also focus on how their divine messages and warnings impacted their lives and the lives of those people to whom they were sent, their communities and/or nations so that we can make some inferences, draw some relevant lessons from them, discard those negative factors, and emulate how to take heed of Allah's warning to mankind.

3.1 Divine Wisdom Vis-à-Vis the Book of Wisdom

Apart from the three statements discussed above (i.e., the first statement refers to the quality of being wise; the second statement refers to scholarly knowledge or learning; and the third statement refers to a wise act), there also prevails the divine gift of wisdom from God to mankind. This gift of wisdom could either be innate or inspired spiritually based on His power of *Kun fayakūn* (be and it is). For example, the Quran gave us an example of this fact when Allah says:

> *Verily, his command, when He intends a thing, is only that He says to it "Be" and it is. (Sura Ya-Sin 36: 82)*

The above Sura and verse is a manifestation of the powers of Allah the Almighty. It depicts the reality that what he wants, he only needs to command a thing once and it will happen.

Actually, when we use words like *wise, knowledge, wisdom* as part of our vocabulary in expressing ourselves during conversations we hold on a regular basis, we often negate the fact that all knowledge and wisdom belong to God, the almighty, all-knowing sole creator of the heavens, the earth, and all that exist therein, and above all else, the wise. The Quran reminds us to "seest thou not that it is Allah whose praises all beings in the heavens and on earth do celebrate, and the birds (of the air) with wings outspread? Each one knows its own (mode of) prayer and praise. And Allah knows well all that they do" (Sura An-Nur 24:41).

Doesn't all of the above provide enough physical and spiritual evidence for man to reflect, understand, and acknowledge the fact that Allah is the sole and ultimate creator with power and knowledge of things that He blessed them with for their respective modes of survival? Among these things are the clouds that give us rain to nurture our vegetation and utilize the water for man's benefit and survival. In this regard, the Quran states to "seest thou not that Allah makes the clouds move gently, and then joins them together, and then make them into a heap? Then wilt thou see rain issue forth from their midst (of clouds), wherein is hail: He strikes therewith whom He pleases and He turns it away from whom He pleases. The vivid flash of His lightning well-nigh blinds the sight" (Sura An-Nur 24:43).

In addition to the creation of the heavens, the earth, and the animals and creatures therein, God created man as his vicegerent on earth. In fact, with all of these bounties that God has provided to benefit His creations on earth, yet still man is unappreciative of these benefits which he takes for granted. The reason being that there exist among men whose greed, lust, and desires of the *nafs* (soul) are inclined to the affinity of this world (*dunyah*) which makes them unappreciative of these benefits and mercies which God has bestowed on them. Also, among God's many names and attributes lies the fact that He is the sole creator and have command over all that prevails in both the visible and unseen worlds. Relative to this statement, the Quran explains: "His is the creation and commandment" (Quran 7.54). Complementary to the abovementioned factors, the Quran testifies:

> *Allah granted wisdom to whom He pleaseth, and he to whom wisdom is granted receiveth indeed a benefit overflowing: But none will grasp the message but men of understanding.* (Quran II 269)

The believing Muslim, therefore, needs to acknowledge the fact that true wisdom is firm and enduring, and discerns God's law in the working of his creation. It looks to the final end of things, whose mystery is only known to God. For example, Luqman, according to the Quran, was a very wise man. The contents of Sura Luqman relates to such kind of wisdom when it states:

> We bestowed (in the past) wisdom on Luqman: show (thy) gratitude to Allah. Any who is (so) grateful does so to the profit of his own soul: but if any is ungrateful, verily, Allah is free of all wants, worthy of all praise. (Sura Luqman 31: 12)

However, not only was Luqman knowledgeable and wise (known as *Hakim* in Arabic), but he was also confirmed to be a man of good practical conduct and/or ethics (*amal*) the right course in life to the utmost of his noble character. These kinds of virtues that were ascribed to Luqman's behavior and character lead to the conclusive belief that his knowledge was correct and practical, but not necessarily complete. The latter quality ascribed to his knowledge is a valid indication of the fact that no man is perfect. However, Luqman's wisdom was also reflected on the lengthy advice he gave to his son, part of which is revealed in the Quran when it states: "And be moderate in thy pace, lower thy voice: for the harshest of sounds without doubt is the braying of the ass" (Sura Luqman31:19).

Luqman was a man whose devotion was to God, and because he ventured to serve Him with sincerity, it made him acquire a high degree of spiritual wisdom and attainment which surpassed that of many men of his generation. In other to venture more into Luqman's spiritual gift of wisdom from God, there is the curiosity for us to explore his spiritual gift of wisdom from an analytical standpoint and ask the question: what is true wisdom? The answer to the abovementioned question is quite befitting to the commentary statements presented in the Book of Wisdom Sura Luqman, which contends that *true wisdom sees God's boundless bounties to men, and how all nature is made to serve man's end. It is due from us to know our place, discern the limits of our knowledge, and see how far above us is God's wisdom and his law. Let us not deceive ourselves. The end of all things will come, but the when and how are known to God alone, to whom be all praise! (Sura Luqman 31:19; c134)*

Our quest to explore some of the main constituents which can be ascribed to the spiritual gift of wisdom has led us to try and ascertain the difference between the spiritual gift of men like Luqman and the innate gift of wisdom instilled in the genes of man as part of his DNA. As regards the former, there prevailed a strong testimony as explained in one of the preceding paragraphs above when God said in the Quran Sura Luqman verse 12, "We bestowed (in the past) wisdom on Luqman." Pertaining to the latter, which is the innate potential of man or his DNA, the Quran reminds us of this fact when God says: "Behold, the Lord said to the angels, I am about to create man from clay. When I have fashioned (in due proportion) and breathed into him of my spirit, fall you down in obeisance unto him" (Sura Sad38: 71-72).

Having clarified the creation of man from two substances: one material clay, a substance of this earthly world, and another divinely associated, the spirit that God Himself breathed unto Adam. Relative to this point is the fact that the spirit which derives from God is a reality that possesses in some measure all the divine attributes. It represents a link, a relation, and connection to God. The Quran reminds us that it was only after this spirit was breathed into Adam that God ordered the angels to prostrate themselves before Adam. The material world is the earthly world that we inhabit, whereas the nonmaterial world is the world of the unseen and/or the spiritual world. Therefore, the *nafs* is a microcosm containing characteristics of both these worlds. According to Islamfrominside.com it is further stated that

the nafs is a "barzakh," a meeting place (a point of overlap, of intersection) where the world of matter and the world of spirit can come together.

The nature of this proportion between the body and the spirit it contains is mentioned in the Quran when it states that

> by the soul and the proportion and order given to it, and its enlightenment as to its wrong and its right, truly he succeeds that purifies it, and he fails that corrupts it. (Sura ash-Shams 91:7-10)

As regards the *nafs*, since it contains both, humans should strengthen the luminous or spirit aspect of the *nafs*. Since the spirit is one reality while the body has many parts, any movement toward man's bodily or clay aspect represents a descent toward dispersion and multiplicity. If the spirit aspect dominates, then order and correct proportion will be given to all of man's existence—the body won't be denied its due, but all things will attain the correct proportion. The Quran also reveals the fact that the *nafs* is one of the places where God discloses himself to man when it states that in order to seek more enlightenment about the significance of this verse we should refer to one of its commentaries, 4524C, which explains that "God's truth always spreads in its own good time across to the uttermost ends of the earth, as it did in the case of Islam. But the intensive spread in the hearts and souls of people is even more remarkable than its extensive spread over large areas. Men like the four companions of the Prophet—and many more—became leaders of men and arbiters of the world's fate."

After these brief explanations of the creation of man, we can now reiterate the two modes of wisdom mentioned in the preceding paragraphs of this chapter as a follow up of God's divine gifts of wisdom to man, including his DNA. However, irrespective of these two modes of wisdom from God (i.e., the spiritual gift of man and the innate gift of wisdom), man must not be complacent, naive, or stay aloof in his relationship with God and in seeking His wisdom. The fundamental aspect of this relationship is to seek knowledge and guidance that will lead to a better understanding of God and ways to adhere to the principles, guidelines, teachings, and practices of both the Quran and the Sunnah of Prophet Muhammad (saw). A testimony to this statement is explained by Dr. Ali Muhammed M. As-Sallaabee (2010) when he states that "Umar ibn Al-Khattab, in terms of spiritual development, relied on two sources: the Quran and the guidance of the Prophet. Furthermore, the Prophet's character also had a profound impact on Umar's spiritual development."

In order to probe more the issue of DNA mentioned in the preceding paragraphs, it is vital to establish the fact that it is a very complex subject matter which exceeds man's imagination and comprehension even in the domains of science and technology. For example, Harun Yahya (2003) pointed out:

> *The DNA molecule, which is located in the nucleus of a cell and which stores genetic information, is an incredible databank. If the information coded in DNA were written down, it would make a giant library consisting of an estimated 900 volumes of encyclopedias consisting of 500 pages each.*

Let us pause for a while and try to imagine who could have originally created a cell with a nucleus to store genetic information of such a magnitude with differing functions beyond man's understanding apart from Allah who created it. If man is honest and truthful to himself, the sophistication of the DNA molecule should have served as one of the evidence of God as the sole creator of the heavens and the earth and all that it contains. Actually, some recent publications related to man's DNA studies published by the *Scientific American* magazine in 1994, confessed:

> *No doubt, if it is impossible for life to have originated for natural causes, then it has to be accepted that life was "Created" in a supernatural way. This fact explicitly invalidates the theory of evolution, whose main purpose is to deny creation. (Harun Yahya, 2003)*

The fact of the matter is that the rapid developments and achievements in the domain of science and technology have rendered man with the fallacy of believing too much in himself, to the extent that he often loses sight of his limitations and shortcomings. Irrespective of his limitations, man's pompousness is largely driven by factors such as his lust and greed for prestige, monetary gain, fame and media publicity that goes with his professional achievements and/or dominance. The nature of this kind of limitation lies with the fact that science and technology are neutral tools. Their neutrality is backed by the reality that science and technology are man's inventions to satisfy his ego, ambitions, and curiosities, which has rendered him with the inability to have full control over their functions. For instance, the invention of aircraft remains one of the most effective and useful modes of world transportation known to man. Yet with all of its sophisticated sensors and radars system, we have witnessed aircraft suddenly losing contact with their tower controls and disappearing while in midair, enroute their destinations. For example, wikipedia.org, along with malaysianairlineflight.com, reports that

> *Malaysian Airlines Flight 370 on 8th March 2014 took off from Kuala Lumpur International Airport and was scheduled to land at Beijing Capital International Airport at 6:30a.m. local time. The aircraft, a Boeing 777-200ER, last made voice contact with Air Traffic Control at 01:19 MYT, 8 March (17:19utc, 7March) when it was over the South China Sea, less than an hour after takeoff. The aircraft disappeared from traffic control radar screens at 01:22 MYT. May the souls of the departed on that flight rest in peace.*

A similitude of scientific technological innovation by man is Frankenstein and the monster that he created, which he later found out he had no control over. If man's aim for perfection in science and technology is limited due to its neutrality, then it is imperative for him to acknowledge the fact that overall creation (with perfectness), power, man's sustenance and life and death, among other factors, are all under the control and prerogative of Allah. The nature of such universal dominance and control over all creations, both in the heavens and the earth, is confirmed in the Quran when it revealed:

Blessed be He in whose hands is dominion, and He overall things hath power, He who created death and life, that He may try which of you is best in deed; And He is the exalted in might; oft-forgiving; He who created the seven heavens one above another, no want of proportion wilt though see in the creation of Allah, Most Gracious, so turn your vision again: seest thou any flow? Again, turn your vision a second time; (your) vision will come back to you dull and discomfited, in a state worn out. (Sura Mulk 67:1-4)

There are numerous lessons to be drawn from the above stipulated verses. First and foremost is for the believer to acknowledge the fact that God is perfect in knowledge and power, and has control over all of His creations in His hands. Secondly, He is teaching mankind that He is the most merciful and forgiving even among those who transgress against His warnings and are willing to abide by the conditions and rules that He stipulates in the Quran regarding repentance(*Tawbah*). In this regard, we will draw some references as indicated below, showing the stance of the believer, the unbelievers, and the transgressors as examples.

3.2

The first example is a reminder to the believing Muslim not to have any doubt concerning Allah's decisions when faced with trials and tribulations in their lives. It is his affirmation and strength of belief in God which will have the tenacity to reinforce the consistency of his unwavering faith and/or *imaan* in Allah. It is this strong faith that the believing Muslim has in his Creator that is contrary to the unbelievers when God says:

But those in whose hearts is a disease, it will add doubt to their doubt, and they will die in a state of unbelief. See them not that they are tried every year once or twice? Yet they turn not in repentance, and they take no heed. (SuraAliImran3:126)

3.3

The second example refers to the nature of defiance of unbelievers during the period when Prophet Hud tried to make them believe in the creator, but they remained adamant and defiance until God's punishment was decreed as a penalty to them. The Quran testifies to this point when it states:

> *And O my people: Ask forgiveness of your Lord, and turn to Him (in repentance): He will send you the skies pouring abundant rain and add strength to your strength: So turn ye not back in sin. (Sura Hud11:52)*

Prophet Hud having addressed the disbelievers and requested them to have faith in God and to turn to Him in repentance, they were still adamant and turned down his call. Rather, their arrogance led them to challenge Hud and then they said: "O Hud, no clear sign have you brought us, and we are not the ones to desert our gods on your word, nor do we believe in you." So when God's decree was issued, He and those who believed with him were saved, and perished were the disbelievers.

3.4

In the third example, reference is made in relation to Sura Zumar in which the transgressors were reminded to seek repentance in order to purify their souls, but despite such a warning those who remained defiant when faced with the wrath of Allah were regrettably anxious to bargain for another chance, which was too late. The Quran attests to this fact when it revealed:

> *Say: O my servants who have transgressed against their souls: despair not of the mercy of Allah, for Allah forgives all sins, for He is oft-forgiving, most merciful. Turn ye to your Lord (in repentance) and bow to His will before the penalty comes on you. After that ye shall not be helped. And follow the best of the courses*

revealed to you from your Lord before the penalty comes on you
of a sudden while ye perceive not(Suraaz-Zumar39:53–55)!

The lesson learned from Sura az-Zumar verses 53–59 reveal the fact that Allah is so merciful that first he has instituted established rules, procedures, and guidelines in the Quran that will help lead mankind toward the straight path. And even when man falters by following his own *nafs* (lust and desires of this world) and corrupts his soul God still has left a room for him to seek repentance. To this end, God, through his infinite mercy and guidance, will send intermediaries or warners to extend his message for man to take heed. Actually, it is when man is in denial to seek repentance after a warner came to them that God will institute a decree for his punishment on man. Since time memorial, such has been the trend and relationship between the unbelievers and those who persistently transgress against Allah's will. Relative to this statement, we will now proceed to give some examples encountered by prophets whose people were in persistent denial of their messages delivered to them. Their denial as unbelievers was exacerbated by the fact they persistently were reluctant to take heed and followed their lust and sinful desires, which led to severe punishments from God.

Actually, it was a common social phenomenon among prophets to experience denial by the people to whom they were sent. The nature of this social phenomenon has also been confirmed by Ibn Kathir (2003) when he explained the following:

> *It is said that the miracle of every prophet was in conformity*
> *with what their people of that time excelled in. For instance,*
> *Moses was given a miracle which could match and excel the*
> *art of magic which his people exercised. Jesus was also sent in*
> *a time when the people were proud of their medicine. He was*
> *given the power of healing a person born blind or lepers or with*
> *chronic illness. He also brought the dead back to life. No form*
> *of medicine is able to heal them so miraculously.*

There are numerous evidence pertaining to these kinds of denial by the unbelievers, who at times would even go to the extreme of challenging a prophet of their time to show them evidence of God's existence. It was a similar kind of encounter and denial with the disbelievers during the time of Prophet Muhammad with the Meccans. In fact, his encounters were so extreme that they waged wars against him on many occasions, and eventually he went into exile to Medina. Moreover, he was sent at a time when the people of Mecca were proud of their literary work and poetry. So God revealed the Quran to him through Angel Gabriel among the literary works and poetry which existed at that time. Apart from the miracle of the Quran which they refused to acknowledge and succumb to the will of God, they remained adamant and still wanted another miracle from the Prophet to show his truthfulness. God split the moon in two separate halves and then rejoined them. The Quran did confirm that "when the last days are near, and the moon is split asunder" (Sura Infitar 54.1). Furthermore, according to Wikipedia.org, it is stated that "photograph from *Apollo 10* in 1969, Rima Ariadaeus, revealed a 300-kilometer-long rift line on the surface of the moon but can't claim it has anything to do with its splitting based on the Quran."

The bone of contention, therefore, lies with the fact that science has its limitations associated with its discoveries and fact-finding missions concerning God's creation of the heavens and the earth. Whereas God, with His infinite grace, mercy, and wisdom, is the creation and commandment," as revealed in the Quran when it states:

> Your guardian Lord is Allah, who created the heavens and the earth in six days, and firmly established on the throne (of authority): He draweth the night as a veil over the day, each seeking the other in rapid succession. He created the sun, the moon, and the stars (all) governed by laws under his command. Is it not His to create and to govern? Blessed be Allah, the cherisher and sustainer of the worlds. Call on your Lord with humility and in private, for Allah loveth not those who trespass beyond bounds. (Sura al-A'raf 7: 54-55)

Actually, the above-stipulated verses 54-55 should serve as a reminder to the believing Muslim and mankind in general that modern science, with all its sophistication, cannot and will not be able to establish a creation like what is described in this Sura. Literally, the real world with beautiful blue sky that we take for granted, along with the sunshine and its associated bounties such as the rain and the air that we breathe, has its appointed time limit under God's commandment and wishes. However, we know from the Quran that this artificial world, together with the planets and all that they contain, will one day come to an abrupt end. But no one knows this day except Allah, for it will be based on his command on an appointed time. The Quran tells us that when it is almost due the sky will split asunder, shattered to pieces before the new Spiritual World is established. The nature of this spiritual world is explained in the Quran when it states that "Metaphorically the portion which seems at present to divide things from the phenomenal world has to be shattered before each soul knows the reality about itself" (Sura al-Infitar 82:1).

The abovementioned discussion is just a reminder that even the Prophet Muhammad *(saw)* did encounter both denial and resistance from the unbelievers.

We will now proceed to give a few examples of prophets who were faced with similar denials from their people but later witnessed their punishment through the wrath of Allah. Among these examples are the following stories.

3.5 Prophet Abraham and His People

The Quran says:

> And relate to them the story of Abraham when "Behold," he said to his father and his people, "What worship you?" They said: "We worship idols, and we remain constantly in attendance on them." He said: "Do they listen to you when you call (on them), or do you good or harm?' They said: "Nay, but we found our fathers doing thus (what we do)." (Sura ash-Shu'ara 26: 71-74).

Abraham's predicament revealed two vital lessons for believers and those who fear God. Firstly, Abraham's innate wisdom, through the guidance of Allah, gave him foresight to reason beyond the level of his people, which compelled him to question their old traditions of worshipping idols. Secondly, his act of wisdom to pose questions to the idol worshippers, including his own father, was an effort by him to enable them to start thinking about their idols in a rational manner, and reject worshipping them as their gods. Even with this kind of critical thinking and analysis by Abraham for his people, his efforts were in vain, for they failed to take heed of his message to them. Abraham then came up with an alternative strategy to dealing with them and their idols. The Quran confirmed this statement when it states: "I shall surely outwit your idols when you have gone away" (21.15). The Quran further revealed that

> Abraham then did he turn to their gods and said, "Will you not eat (of the offerings before you)? What is the matter with you that you speak not (intelligently)?" Then did he turn upon them, striking (them) with the right hand. Then came (the worshippers) with hurried steps and faced him. He said: "Worship you that which you have (yourselves) carved?" (Sura as-Saffat 37: 91-95)

The idol worshippers, having seen the intense damage that was done to their gods, were in deep anguish, and to their surprise, the Quran contends, "They then asked Abraham: 'Have you done this to our gods?' He replied: 'It was the biggest of them that did it. So ask them if they are able to speak intelligently.' So they turned to themselves and said, 'Surely ye are the ones in the wrong.' Then they were confronted with shame. They said, 'Thou knowest full well that these (idols) do not speak'" (Sura Anbiyaa: 21:62-65).

Based on the evidence of these verses, we can again derive ample evidence of Abraham's wisdom outweighing their minds to understand whether they were true gods; if they were, they would not have suffered this kind of humiliation. The magnitude of their anger and frustration led them to devise a plot to cast Abraham into a furnace of firewood that they will prepare against him. The confirmation of this statement is confirmed by Ibn Kathir (2003) when he explained that

> they then shackled Abraham in chains, and he remembered Allah and praised him with these words: There is no God worthy of worship but you. You are free of all imperfections, O Lord of the worlds! You deserve praise, and the power is for you; and you have no partner. They then placed Abraham on the catapult, shackled in chains, and threw him in the fire. He further praised Allah and said, "Allah is sufficient for us, and how good a protector He is!"

In this regard, the Quran further confirmed that "they said, 'Burn him and protect your gods, if ye do (anything at all)!' We said, 'O fire! Be thou cool, and a means of safety for Abraham (Sura al-Anbya 21: 68-69)!'" As they could not get rid of Abraham by open punishment, their secret plans also failed them throughout. It was not he that lost but they the idol worshippers. The Quran contends that Abraham said:

> "And what, O ye Messengers, is your errand (now)?" They said, "We have been sent to a people (deep) in sin to bring on, on them a shower of stones of clay (brimstone) as a mark as from thy Lord for those who trespass beyond bounds." Then we evacuated those of the believers who were there, but we found not there any just Muslim persons except in one house (the house of Prophet Lot). And we left there a sign for such as fear the grievous penalty." (Sura Adh-Dhariyat 51:31-37)

In relation to the message that Abraham received concerning the people of Lot, we will now proceed to discuss their defiance and eventual destruction in subsection 3.6 below.

3.6 Prophet Lot and the Defiance of His People Against His Warnings

Lot was the nephew of Prophet Abraham. The denial of Lot's warning to his people and the punishment they were afflicted with was a terrible incident which took place during the life of Abraham. In this regard, Lot went to the city of Sodom after Abraham had asked him to do so. Actually, its people were the most immoral and insolent in nature. Ibn Kathir (2003) stated that the people of Sodom were the first in human history to practice homosexuality. Lot tried to explain to them to heed to Allah's command and to worship Him alone, without associating any partner with Him. He tried to forbid them from their evil, unnatural practice and abhorring act. Despite his warning, they ignored and rejected his appeal, and persistently continued with their erroneous indecency and practice. The evil of this practice is explained in the Quran when it states, "That we also (sent) Lot: He said to his people: 'Do ye commit lewdness such as no people in creation (ever) committed before you? For you practice your lust on men in preference to women: ye are indeed a people transgressing beyond bounds." And his people gave no answer but this: They said, "Drive them out of your city: these are indeed men who want to be clean and pure! But we saved him and his family, except his wife: she was of those who lagged behind. And we rained down on them a shower (of brimstone). Then see, the final evidence of those who indulged in sin and crime (Sura Araf: 7: 80-84)!"

3.7 Prophet Saleh and the Famous Tribe of Thamud Who Rejected Faith

The Thamud people were Arabs who lived between Hijaz and Tabuk. They lived after the people of the Ad and worshipped idols just like the Ad did. Evidence from the Quran revealed that to the Thamud people God sent one of their own brethren, Prophet Lot. He told them: "O my people! Worship Allah; you have no other god but him. Now has come to you a clear (sign) from your Lord! This she- camel of Allah is a sign to you. So leave her to graze In Allah's earth, and let her come to no harm, or you shall be seized with a grievous punishment." However, because of their stubbornness, disobedience, and lack of faith in God, they decided to be rebellious. "Then they hamstrung the she-camel, and insolently denied the order of their Lord, saying: "O Salih! Bring about thy threats, if thou art an apostle (of Allah)!" So the earthquake took them unaware, and they lay prostrate in their homes in the morning! So Salih left them, saying: "O my people! I did indeed convey to you the message for which I was sent by my Lord: I gave you good counsel, but ye love not good counselors" (Sura al-A'raf 7:77-79)."

In view of the foregoing examples, it is crystal clear that the unbelievers remained defiant and arrogant toward the prophets who came to them as warners. Their mistakes are numerous and sometimes associated with them following their lust, the old tradions of wrong doings, evil practices of their ancestors, the misconception of regarding them as humans like themselves, and often the ignorance of challenging them to show them a sign and/or proof as evidence. Despite all of these examples of the past, even today some men are still in defiance to submit to the will of Allah. Man's insubordination and failure to adhere to the warnings and guidelines of Allah and his prophets could lead to serious or devastating consequences.

Other lessons derived from the above stated examples do manifest the fact Allah usually gives some form of clear warning before imposing his wrath on mankind. This fact is revealed in the Quran, which contends that.

> when we decide to destroy a population, we (first) send a definite order to those among them who are given the good things of this life and yet transgressed; so that the word is proved true against them: then (it is) we destroy them utterly. (Sura Bani Israil 17:16)

Having discussed God's divine wisdom on His prophets and the power of His wrath on those who failed to take heed of the messages given to them by His warners, we will now proceed to discuss man's inclination for spiritual wisdom as a source of guidance.

Man's Inclination Toward Spiritual Wisdom as a Source of Guidance

I T IS MY earnest belief that man's quest and search for religious and spiritual wisdom will not surpass what is embedded in the Holy Quran, also known as the Book of Wisdom, and that of the Sunnah (the teachings of the Prophet). In relation to both the Quran and the Sunnah, efforts to conceive knowledge about them is one thing, but having their understanding is quite another. In relation to the latter and according to Islam and psychologyblogspot.com (June 12, 2011), it was narrated from Zaid bin Thabit that the messenger of Allah said:

> *May Allah cause his face to shine, the man who hears what I say and conveys it (to others). Many of those who have knowledge but no understanding, and many who convey knowledge to those who have more understanding of it than they do. (Sunnah Ibn E-Majah, Book of Sunnah, Hadith no. 230, classified as Sahih by Allama Albani)*

We can derive from the abovementioned *hadith* (saying and/or teachings of the Prophet) that emphasis is laid on both the acquisition and dissemination of divine spiritual knowledge supported by a prayer from the Prophet with a plea for Allah's reward to make shine the face of spiritual facilitators such as the prophets, their companions, the rightly guided spiritual leaders and *imams*, including people of Islamic knowledge and wisdom. Actually, from a religious perspective, the Quran, as a Book of Wisdom, its inspiration and guidance will benefit only those men of understanding and guidance from Allah. The reason attributed to this statement is based on its divine revelation from God (through Angel Gabriel) to Prophet Muhammad (saw), who was unlettered. This testimony reaffirms the fact that all knowledge belongs to Allah, and He gives it to whomever He wills. For instance, the Quran did make so many proclamations almost some fourteen hundred years ago that came out to be true and still in conformity with modern science.

The islamiclandmarks.com in Egypt confessed to the fact that "The body of Pharaoh Ramses II was discovered in 1881 in a mummified form among the group of royal mummies that had been removed from their original tombs for fear of theft." The nature of this startling discovery leads to the opportunity for Dr. Maurice Bucaille, a French national and scientist, to eventually conduct a study on Pharaoh's mummified remains. However, his findings were quite astonishing when he revealed his final analysis which stated the fact that

> the remains of the salt stuck in his Pharaoh's body were shinning evidence that he had drowned and his body was retrieved from the sea.

The abovementioned confirmation which came from a French Christian scientist wasn't at all surprising due to the fact that the Quran is a revelation from God and was perfected and given to Prophet Muhammad(saw) as a mercy and guidance to all of mankind. A related factor that has some relevance to this statement in our modern-day world revolves around the manner in which Dr. Maurice Bucaille was puzzled over a question. "How did this body, to the exclusion of other mummified bodies of other ancient Egyptians, remain that intact although it was recovered from the sea?" he asked himself. While attending a medical conference with a galaxy of Muslim anatomists, he proclaimed, "I believe in this Quran. When God guided me to undertake a study of the Quran, my inner soul cried out that Al-Quran was the Word of God revealed to his Last Prophet (saw)." Complementary to this fact is the reality that the Quran made the underlying statement attested by Dr. Bucaille, which is in conformity with his significant findings in relation to Pharaoh's mummified remains. Related to this finding which came as a reminder to mankind that the Quran, almost some fourteen hundred years ago, proclaimed this fact regarding Pharaoh's remains, when God says:

> *This day shall we save In your body, that you may be a sign to those who come after you! But verily, many among mankind are heedless of our signs. (Sura Yunus 10: 90-92)*

Now, if we ponder for a while and reflect about Pharaoh's remains in connection with the Quranic proclamation and the significant findings of Dr. Bucaille, it does reveal a perfect match of the above mentioned Quranic verses almost fourteen hundred years ago. The nature of this match cannot be coincidental but it is a reality of the powers attributed to God and His infinite knowledge and wisdom, one of which is *Kun fayakūn*, which denotes the fact that when he wants something to happen, he just says "Be" and it is. Notwithstanding, this spiritual reality that God brought to mankind is evidence of His powers and how He is in control of what He created both in the heavens and on earth. In this regard, isn't Pharaoh's case to mankind enough evidence for us to accept the existence of a God and to submit to His will (as a Muslim)?

In order to throw some light on our readers, a Muslim is regarded as someone who accepts the fact that there is a God, and at the same time submits to His will. This clarification is relevant to our discussion to put it within its proper context and to clarify the current Islamophobia that tarnishes the image of Muslims and Islam in general. The brute nature concerning such negative rationale pertaining to the so-called propaganda about Islamophobia is propagated by a host of factors; namely, the misguided concept of some negative differences and ideologies that are innovated by some religious clerics, scholars, sects, and those who falsely disguise themselves under the name of Islam and commit evil and erroneous, shameful, and unacceptable acts of hate and violence through suicide bombings, mass indiscriminate killings, and committing genocide and the like. The rationale behind our condemnation of this kind of irrational and unacceptable behavior by those perpetrators who commit such cowardly acts is they are brainwashed, which makes them sick in the heart by allowing themselves to succumb to the dictates of others and to reduce themselves to the lowest of the low among the human creation.

As a reminder to Muslims, Allah has reminded us that the best among us are those who fear Him, strive to be always truthful, patience, righteous, and enjoin what is right and forbid what is wrong, adhere to promote justice and do good deeds at all times. These are the virtues of a believing Muslim, which will now bring us to the point to sincerely ask the question: would a believing and righteous Muslim kill indiscriminately innocent children, women, the elderly, and many other people in civil society who are innocent and don't have anything to them that warrants their mass murder? These are some of the harsh realities and questions pertaining to the brute acts of such people who are suffering from the diseases of the heart that need to be resolutely asked and answered.

The nature of such barbaric acts by such irresponsible people takes us back to the way and manner someone like Pharaoh oppressed his people, which can also correlate to the violent acts of these perpetrators who kill innocent civilians indiscriminately, including their other victims, behind closed doors. However, just like Pharaoh, it is just a matter of time and they will have to inevitably account for their wrongful and sinful deeds, both in this world and the hereafter.

The nature of such accountability as manifested by God in the Quran brings us back to further examine the Quranic as well as the scientific evidence pertaining to Pharaoh. Moreover, some of the scientific revelations contained in the Quran came long before modern science which now ascertains such revelations as valid. In this regard, Dr. Maurice Bucaille, a born Christian and a French professor, was searching for a holy book that is in harmony with modern science. He later made a discovery of Pharaoh's mummy, which he and other renowned scientists examined thoroughly. Dr. Bucaille then confessed that it made them deem it quite unthinkable for a man of Muhammad's time to have been the author of such statements on account of the state of knowledge in his day. Such considerations are part of what gives the Quranic revelation its unique place, and forces the impartial scientist to admit his inability to provide an explanation which calls solely upon materialistic reasoning. Complementary to the abovementioned statement, Dr. Maurice Bucaille (1978), in his book *The Bible, the Quran and Science*, reiterated the fact that

> *a totally objective examination of the Quran in the light of modern knowledge leads us to recognize the agreement between the two, as has been already noted on repeated occasions.*

Another wonder of the Quran which modern science has endorsed to be in conformity to their findings is in relation to the convergence of two different seas, where exist a barrier. Relative to this statement, the Quran states that

> *Allah has let free the two bodies of flowing water, meeting together: Between them is a barrier which they do not transgress. Then which of the favors of your Lord will you deny. (Sura ar-Rahman55:19-21)*

In relation to the abovementioned verse, it is still a wonder how two bodies of seawater, salty and sweet, converge yet stay separated by the formation of an unknown natural barrier between them. This is one of those mysterious wonders that remain a challenge to mankind. This scenario for man remains a wonder, but in reality it is one of the favors of Allah. We are aware of the fact that seawater is a sanitizing agent, while freshwater is sweet and palatable to drink. The revelation in the abovementioned sura and verse of the Quran revealed almost fourteen centuries ago, way before modern science came up with such evidence, is another match that is in conformity with Allah's proclamation in the Quran. For example, marine captain Jacques Cousteau, a French scientist who conducted the study of the two seas (the Atlantic and the Mediterranean seas), also attests to the fact that there is a barrier at the convergence of the two seas as revealed by the Quran.

Now the examples of these two different types of seawater converging will be accepted as part of Allah's favor and mercy to mankind by Him latently imposing a barrier between them in order to prevent them from mixing and polluting each other. We know based on modern science that water has a capillary action which allows it to move and flow freely. The spiritual mystery that is blocking these two seas from mixing at their point of convergence is still a wonder to mankind and modern science. In fact, if the two seawaters were allowed to mix together it may have led to the destruction of marine life species and man's dependence on them for his survival.

At least, we have illustrated an example of Allah's favor and mercy to mankind, now let us also venture to discuss Allah's wrath on those who disbelieve and/or transgress against his warnings, like Pharaoh, who denied the warnings of Prophet Moses, which led to his drowning in the Red Sea. These two kinds of divine wonders by Allah (the barrier established between two different seas and/or rivers, and the splitting of the Red Sea by Prophet Moses to drown Pharaoh) are way different in magnitude from what man conceives as wonders of the world such as the pyramids of the ancient times of Egypt. Although the pyramids which survive up to modern times are man's own creation and are admired for their sophisticated nature, they are of less significance compared to the divine wonders of Allah as explained above.

Another example of Allah's divine creation is that if man could ponder for a while and look at the size of planet Earth on which the pyramids and other wonders of the world are erected, then he will be able to realize and acknowledge his inability to create something like planet Earth, the sun, the moon, and the stars, among other creations of Godin fact, all of God's creations are explicitly stated in the Quran, which we will also discuss in this chapter. Besides, God has repeatedly challenged mankind to produce at least a sura or chapter like the Quran if they doubt it. These challenges that beckon to mankind are revealed in various suras of the Quran, but we will just restrict it to the undermentioned Sura and verse when Allah said: "And if ye are in doubt as to what we have revealed from time to time to our servant, then produce a sura like thereunto; and call your witness or helpers (if there are any) besides Allah if your (doubts) are true" (Sura Al-Baqarah 2:2).

Another revelation in the Quran which is now confirmed by modern science is the story of Prophet Sulayman and the ants, of which the Quran states:

> And before Solomon were marshaled his hosts of Jinns and men and birds, and they were all kept in order and rank. At length, when they came to a (lowly) valley of ants, one of the ants said: "O you ants, get into your habitation lest Solomon and his hosts crush you (underfoot) without knowing it." (Sura An-Nami 27:17-18)

The point to note here regarding the above stated verse in Sura Nami is the hidden knowledge that Solomon inherited from Prophet David as his heir, both in prophethood and kingdom. In this regard, they were taught the speech of the birds, and he understood the language of all kinds of birds. He was given huge armies of men, jinn, birds, wild animals, and the knowledge and science of other things, and the ability to understand the other silent creatures.

Allah counted this as one of the manifest bounties upon Solomon, hence his ability to understood what the ant said to his fellow ants in and around the anthill valley. In fact, this is why when Solomon heard the ant alert his fellow ants of him being around their vicinity, he smiled, amused at her speech; and he said: "O my Lord! So order me that I may be grateful for your favors which you have bestowed on me and on my parents, and that I may work the righteousness that will please you; and admit me, by your grace, to the ranks of your righteous servants." This hidden language of communication by ants remained a mystery until now but has been confirmed by modern science. Relative to this fact, quranandscience.com pointed out that

> modern science just in 2009 had their scientists make a startling discovery when they completed their research on ants and listened to them talking to each other. Similarly, their findings were also reported on the Sunday Times and ABC News.

The above stated findings mark another testimony to the fact that the Quran is actually the voice of God revealed about fourteen hundred centuries ago when scientific research was nonexistent. These findings also reaffirm the fact that the Quran, with some of its scientific revelations, came way before modern science.

Another finding about the Quran is its mathematical mysteries when it comes to its mystics regarding numbers. For example, the words *man* and *woman* are each mentioned twenty-three times in the Quran. By adding these two numbers together we get forty-six. Amazingly, this figure corresponds to the total number of chromosomes of which the human body is made up. Similarly, we know that in the Quran *forgiveness* and *punishment* are mentioned 117 times. If we double the number for *punishment*, it will give us 234 in total. This is both meaningful and significant results, because as Muslims God asked us to forgive more than to take revenge. Moreover, it also reinforces the fact that God is merciful and oft-forgiving, hence his request for us to seek repentance from him when we either commit a sin and/or transgress, as the case may be.

In view of the abovementioned factors, let us try and discuss what is implied as the Book of Wisdom in the Quran. The answer to this question is revealed in various parts of the Quran. Therefore, efforts will be made to highlight a few examples in this chapter.

4.1 Reconciling the Book of Wisdom as a Source of Spiritual Attainment and Guidance for Man

The search for spiritual wisdom is embedded in the Holy Quran, also known as the Book of Wisdom. The authenticity of this claim is revealed in various suras of the Quran. For example, in Sura Luqman we can refer to commentary #183 of its introduction which states that "the Book of Wisdom is a guide and mercy to men, and teaches them how to attain bliss. God's mercies are infinite; how can man deny them?"

These are verses of the Wise Book, a guide to the doers of good, those who establish regular prayer, give regular charity, and have (in their hearts) the assurance of the hereafter. These are on (true) guidance from the Lord; and these are the ones who will prosper. (Sura Luqman 31:1-5)

The concept of guidance that is of paramount importance for the Muslim is the plea that every day, when praying to Allah, he asks Him to Guide him to the straight path. In other words, a critical reflection of this constant plea by the Muslim during the opening part of each of his five daily prayers is a reflection of the reality that his success for guidance can only come from God. However, we need to clarify the point that all forms of Allah's creations are endowed with some form of innate guidance, and they include mankind, animals, and plants, among other things. We have explained the nature of this type of guidance in detail in chapter 6 and in the summary and conclusions. In fact, "there is no single thing among His creation that does not celebrate the praises of Allah, though we do not understand their praise" (Sura Al-Isra 17.44). Therefore, this innate fundamental guidance is something that we all are endowed with from Allah, but the fact of the matter is that we constantly yearn to attain more of its advanced and higher stages.

Similarly, Sura *Ta-Ha*, which denotes mystic letters abbreviated as TH, contends the following:

We have not sent down the Quran to thee to be (an occasion) for thy distress, but only as an admonition to those who fear (Allah). (Sura Ta-Ha 20:2)

We can briefly discern from the abovementioned verses that the Quran, full of wisdom, is sent down as a guide for the doers of good, the righteous, and those who fear Allah. During its revelation, prophets were sent periodically as warners to different tribes, people, and nations on differing times and places, except for Prophet Muhammad, who was sent to the people of Mecca, Medina, and all of mankind. To this end, the Muslim needs to acknowledge the fact that all of the prophets had inspiration from Allah. This valid explanation is manifested in the Quran when it states as follows:

> *We have sent thee inspiration, as we sent it to Noah and the messengers after him; we sent inspiration to Abraham, Ismail, Isaac, Jacob, and the tribes, to Jesus, Job, Jonah, Aaron, and Solomon, and to David we gave the psalms. (Sura an-Nisa 4:163)*

The crux of this inspiration from Allah to the prophets led to the unique revelation of the Holy Quran to Prophet Muhammad through Angel Gabriel. It is the Book of Wisdom. When followed spiritually by his servants, it will lead them to *the truth and guidance on the straight path.* The spiritual guidance pertaining to the straight path is embodied in the opening chapter of the Quran, Al-Fatiha, also generally referred to as the Mother of the Quran (Umm Al-Quran) which states: "Show us the straight path. The path of those on whom You have bestowed Your Grace; Thou whose (portion) is not wrath, and who go not astray" (Sura al-Fatiha 1: 6-7).

Before we proceed further with our discussion, we will venture to explain the many names of Sura Fatiha. Apart from the abovementioned verses of Sura Fatiha, Muslims have also come to realize and acknowledge the many spiritual names and benefits we inherit as a legacy from the Prophet (saw). To begin with, Sura Al-Fatiha is considered as the greatest sura of the Quran. Within this context is the fact that this great sura has enormous benefits and virtues, including its amazing and miraculous use in spiritual protection and healings. Complementary to these vital benefits, it is imperative that we try and spell out some of these spiritual names and benefits that are associated with it as stipulated below:

First, Al-Fatiha denotes (the opening), and it name is derived from Sura Al-Fatiha, which in essence marks the opening or commencement of the Quran. The Sura is also used as a preceding sura followed by another sura or verse for each *raka* (the standing position) in a given prayer. For example, the *fajr* (early dawn) prayer is two *rakats*; therefore, each of these two *rakats* must be preceded by a Sura Fatiha and followed by a sura or verse.

Second, it is referred to as Umm al-Quran, "Mother of the Quran." Normally, the sura starts with the verse which says "all praises and thanks are due to Allah, the Lord of the worlds," or in Arabic "*Alhamdu lillahi rabbilalameen.*" The sura also contains the Seven Oft Repeated Verses and the Great Quran. The reason to ascribe Sura Fatiha as a divine symbol of the whole Quran is based on an authentic *hadith* by Abu Hurairah.

Third, it is referred to as Umm al-Kitab, Mother of the Book. This name is derived mainly due to the fact it is the first chapter written in the Quran. This fact is also confirmed in Al-Buhari, the Book of Tafsir, in his *sahih.*

Fourth, Sabul-Mathani, also named the Seven Oft Repeated verses. Notably, these verses are frequently recited in every *raka* of the prayer, as mentioned in the preceding paragraphs above. The Quran also mentioned this fact when it states: "And we have bestowed upon thee the Seven Oft Repeated Verses, and the Grand Quran" (Sura Al-Hijr 15: 87). The Seven Oft Repeated Verses are usually understood to be the opening sura (the Fatiha) which is regarded as a summary of the whole Quran.

Fifth is Al-Hamdu lillah (praisebe to Allah), which is associated with the reason why it is also named *Al-Hamdi*, the praise. Notwithstanding, the attribute attached to this name is due to the fact that the word *hamdi*, just as in Sura Al-Baqarah, contains mention of the cow. For the benefit of our readers, the spiritual name attached to Sura Al-Baqarah is the cow.

Sixth is As-Salah (the Prayer), and the reason for associating this name with Al-Fatiha is because its recitation is an obligatory condition for the validity of the prayer. The word *salah* in Arabic is prayer.

Seventh is As-Shifa, also Ash-Shifa (the Cure). The reason is based on an authentic *hadith* by Abu Sa'id that the Prophet (saw) said that "the Opening of the Book is a cure to every poison," implying that it is a *dua* (prayer) for cures and healing.

Eight is Ar-Ruqyah, also Ar-Ruqya, the spiritual cure. This is also based on the authentic *hadith* of Abu Sa'id in Bukhari that he recited Sura Fatiha to cure a person who was bitten by a scorpion. The Prophet asked him, "And what made you know that it was a *ruqya?*"

Ninth is Asas al Quran (the foundation of the Quran). This is based on *hadith* by Ash-Sha'bi confirmed by Ibn Abbas that the "foundation of Al-Fatiha is 'Bismillah,'" which denotes "I begin in the name of Allah." The word *bismillah* in its full verse reads *Bismillah, ar-Rahman, ar-Rahim,* denoting "I begin with the name of God, the Almighty, the most merciful." This verse is in the majority of the suras in the Quran with few exceptions. Moreover, in Islam, it is also a spiritual ritual for a Muslim to say *bismillah* before embarking on the task of his daily life pursuits.

In view of the foregoing discussions, it is a crucial factor for the Muslim to note that the way to the straight path is to follow the instructions and guidance in the Quran and to adhere to the revelations and practice of the way of Prophet Muhammad (His Sunnah). The former statement is reflected in the Quran when it contends the following:

> *O mankind! The Apostle hath come to you in truth from Allah: believe in him, it is best for you. But if you reject faith, to Allah belongs all things in the heavens and on earth, and Allah is all knowing, all wise. (Sura an-Nisa 4:170)*

These words of truth, guidance, and wisdom are for men who reflect, fear Allah, and have both the understanding and wisdom of His creations and revelations of those books given to some of the prophets, such as the Tawrat to Prophet Musa and the Quran to Prophet Muhammad propagated, among other factors, the oneness of Allah. For instance, the Quran stipulates:

> *O you who believe: guard your own souls. If you follow (right) guidance, no hurt can come to you from those who stray; the goal of you all is to Allah. It is he that will show you the truth of all that you do. (Suraal-Maidah 5:105)*

The truth of all that we do should be a reflection of our sincerity to believe in and worship Allah, which must encompass taking care of His creations, piety, and practicing righteous deeds just for His sake. This piety toward Allah and His creations must also include the fulfillment of our religious obligations to Him, including our dutiful respect toward our parents, and in particular our mothers. This piety, if we are to practice it for the sake of Allah, should enable us to serve our communities, such as the disabled, the weak, the poor, the orphans, and our leaders, so long as they fear Allah and are just and righteous in their deeds. Relative to these issues and those mentioned above in this chapter are pertinent to similar views expressed by Dr. Ali-Mohammad M. As-Sallaabee (2010) when he mentioned that

> *Umar ibn Al-Khattab, a prominent companion of the Prophet (saw), believed that piety was displayed not through affection, not through lowering one's head and speaking in an almost inaudible tone, but through sincerity and righteous deeds.*

Man's sincerity and righteous deeds can be facilitated through our belief in Allah and fearing His punishment when we transgress. We have stated in subsection 2.3 that Allah has created mankind into tribes and nations so that we can understand each other. If we reflect on the prevailing status of man from a global perspective, we see a lot of social unrest where man's lack of understanding for each other has negatively overwhelmed societies at the individual, local, national, and international levels, posing threats of instability at each level. To this end, the UNHCR reported that

> *we are now witnessing the highest levels of displacement on record. An unprecedented65.3 million people around the world have been forced from home. Among them are nearly 21.3 million refugees, over half of whom are under the age of 18. There are also 10 million stateless people who have been denied a nationality and access to basic rights such as education, healthcare, employment and freedom of movement. (UNHCR.Org)*

The abovementioned figures revealed by UNHCR represent the brutal and evil nature of man who lusts after and is greedy for power, authority, wealth, and domination of the rich over the poor, the strong over the weak, and the privileged over the underprivileged, among other factors. Based on the abovementioned statistics, it is ironic to see that we are witnessing a world that is in disarray due to differences in political, religious, racial, tribal, and other related factors which contradict Allah's message to mankind to have understanding for each other so that peace and love can prevail on earth. Unfortunately, man so far is unable to nurture an understanding that will promote a peaceful coexistence among men and nations, both nationally and globally, without any exception whatsoever. Presently, man's prime vehicle to manage our societies is politically driven, which up till now has been jeopardized by his failure to fear Allah and to fully submit to His will and refrain from the temptations of greed, intolerance, injustice, and aggressive hostile behavior toward each other. For example, we are witnessing the lack of sympathy, empathy, and impartiality propelled by his lust and desire for the temptations of the life of this *dunyah* (world), which is short-lived.

4.2 The Book of Wisdom That Makes Things Clear

It is important for the Muslim to acknowledge the fact that the Book of Wisdom can enhance his spiritual enlightenment, clarity to attain *tawheed* (the oneness of God), *iman* (faith or belief), *taghwah* (consciousness and cognizance of Allah), and the regular practice of good deeds. In this regard, the Quran in Sura Naml explicitly states:

> that these are verses of the Quran, a book that make (things) clear, a guide and glad tidings for the believers, those who establish regular prayers, and give in regular charity, and also have (full) assurance of the hereafter." (Sura an-Nami27: 1-3)

Furthermore, the Quran reaffirms its message regarding the clear signs that God revealed in it for mankind when he says: "Asura which we have sent down and which we have ordained: in it have we sent down clear signs in order that you may receive admonition" (Sura an-Nur 24:1). It is also stated in the Quran that:

> For those who give in charity, men and women, and loan to Allah a beautiful loan, it shall be increased many fold (to their credit), and they shall have (besides) a liberal reward. (Sura al-Hadid 57:18)

However, it is imperative to note that those who wish to be among the prosperous of this *dunyah* (world) must fear Allah, adhere to his commands and assist the poor and the needy and adhere to the practice of righteousness and good deeds just for His sake and as a loan to Him. The bone of contention here is to avoid the negative practices of some Muslims whose perception about Islam is tied to praying at their own lust and convenience, thereby subjecting them to a state of complacency to an extent whereby they will find it difficult to adhere to the recommended regular praying times. Such kind of behavior is contrary to a wise act, and will not aid this category of Muslims in attaining a spiritual path of purity as anticipated in Islam. Therefore, in order to avert this kind of negligent behavior, the emphasis here is for Muslims to seriously acknowledge the very importance of performing regularly the five obligatory prayers on time. Similarly, some Muslims pray but sometimes fail to take heed of the importance of *zakat* as instructed in the Quran, which states:

> And establish prayers and give zakat, and whatever good you put forward for yourselves, you will find it with Allah; surely Allah sees what you do. (Sura Al-Baqarah 2:110)

Hence, zakat is an important aspect of the religion of Islam. It is necessary to make a brief explanation about it. *Zakat* is a monetary devotion and an *ibadah* (service or servitude or to worship) that has been ordained in the *shariats* of the *ambiya* (the prophets, peace be upon them). In addition, the word *ibadah* refers to Islamic jurisprudence. *Zakat* is one of the five pillars of Islam. Furthermore, the word *zakat* denotes "to increase." Technically, it means to purify one's position of wealth by distributing a prescribed amount which has to be given to the poor as a fundamental *ibadat*. *Zakat* is attributed to the individual and is not a government tax, but its main purpose is to keep those who are wealthy clean monetarily from sins.

In fact, in Sura al-Munafiqun 63:10 discussed above, God has reminded Muslims in very clear terms when he says: "Spend something (in charity) out of the substance which we have bestowed on you before death should come to any of you..." The importance of this statement is a crucial reminder that the end of all things will come but the when and how are only known to God the Almighty. Relative to this statement, it is important for Muslims to sew the spiritual seeds of good deeds, such as the performance of regular prayers, giving out charity, and assisting the orphans, the poor, and the needy as part of their routine behavior, among other things. Most important of all is for Muslims to fear Allah, submit to His will, and to remember that our lives are short-lived and we will eventually meet Him to account for our deeds in this *dunyah* (world).

Actually, deeds are also associated with those which Allah has commanded his servants to do, such as obligatory and voluntary deeds. Dr. Ali Mohammad M. As-Sallaabee (2010), referred to Dirasat Fi Ahd An-Nubuwwah Wal-Khilaalah Ar-Raashidah (pg. 273), explained when Abu Bakr, shortly before returning to his Lord, had to meet in private with Umar in order to impart to him important advice. He said:

> *O Umar, fear Allah, and know that Allah has deeds which He commands His slaves to do by day, deeds which He does not accept if they are performed at night. And He has deeds which He commands His slaves to do by night, and He does not accept them if they are performed by day. And He does not accept voluntary deeds until obligatory deeds are first performed... Verily, Allah has mentioned the inhabitants of paradise, and He mentioned them by the best of their deeds, and He overlooked the worst of their deeds...Indeed, Allah mentioned the people of the Hellfire and He mentioned them by the worst of their deeds and He rejected the best of their deeds.*

The abovementioned advice from Abu Bakr to Umar is worthy of note for Muslims to understand the fact that after submitting to the will of Allah it is imperative for them to venture to perform good deeds, learn the Quran (the Book of Wisdom), and venture to comprehend its contents. They should also learn to live their lives according to the clear messages and teachings of the Prophet, both of which are intended to benefit them shape both their personality and character as role models in their communities. Furthermore, Muslims should consistently endeavor to seek knowledge of the Quran through proper guidance of a teacher and/or sheikh in order to gain wisdom and to understand the fundamentals of *tawheed* (the oneness of God). Through this medium of seeking knowledge, and with Allah's guidance, they may be able to increase their *imaan* and *taghwah*, control their lust and desires of this world, and purify their souls before they meet with their Lord.

For the interest of our readers, the Arabic word *iman* means faith or belief, and *taghwah* means consciousness and fear of Allah, including truth of rational reality and piety. However, when we talk of *taghwah* it is quite apparent that among men there are those who don't belief in Allah, the Resurrection, and Day of Judgment. Generally speaking, these categories of people are usually driven by their lust and desires of the love of this *dunyah* (world), to an extent where they disregard anything to deal with the hereafter. Notwithstanding, they are of the notion that their life in this world ceases to exist after they die, and as such can't be rejuvenated in the hereafter. Regarding such people who are in doubt of the Day of Resurrection, God gave them a clear sign with a reminder of how he created mankind. This reminder is explicitly stated in the Quran when God says:

> O mankind! If ye have a doubt about the resurrection (consider)
> that we created you out of dust, then out of sperm, then out of a
> leechlike cloth, then out of a morsel of flesh, partly formed and
> partly unformed, in order that we may manifest (our power) to
> you. (Sura Hajj 22:5)

Apart from this magnificent explanation about life, death, and the hereafter, God also sends a reminder to mankind confirming his promise that man cannot escape death irrespective of their status, wealth, knowledge, and other worldly attributes that we strive and yearn for on a daily basis. In connection with this statement, the Quran reaffirmed the following:

> Every soul shall have a taste of death, and only on the Day of Judgment shall you be paid your full recompense. Only he who is saved from the fire and admitted to the Garden will have attained the objective (of life), for the life of this world is but goods and chattels of deceptions. (Sura Ali Imran 3:185)

In another *ayah* of the Quran God reminds mankind of the material competitions of this world which dominate their time in a manner that they overlook their main purpose in life. This reminder is revealed in Sura Takathur, which states: "The mutual rivalry for piling up (the good things of this world) diverts you (from the more serious things) until you visit the graves" (Sura at-Takarthur 102:1–2).

In fact, some vital lessons to be learned from this section of our discussion are the clear manifestations of the wisdom embedded in the Quran and its guidance for the believers to work toward a path of spiritual and moral purification of their souls. However, the nature of such guidance will be beneficial only for those who submit fully to the will of Allah and are willing to read and understand the contents of the Quran, discern the real purpose of life, including its deceptive nature, take heed of Allah's warning of the trials and tribulations that go with life, the inevitability of death, and Judgment Day.

In order to conclude the subsection of this chapter, we will give *the scenario of two types of Muslims* and allow you the privilege to decide which one of them is making the right effort to fulfill his purpose in life. *Muslim type A* acknowledges the fact that there is a God. He is neglectful of his prayers because he values deeply the life of this world with its goods and chattels of deception, doesn't care much about his neighbors and the welfare of the people of his community until he encounters death. *Muslim type B,* however, is the type who fears Allah, submits to his will, prays regularly, and gives out charity to assist the poor and the needy. Moreover, he is mindful of not committing sins, knowing fully well that death strikes him without notice. Which of the two individuals would you rather advocate to be in your life?

The objective of stating the abovementioned scenario of two types of Muslims is to highlight the fact that the lust and greed for money and goods and chattels of deception of this world do not guarantee happiness. The fact of the matter is that we can only find true happiness by striving to be closer to Allah. Moreover, when we talk about the Muslim striving to be closer to Allah, we imply that he is the type who fears Allah, submits to his will, adheres to his guidance by following both the Quran and the Sunnah, and always seeks to remain righteous and perform good deeds.

We have witnessed celebrities who attained fame and wealth at a very high level but didn't acquire happiness to an extent that they preferred to die than to live. The crux of the matter is for man to realize that true happiness could be attained through fear of God and submitting to his will. Once the Muslim submits to the will of Allah, relinquishes the material and social temptations of this world through his ability to distinguish and differentiate needs from wants, *halal* (lawfully permissible) from non-*halal* (lawfully not permissible) based on the Quran, Sunnah, and Islamic Law and/or jurisprudence. The adherence to these Islamic fundamental principles has the tendency to purify the body and soul of a devout servant, and could eventually bring about true internal happiness.

The fact of the matter is that such a category of Muslim who adheres to these fundamental principles will feel the increase of his affinity to serve Allah, making him get closer to his creator with a feeling of his heart at rest. When the soul is at rest, the Muslim will put more emphasis in the planning for the hereafter than in this world. He will be in a position then to acknowledge the fact that planning in this world would imply that he will have to exert most of his energy and reasoning efforts on worldly gains and affairs, which has a futile ending. The reality that is associated with the futile end of whatever we may achieve in this world, be it worldly goods, taking pride in acclaim, are all short-lived due to the fact that everything will come to pass except the kingdom of Allah. Moreover, all of the things that we attained in this word will be left behind the day we depart from this world.

These statements are just mere reminders that we are not angels but mere mortal beings, and are prone to perish from the face of this earth based on an appointed time and place fixed by God. However, one must not misconstrue these harsh facts and realities of life with the impression that man shouldn't venture to strive hard for his living in order to sustain both himself and his family. What the Muslim must not do is, after he acquires wealth or status in society, with every little thing that he gets of worldly means make him directly or indirectly grow in negligence, arrogance, self-importance, and pompousness, among other negative factors and influences. The reason being that worldly success implies that it preoccupies you from operating in accord with divine directives, which will sway you to oppose God's Will.

Contrary to the efforts of the Muslim to limit his planning to this world, he can still plan but extend it to cover that of the next world. This will consist of arranging his worldly affairs to a degree that will facilitate him to prepare spiritually for the next world. For instance, the Muslim whose work enables him to be financially successful, granted he attains his wealth via *halal* (permissible) means, could choose, for example, to reinvest part of his money toward the building of a *masjid* (mosque) or an orphanage, planting fruit trees that will benefit his community, the provision of a well or borehole to benefit his neighbors, and similar worthwhile ventures that are in conformity with Islamic teachings and rewards both in this world and the hereafter.

Some of the signs of a Muslim who conscientiously minimizes his reliance on worldly means (*zahid*) are twofold: on the one hand when the world gives them nothing, and on the other hand, when the world gives them something. The former is marked by his contentment to tranquil relaxation, while for the latter it is marked by his efforts to selflessly give it out to others. To this end, these are the visible signs that are noticeable to indicate that love of this world has left the heart when the individual servant gives things away when he has them and is tranquilly at rest when he doesn't.

Furthermore, it is through this spiritual submission that the Muslim will eventually come to realize that the best ways to connect with God is to prostrate to him in *sujood*(prayer) and/or to sing his praises together with other believing servants or especially when in solitude. Allah reminds us of this spiritual submission in the Quran when he says: "O ye who believe: Let not your riches or your children divert you from the remembrance of Allah. If any act thus, the loss is their own" (Sura al-Munafiqun 63:9). It is imperative, therefore, that man take heed of the temptations of this world and work toward the building of a solid spiritual foundation through his sincere worship to serve and obey the guidance of Allah. Complementary to this statement, the Quran states: "Nay heed him not, but bow down in adoration and bring yourself the closer to Allah" (Sura al-Alaq 96:19).

Having discussed how the Book of Wisdom came with clear suras and verses to promote man's knowledge, clarity in wisdom enables the Muslim to nurture and establish closer links with God and to attain true happiness, among other things. We will now proceed to explain how the acquisition of spiritual knowledge may be utilized to distinguish right from wrong and the fear of Allah.

4.3 The Wisdom of Spiritual Knowledge as a Guide to Enable Man's Conscience to Distinguish Right from Wrong

The acquisition and/or the attainment of spiritual knowledge could serve as a vehicle to promote moral guidance and the fear of Allah. This is because man's attainment of spiritual knowledge combined with his fear of Allah should equip him to utilize his conscience as a moral guide and/or GPS to discern the prevailing circumstance he is confronted with, and to make informed decisions on matters that are right or wrong. Actually, the Muslim who claims to submit to the will of Allah and attain a high level of spiritual knowledge and understanding should strive to live by example of righteousness, good deeds, and refrain from committing sins which he will account for in the hereafter. The fact of the matter is that man is in a haste to complete his task of the day, go to sleep, wake up, and continue with where he stopped with his task the previous day, or set forth on a new task. After work, in the evening, it is the belief of some men that they need to occupy themselves in the evening and at night with social entertainment such as dining, watching movies, drinking, and partying in nightclubs, or organizing traditional social functions such as drumming and dancing (in which a lot of money is spent lavishly). However, there is nothing bad about entertaining oneself to be happy and joyful. The crux of the matter is the acts and intentions that go with it until it becomes a habit of life. Seemingly, what man failed to acknowledge when everything is going well with him (he tends to see life as an ongoing everlasting trend) is to forget that he has one life to live. In this regard, he is consumed with the above template of social life, forgetting the fact that life is nothing but a measurement of time. The reality is that every day we accomplish yearning for the next makes us older and closer to the life time frame that God has set for us. The nature of this life time frame varies from individual to individual, just like how we are endowed with differing fingerprints that are unique by themselves. It will imply, therefore, that each passing day draws us closer to death and the accountability of our deeds in this world.

Man also tends to take this world, his life, and all of the bounties that God gave us for granted. In this regard, we start counting our existence in this world using the number of years as our most precious indicator. For example, if someone lives for even one hundred years measured against time, relatively it is like a grain of sand taken away from the earth, which makes it very insignificant. The nature of such insignificant life time frame when translated into days equals 36,500 days. In reality, man's anxiety to crave for the next day which might not materialize for some is due to anxiety, haughtiness, and ignorance and uncertainty of what tomorrow might bring for him. Notwithstanding, using this concept to evaluate our existence on earth is just a number of counted days that is so insignificant relative to time.

The fact of the matter is that, either intentionally or unintentionally, man tends to ignore this very serious and profound reality of death that is in us and with us, accompanying us like our shadows every second and minute of the clock, and can strike us at any moment of our lives. This is the reason why it is called death, for surely it does always come by surprise.

Another factor worth considering by the believing Muslim is to live his life as he will depart from this elusive and deceptive world that we so love more than anything else, and to an extent that we don't want to part from the temptation that comes with it. The reality of this statement is justified by man's greed, lust, and desires of this world. In fact, it is our desire for things that we accumulate as material accomplishments, such as our houses, cars, televisions, money, which makes us compete for them in order to satisfy our ego. Based on the author's experience of living in both developed and developing countries, the underlying fact of man's craving for these material gains is one of the basic causes to trigger his ego toward the generation of grudge, envy, jealousy, hatred, and the like, all of which are associated with the diseases of the heart that need to be cured.

Actually, the importance of time and how it can sway man to be in loss is revealed in the Quran when God says:

> By (the token of) time (through the ages), verily man is in loss, except such as have faith, and (join together) in the mutual teaching of truth, and of patience and constancy. (Sura Asr 103:1-3)

Candidly speaking, the Muslim should pause for a while and grapple with the reality that by wasting today's time he has actually destroyed the opportunities of yesterday. Therefore, it is vital for the Muslim to cherish each second, minute, and hour of the day, for each day that passes will never return again. The fact of the matter is that if the Muslim was to revert to the above template of social life and utilize it with a life spent in solitude and praise of God, then he will have more serenity, inner peace, and true happiness to himself and could then transfer this positive energy to people around him.

In view of the above discussion, it is to the interest of the Muslim to live each day as if it is his last. He should also avoid the gatherings of killers of time and utilize that time to seek knowledge and wisdom from spiritual scholars, and to engage in the praise of God. It is imperative, therefore, for the Muslim to redirect and/or channel his doubts through God for spiritual guidance and ultimate solution, for he is the sole provider of his daily sustenance. Once the Muslim has adopted this spiritual path to cleanse his soul, he should refrain from listening to idle mouths, avoid lingering with idle hands and bodies for the fear of God and the last day so that he can be successful. In fact, this spiritual path to cleanse the Muslim's soul will enable the mind to appropriate things and matters to their proper sizes. It will give him the wisdom to view his failures as part of the test of life, knowing full well that they will vanish in clouds of new dreams that bring joy and happiness. As for the Muslim, the tests of life are numerous and sometimes painful and distressful. But God is with those who are patient and can persevere to muster such difficult times in good faith and in consistency. In this regard, we can refer to the Quran when it explains:

So verily, with every difficulty, there is relief: Verily, with every difficulty there is relief. (Sura al-Inshirah 94:5-6)

Furthermore, Muslims who believe and fear Allah should make it a habit to read the Quran, but more so often especially in times of distress and difficulties so as to uplift their hearts and soul to find happiness and sanctuary in him who knows and sees all things. A path toward this direction during the Muslim's difficult moments is to go on repentance and conduct praises of Allah in solitude.

In fact, the abovementioned verses serve as a reminder to the Muslim that time changes everything, and any problems or challenges he is confronted with is bound to pass with time. Similarly, it is men with faith and wisdom who will acknowledge the reality that all worldly things shall indeed come to pass. Actually, people who believe in God and are rightful and fearful of His recompense will endeavor to refrain from evil deeds and sinful acts. Their fear of God and the day of reckoning are strong reminders to make them realize the fact that each day passing is taking them closer and closer to Allah, as explained in the preceding paragraphs. Complementary to this statement is the reality of the day of reckoning mentioned in the Quran when it states that "closer and closer to mankind comes their reckoning, yet they heed not and they turn away" (Sura al-Anbya: 21:1).

In subsection 4.2 we have discussed in detail about the day of reckoning. Therefore, we will only reiterate the fact that no matter how much man tries to ignore this reality it is inevitable that it will take place at an appointed day and time only known to Allah. Generally, man is in denial or often in doubt of the mysteries of the unknown. Usually, it takes men of faith who fear Allah and believe in Him to have the understanding that He created the heavens and the earth, including the angels, jinns, and the mysteries of the unknown. Ironically, it is a reality that one day God will end the creations the heavens and the earth, and on that day Allah reminds us in the Quran that mankind will be awake to account for his own deeds. However, the irony remains that man is not only in denial of God's creations but is in constant denial of his wrongful and sinful acts. The reason is because wrongful and sinful acts are shameful to its doer, especially in a society where moral values and ethical guidelines are established as part of the norms of the day. Generally, it is due to this reason, among other factors, that people who do wrong will often try to hide their negative deeds as a cover-up so that their actions are concealed to those close to him and society at large. Man's insidious nature dictates him to try and conceal the truth, forgetting that God is aware and knows (every) word (spoken) in the heavens and the earth. He is the almighty, the merciful. Furthermore, man's deeds are recorded by angels in the book of deeds for every living individual. In order to validate this statement, the Quran testifies that "for us will be their return, then it will be for us to call them to account" (Sura al-Gashiyah 88: 25-26).

In relation to man's accountability for the rights and wrongs he did in this world will be traumatic on that Day of Reckoning, for God has reminded him that not even an atom of his deeds will be left out. As we try to scrutinize the wisdom behind the individual fear of God and to submit to His will, the more we unveil evidence in the Quran that man's actions are propelled by the good and evil deeds he displays in his lifetime, of which God will use to decide his faith on the Day of Reckoning. In this regard, the Quran further explains:

> On that Day will men proceed in companies sorted out to be shown the Deeds that they (had done). Then shall anyone; who has done an atom's weight of good, see it. And anyone, who has done an atom's weight of evil, shall see it. (Sura az-Zalzalah99:6-8)

Generally speaking, man's insidious nature to cover up his sins and wrongful acts in a deceitful manner to mislead people is one thing, but his failure to acknowledge such kinds of acts and seek repentance from Allah is another thing. As for the Muslim, repentance, therefore, must emanate from within the heart, thereby empowering the inner conscience of his mind to first acknowledge the fact that a wrong and/or a sin has been committed by its doer. Once this acknowledgment is established, it is vital for him to seek forgiveness from both his victim and Allah, depending on the nature of circumstances which might dictate whether to restrict it to the former or the latter. Ironically, if due to pride or ignorance the Muslim fails as an individual to acknowledge his wrongs and/or sins and seek the appropriate type of forgiveness and repentance, it might lead him to the temptation of perpetually continuing to repeat the same mistakes or even engage in more erroneous and sinful acts. However, there is always a thin borderline between good and bad, and right and wrong to an extent that the moment the individual crosses any of these borderlines in a negative manner it will become apparent to him, either consciously or subconsciously, that he is in the transgression zone. The transgression of the individual, therefore, is due to his own deeds, arrogance, stubbornness, and insubordination against the prescribed guidelines and laws of Allah. The nature of such a transgression zone is not pleasing to Allah, but remains a breeding ground for Satan. The

Quran reminds mankind about the evil intentions and misleading whispers of Satan when it states:

> O you children of Adam: Let not Satan seduce you, in the same manner as he got your parents out of the Garden, stripping them of their raiment, to expose their shame, for he and his tribe watch you from a position where you cannot see them. We make the evil ones friends (only) to those without faith. (Sura al-A'raf 7:27)

The fact of the matter for which the Muslim should be aware of is to adhere to the above instruction of the Quran, as revealed in Sura an-Nahl, verses 98 to 100, in order to repel the temptations of Satan. This instruction is as crucial as a tool to combat the evil whispers of Satan, because when the Muslim deviates from God's path his alternative is to falter, transgress, and sin, all of which will make him fall into the trap of Satan. Actually, the Muslim should also take heed of Umar ibn Al-Khattab's (one of the rightly guided caliphs of Islam) way of deterring Satan. Once Satan is successful in making the Muslim commit a sin, the more likely it is for him to succumb to the whims and dictates of Satan to repeat the same type of sin. Moreover, Satan's objective is to distance the Muslim from his sole duties and responsibilities toward the fundamental pillars of Islam and join the ranks of those who go astray. The reason being that whatever God and His Messenger dislike for the Muslim to do, Satan will whisper the contrary to him in order to make him falter and sin. For instance, it is a fact that Satan will do his utmost best to make the Muslim miss or neglect his prayers, fasting, charity, humility, and every act of good intention or deed he has on his mind to submit to the will of Allah. Another example might be a circumstantial situation where the Muslim encounters a severe problem and/or disagreement with his fellow Muslim brother, family member, or friend and wants to reconcile with any one of these parties. Satan will work relentlessly to deter them from making peace. It is imperative, therefore, to note that such is the intention and power of Satan, which makes him an enemy not only to the believers but to mankind in general.

In order to continually refrain from such a transgression zone, the Muslim must be in a constant state of fearing Allah and fully submit to His will at all times. Actually, he can attain this kind of protection from Allah by fully adhering to the five fundamental pillars of Islam both in good times and during the times of trials, tribulations, and adversities, among other factors. Complementary to the adherence to the five pillars of Islam, the Muslim should also pray to Allah to help him remain humble through obstacles and failures, and guide him toward the straight path and to gain victory in all of his life's endeavors.

The reason for the Muslim to learn to stay humble and be consistent in his faith with Allah when faced with calamities is to reinforce his *iman* (faith in Allah). The Quran reminds of the kind of man whose comfort in Allah is realized when things are going well with him and feels distress and turns away from Him when calamities befalls him. God says:

> There are among men some who serve Allah, as it were, on the verge. If good befalls them, they are therewith, well content, but If a trial comes on them they turn on their faces; they lose both this world and the hereafter. That is loss for all to see (Sura Hajj 22:11)!

Due to the fact that man's modern way of life is grossly dominated by the social media activities engulfed with a lot of defaming, suspicion, and gossip, to say the least, the Quran reminds the believing Muslim to refrain from defaming, suspicion, and gossip among each other and mankind when it states:

> O you who believe: let not some men among you laugh at others. It may be that the (latter) are better than the (former). Nor let some women laugh at others. It may be that the (latter) are better than the (former). Nor defame nor be sarcastic to each other by (offensive) nicknames; ill-seeming is a name connoting wickedness (to be used of one) after he has believed, and those who do not desist are (indeed) doing wrong. (Sura al-Hujurat 49: 11)

In view of the foregoing discussion, it is imperative for the Muslim to venture and continually pray to Allah for his protection and guidance and to bless his words that they may bear fruits of truth and joy and to silence him from gossip. It is also ironic to see man's valuable time being dominated by the use of social media where parents don't even have time for each other, much less their children. It is sad to enter a household these days just to find each member of the family glued to his or her cell phone, distancing them from each other. To be more precise, the days when families used to sit together and discuss affairs that are beneficial to their welfare are gone and replaced by the escalation of modes of messaging through texting, tweets, and emails due to our addiction to the fast pace of electronic developments.

Nowadays, man is gradually losing the art of verbal communication, whereby we have developed the arrogance of impatience not to tolerate the indigenous and ancient art of dealing with each other. Rather, on the contrary, some people will abruptly close your verbal conversation with them and will request you to text, tweet, or email whatever you want to say to them, and they see these modes of communication as part of the norm of society without noticing the negative damage it is causing on human communication relationships. Based on my observation of some families and society in general, the current disintegration of the family is a reflection of some of the prevailing social turbulence we are witnessing in schools, communities, and society at large. For the discipline of the child should start at the home level where parents inculcate all of the basic moral and social values needed to make the child have a holistic view of his civic responsibilities, both at home and in his/her community.

The nature of this kind of discipline inculcated in the mind of the child will then eventually shape his/her moral and social behaviors at school and society at large. The Muslim, therefore, should also constantly pray for Allah to instill in him and his family the habit of engaging in regular prayers and to sing his praises collectively and in solitude.

Due to these temptations associated with some of the negative effects of social media and cellphone abuses, the Muslim parent should also pray and seek for Allah to favor him with alertness to recognize positive opportunities yet endow him with patience and consistency to concentrate his strength in doing right, refraining from all wrongful and sinful acts, and to guide him toward the straight path.

In view of the foregoing discussion, the bone of contention here is to acknowledge the fact that evil deeds, as my late father (Alhagi Nyang Njie) used to say, are often characterized by wrong, unjust, or unlawful behavior to an extent that the act itself is afraid of the doer. Consequently, it does imply that the act of each evil deed will instantly distance itself from the doer and deter him from rational thinking to acknowledge the reality of the prevailing situation. This kind of situation which impairs the effective rational thinking and behavior of the individual makes him continue to enjoy the predicament he is in, to an extent that he does not see the immediate repercussions of his evil deeds. Because of this lack of immediate repercussion, the individual is therefore enticed to follow the lust and desires of his *nafs* (soul), forgetting the fact that each repeated evil deed keeps piling up as a sinful act. Ironically, it is the pilling up of such evil deeds that will eventually accumulate as a force with an intention to destroy no one but the evildoer, and the nature of such act of destruction to the evildoer is linked to Allah's justice.

Apparently, my father's words of wisdom to me were so effective to the extent that they impacted me psychologically, to the point where I was afraid to do any form of evil deed to any person. My father's advice to me also serves as an indication of the traditional role parents could tale in disciplining their children.

I can vividly remember those moments that we shared as a family. They still linger in my mind, echoing reminders like the ticking of the clock for every second. The way my mom and dad raised us traditionally was in such a way that their modes of communication were not always verbal yet still their messages were always received and adhered to effectively and efficiently. For instance, while seated with them and a visitor come in the house, just by eye contact with either of them we, the kids, knew we needed to excuse them to have a private conversation with the guest. Actually, this mode of nonverbal type of communication was so effective during our childhood days until adulthood, but it is no longer in use due to the modernization of ways of raising our different families in the Gambia. Although this mode of traditional aspect of raising a family was effective, it was not devoid of the inculcation of religious Islamic teachings, which also were meant to educate the child at an early stage to acquire those moral and civic ethics that eventually lay the foundation of good character in his social development. Moreover, having parents educate, engage, and encourage their children in an interactive and conducive atmosphere is way better and more beneficial psychologically to both than the negative prevailing situation which prevails in some homes where the television and social media are distancing them more and more, with detrimental effects and consequences.

Apart from these words of wisdom that my father inculcated to our family, it is also of paramount importance for the Muslim to note that whatever kind of deeds he does, good or bad, Allah is still a witness to it, and will reward good deeds but will punish the individual for evil deeds. Therefore, man needs to acknowledge this fundamental basic fact of life that Allah's justice is strict but in favor of man, yet His grace is beyond calculation. For it is when man is faced with the wrath of Allah will he then come back to his senses and start to repent and ask for his forgiveness. As regards an individual who continually fails to desist from his wrongful deeds until faced with the wrath of Allah, the Quran explains

> *On no soul do we place a burden greater than it can bear: Before us is a record which clearly shows the truth: they will never be wronged. (Sura al-Mu'minun 32:62-67)*

Notwithstanding these two examples of evil doers, it is apparent that the former, who is ignorant of his sin and having acknowledged it seeks repentance, whereas the latter knowingly commits a sin and persistently keeps repeating it until Allah's wrath befalls him to account for his deeds and will groan in supplication for mercy. Furthermore, we can derive from these statements that for such evil doers their hearts are in confused ignorance of guidance compelling them to follow their lust and desires until they meet up with the punishment or wrath of Allah. However, the Muslim should also bear in mind that even those believing servants who have received the good things from God should know that they will be tested. However, when such periods of trials and tribulations arise they need to exercise patience, consistency in their belief in God, and should not be the type who will groan in supplication like the evil doers. Rather, they should engage in praise of their Lord, keep steadfast in their prayers, and also seek repentance and forgiveness for their shortcomings, knowing that after every hardship there will be ease. It is this kind of attitude that a believing servant should adopt when faced with trials and tribulations.

Another example relates to the kind of people who fail to acknowledge the signs of Allah as guidance and the truth until they are faced with their Lord and want to cry and bargain for another worldly chance to repent and do good deeds. In fact, the Quran reminds us of people of this caliber. Their soul will say:

> If only Allah had guided me, I should certainly have been among the righteous." Or (least) it should say when it (actually) sees the penalty: "If only I had another chance, I should certainly be among those who do good deeds!" (The reply will be), "Nay, but there came to thee my signs, and thou didst reject them: though wast haughty, and became one of those who reject Faith." (Surar 39: 57-59)

Regarding the first sentence, we might be inclined to say, "I wish I had received warning or guidance." But this would not be true, because the warning and the guidance are being conveyed in the cleanest manner in God's revelations. However, it is also anticipated here that there is the call to repent and the warning about the hereafter. The rest of the following statements imply that when we stand face to face with the penalty of our own deeds we might say, "I wish I had another chance." But not one but many chances are being given, especially when we are told that when a servant transgressed against his soul despair not of the mercy of Allah: for Allah forgives all sins, for he is oft-forgiving, most merciful.

Due to the fact that man is infallible, weak, fragile, and liable to transgress and make mistakes, God made sets of guidelines, rules, and procedures in the Quran to warn and guide mankind for his own benefit and prosperity. Hence, the very reason why God, because of his grace and mercy, sends warners to various generations to desist from their sins and wrongful acts, seek repentance, and change if possible. However, God does send his wrath in the event that man remains in denial and in subordination to his signs. We have discussed this issue extensively in chapter 3.5 to 3.7.

The reality, therefore, is for man to utilize his inner conscience to evaluate his motives of right and wrong deeds pertaining to his daily life pursuits. Pertaining to this statement, the author is of the belief that conscience is that inner compass which guides man to discern and recognize right from wrong, and always warns him to adhere to what is right and abstain from engaging in wrong deeds. This reality is based on the fact that man is the author of his own character, and it is his character that shapes him as an individual. The shaping of one's character should be a vital prerequisite of every Muslim. The reason being that every believing Muslim should make a great deal of effort to emulate Prophet Muhammad (saw), whom God praised extensively based on his noble and unique character beyond all of mankind. The confirmation of his noble and unique character is revealed in the Quran when it states:

> And verily for you (Muhammad) is a reward unfailing: And you (standest) on an exalted standard of character. (Sura Al-Qalam 68:4)

Furthermore, the positive and unique manner in which the Prophet always conducts himself throughout his life's endeavors is revealed in the Quran when God says:

Indeed in the Messenger of Allah you have the most beautiful pattern of conduct. (Sura Al-Ahzab 33.21)

Due to the exemplary character of Prophet Muhammad, his fear of Allah, his worship, the revelations to his people, the disbelievers, and mankind in general, was pertinent during his time and above all still relevant to our times. Hence, his advice to Muslims during his last farewell *khutbah* in Mecca remains a manifestation of one of his prophecy when Allah revealed to him the following:

> *"This day have I perfected your religion for you, completed my grace upon you, and have chosen Islam for you as your religion." The Prophet then proceeded and says, "People! No prophet or apostle will come after me, and no new faith will be born. Reason well, therefore, O people! And understand words which I convey to you.* I leave behind me two things, the Quran and my example, the Sunnah, and if you follow these you will never go astray." (Reference: islamreligion.com)

The Prophet's farewell *khutbah* was in 10 AH, during the *Hajj* of the year 632 CE, the ninth day of Dhul-Hijjah, the twelfth month of the lunar year, at Arafat, the most blessed day of the Muslim year.

The fact of the matter is that we should pause for a while, ponder, reason, and try to comprehend the two vital things that Prophet Muhammad left for Muslims (the Quran and the Sunnah) and guaranteed that those who adhere to it will never go astray. Moreover, not only was he sent to Muslims but to all of mankind. Relative to this fact, the Quran revealed:

> *We sent thee not, but as a mercy for all creatures. (Sura al-Anbya 21: 107).*

Actually, Muslims have also been warned explicitly by Prophet Muhammad in his last *khutbah* in Mecca that "no prophet or apostle will come after him." Therefore, Muslims are lucky to have witnessed the last vital message of guidance to his audience at that time in Mecca.

The crux of the matter, therefore, is for Muslims to adhere to the revelations of the Quran and the practices of the Prophet (his Sunnah). Apparently, Muslims who abide by these dual applications (Quran and the Sunnah) as a means to sincerely worship Allah are on the right path of guidance. However, there are also among them some Muslims who downplay the Sunnah of the Messenger of Allah and don't practice it at all. This latter category of Muslims needs to be reminded of the fact that Allah created man first to worship Him and second to serve as His vicegerent on earth.

> According *to the Random House Webster's School and Office Dictionary (2001), the word* vicegerent *could be interpreted in twofold: (i) a deputy to a sovereign and (ii) a deputy to a magistrate.*

In view of the foregoing discussion, we can then say that when God created the first man Adam He wanted him and all of the children of Adam to be his vicegerent on earth. The crux of the matter, therefore, is for man to try and understand some of the salient factors about who is God, what are His signs, attributes and above all, the conditions that He commanded man to adhere to as His Vicegerent on earth? In relation to such conditions, we have in chapter 3.5 explained God's divine wisdom on His prophets and their warnings to the communities and people that they were sent, such as Abraham, Lot, and Salih. We have also explained in the same chapter how God's Wrath is imposed on those communities and people who failed to take heed of their prophet's warnings. We have also explained in subsection 2.3 that a Muslim is one who submits to the will of Allah and must adhere to the teachings of the Quran and that of the Sunnah of the Prophet Muhammad (saw). Similarly, in subsection 3.1 we discussed the divine wisdom of Allah; the wisdom in the Quran; His many names and attributes, such as Allah the All Knowing, Sole Creator of the Heavens, the Earth, and All Therein, the All Wise, the Merciful; and how He created man first from dust, and in subsection 4.2, from a drop of sperm in our mother's wombs.

The mere fact that God and all of His creations prevail in a pure state of existence warrants for man, as His vicegerent on earth, to harness this purity and to try and preserve it at all times. In this regard, the Quran states that "the Lord has decreed that ye worship none but Him" (Sura Bani Israil 17:23).

As far as the Muslim is concern, the way to preserve this purity is through Islamic practices as revealed to the Holy Prophet Muhammad, constituting the Quran and his way of life (the Sunnah). But what is Islam? First of all, it is imperative at this juncture to refer to the Prophet's last *khutbah* in Mecca as discussed in the preceding paragraphs of this chapter. When he neared the summit of Arafat came the revelation from God, which he delivered and said, "This day have I perfected your religion for you, completed my grace upon you, and have chosen Islam for you as your religion" (Sura al-Maidah 5:3).

This proclamation by the prophet sets the legitimacy of Islam as a religion for Muslims to follow and practice as a way of life. Furthermore, in an effort to clarify what Islam entails, Dr. Muhammed Al-Hashimi (2005) contends that "Islam, being a complete code of life, encompasses all aspects of human life and guides mankind to the path of success here and in the hereafter."

In another explanation about what Islam is about, Abdul Rashid Architect in his book *Deeni Ma'lu'mat, Religious Knowledge* (2013) explained that

> Islam *is an Arabic word which means obedience and peace. Islam thus means complete submission to the will of God and to be at peace with all the creations of God. In other words, the fundamental purpose of Islam is to bring back mankind to its creator and to improve the quality of human relationships. Islam emphasizes that men and women are equal before Allah and only righteous deeds elevate one person above the other. Islam reinforces the concept of humanity and respect for individual liberty. It also reminds man of his fundamental right of being free to choose his religion. It is clearly stated in the Holy Quran that there is no compulsion in religion.*

Having given some definitions of what Islam means, it is also vital to understand its proclamation as a religion. To begin with, let us ask the question, what is religion? In order to answer this question, we will refer to Abdul Rashid Architect (2013) when he explained that "religion is a divine system of worship to establish a relationship with Allah (God), and rules of conduct that enable human beings to achieve and lead a peaceful life."

Islam, however, is a universal religion and stands as one of the most predominant religions in the world. Today, we are witnessing people entering the religion of Islam in vast numbers. In fact, witnessing the massive number of people embracing Islam is nothing strange but rather the fulfillment of God's revelation, which is manifested in the Quran when He says: "When comes the help of Allah, and victory. And thou dost see the people enter Allah's religion in crowds. Celebrate the praises of thy Lord and pray for His forgiveness: for He is oft-returning (in grace and mercy)" (Sura an-Nasr 110: 1-3).

Another vital testimony as regards Islam is the fact that as a religion its vibrant teachings remain as relevant today as they were during the lifetime of Prophet Muhammad (saw), which has touched and influenced the hearts and minds of so many, thereby making it a universal religion.

In view of the above proclamation (in Sura an-Nasr verses 1–3) by Allah, reminding mankind of the inevitable spread of Islam, it serves as a stern testimony that His words pertaining to the Quran and Prophet Muhammad left for Muslims as his Sunnah are true Islamic directives and/or revelations from Allah.

Based on the abovementioned facts from the Quran, there is ample evidence that Prophet Muhammad was instructed by God through divine revelations to explain the Quran to his people and mankind in general, having brought adequate evidence from the Quran that Muslims must first submit to the will of Allah, comply with the revelations of the Quran and that of the Sunnah of Prophet Mohummad.

Frankly speaking, I just don't understand the reason why some Muslims are reluctant or in denial of and disobedience to the practice of the Sunnah of Prophet Muhammad. However, I do believe that

Muslims should adhere to the two recommended things (the Quran and the Sunnah) that the Prophet said, *"whoever follows it will not go astray"*; in order words, it will help Muslims to adhere to the straight path and to continually purify their own souls.

Ironically, I do believe that those Muslims who are in disobedience with this crucial statement and reminder of the Prophet's last *khutbah* during *Hajj* in Mecca are also disobeying God's revelations, who inspired him to proclaimed Islam as a practicing religion for Muslims. In addition to the abovementioned obligatory warning by Allah to believers, the Quran further states: "It is not fitting for a believer, man or woman, when a matter has been decreed by Allah and His Messenger to have any choice in the matter. If anyone disobeys Allah and His Messenger, he is clearly astray and/or on the wrong path" (Sura Al-Ahzab 33: 36).

The bone of contention regarding the foregoing statements is the fact that when Allah and his Messenger decree something for mankind then there is always a benefitting factor(s), even if not realized by the individual(s). In addition to this statement are the numerous benefits rewarded both in this world and that of the hereafter for those righteous Muslims who obey Allah and his Messenger. Muslims, therefore, should take heed of the importance and purpose of life, which so often man tends to attribute to the deceiving nature of materialism, such as the accumulation of wealth, luxury items such as cars, houses, jewelry, to name a few. In fact, Allah did remind us of the greed and lust that man has attached to materialism and the accumulation of wealth when the Quran states that "the mutual rivalry for piling up (the good things of this world) diverts you (from the more serious things) until you visit the graves. But nay, you soon shall know (the reality)" (Sura at-Takathur 102: 1-3).

Similarly, some of the other things of this world which divert us from attending to matters of more serious concern are also associated with man's quest for fame, leadership, power, and blameworthy knowledge (such as the science of magic and talismans), all of which are also things that the *nafs* (soul) yearns for in so many ways. These temptations of the *nafs*, among other things, had led many, ranging from man's past generation up till now, to falter and go astray. As regards the righteous Muslim who obeys Allah, Dr. Ali Muhammad M. As-Sallaabee (2010) contends the following:

> *One day, Umar ibn Al-Khattab said to his companions, "Wish for something." One of them said, "I wish that this house was filled with gold so that I could then spend it all in the way of Allah and on charitable causes." Another man said, "I wish that it was filled with precious gems and jewels so that I could then spend it all in the way of Allah and on charitable causes."*

The abovementioned narration about Umar revealed that his distinctive spiritual values differ greatly from his companions whose intentions were to spend in the way of Allah. The nature of his difference was manifested after Umar attentively listened to them and finally asked the same question: "Wish for something." And his companions reply, "We do not know what to wish for again, O leader of the believers." Umar then said, "I wish that this house was filled with the likes of Abu Ubaydah ibn al-Jarah, Mu'adh ibn Jabal, Saalim the freed slave of Abu Hudhaifah, and Hudhayfah ibn al-Yaman, so that I can use them for the obedience of Allah (i.e., so that I can make use of their time, talent, abilities, and strengths in order to further the cause of Islam)." In the case of his companions, their intentions were good, for they would have loved to get a house full of gold, precious gems, and jewels which they will spend in the cause of Allah and on charitable causes of which they will get the rewards of their good deeds. Umar's intention has a much wider dimension due to the fact that as much as he will be rewarded by Allah for using his strength, talent, abilities, time, wisdom, he was cognizant of the belief that a much greater reward from Allah awaits him by guiding his companions to work together with him to spread Islam. He knew that this kind of joint effort together with that of his companions will yield a multiplier effect of promoting Islam as a religion, and has much greater benefits and rewards. What a genius and effective leader Umar was. In fact, another gist of the above narration depicts that he was a democratic type of leader who was charismatic, led his people by example, and above all showed them that his commitment to love and sacrifice for the love and sake of Allah to propagate Islam was a paramount factor as a believer.

Actually, these character traits exhibited by Umar should remind us of the fact that he and the other three *sahabas* Abu Bakr, Uthman, and Ali were the top companions and followers of Prophet Muhammad, who was their mentor in Islam. Actually, Prophet Mohammed's noble character was unique among mankind, and we discuss it in the latter part of chapter 8. Among these virtues is the magnanimity of his character, and his love for mankind was fully recognized even in his lifetime, and his name stands highest among the heroic leaders of mankind. Therefore, in view of this statement, it is blatantly clear that the Quran has manifested that the magnanimity of the character of Prophet Muhammad (saw) has remained as a model for the rest of mankind. Apart from this fact, which should have been the perfect template for both individuals and leaders to follow, rather it is ironical to acknowledge the reality of a world dominated by greed, materialism, anger, jealousy, hatred fueled by factors such as politics, religion, racial and national identity differences, to name a few. On top of these factors, and based on my experiences of the world that we inhabit, there still exist among mankind some who are prone to succumb to the lust of this *dunyah* (world) and that of its temptations and desires for wealth, power, and authority domination.

Relative to the above narration, we also gave an example of a believer like Umar ibn Al-Khattab as a leader who was just, served his people with love and fear of Allah, and was completely the opposite of other notorious leaders such as the likes of Pharaoh and Thamud, whose lust for fame, greed, and power led to their divine destruction, including their armies and/or followers.

Contrary to those who had power and abused it, such as Pharaoh and Thamud, are constant reminders to mankind that God doesn't like leaders who oppress the people of the land. Rather, God favors leaders who are just and righteous and not greedy such as the likes of Pharaoh and Thamud. We are reminded in Sura at-Takathur verses 1–2 that "mankind is engaged in mutual rivalry for piling up (the good things of this world) which diverts us (from the more serious things); until we visit the graves."

In addition to these factors which the *nafs* yearns for, man is also addicted to status, prestige, and power and their related evils, which has often led man to even kill, harass, belittle, and castrate his fellow human being without any regret or remorse just for the love of this world (*dunyah*), which is very misleading and short-lived. The irony is that some of today's parents who are descendants of past generations who believed in the Abrahamic faiths (Jews, Christians, and Muslims) haven't succeeded in the inculcation of those civic, moral, ethical, and religious disciplines and practices that govern the core elements of the oneness (*tawheed*) of God. In view of these harsh realities of the world that we live in, coupled with the author's long periods of stay in Africa, Germany, England, and America, a lot of families today just bear the symbolic names of these religions as Jews, Christians, and Muslims but are not actually practicing the norms and values of their respective religions.

Another factor associated with this argument lies in the fact that in all of the books of these Abrahamic faiths we are reminded that when societies in the past were spiritually ignorant of the divine revelations of God it tends to make them follow their own lust and desires, thereby ignoring what their prophet of that time told them about God. We have discussed adequately in this book how when such group of people failed to take heed they were subjected to either punishment or destruction through natural disasters. In this regard, those who repented, embraced the way of God, and stayed righteous were forgiven.

Based on the foregoing example, it is imperative that we draw some correlation with these kinds of societies that prevailed in the past and see if we in today's societies, be it in developed or developing countries and irrespective of one's faith, be it Jews, Christians, or Muslims, lies the reality that the children of Adam are invoking the same cry of sufferings and insecurity among other factors. Sometimes, it is the mode of suffering and its magnitude that varies, such earthquakes, tsunamis, volcanic eruptions, wildfires, indiscriminate mass killings, terrorism, genocide, poverty, malnutrition, and the persistent pattern of slavery in Libya, among other factors. The continued arrogance and power dominance of man tends to make him feel that he is in control and can exploit, oppress, and manipulate his fellow human beings without justice and accountability for his deeds in the hereafter. Relative to this statement, mankind is being reminded in the Quran of our vulnerability on the planet that we are systematically eroding, together with other serious mischief as explained above. The Quran gave us a warning of how abruptly God can end the earth and the universe when it reveals that

> *it will be no more than a single blast, when lo! They(mankind) will all be brought up before us. (Sura Ya-Sin 36:53)*

The bone of contention here is to acknowledge the fact that there are ample reminders in the Quran about the futility of the negative pleasures and material gains of this world, and their palpability and insignificance in some cases (except those that are spiritual as ordained by God) diverts man away from the worship of God and remaining righteous. In relation to the futile nature and how short-lived man's life is in this *dunyah* (world), which he takes for granted as a lasting phenomenon until death takes him by surprise. However, the futile nature of this life depicts both the similitude and vulnerability of man's naivety, who is tempted to disregard how palpable and insignificant the realities of this material world that we adore and yearn for so desperately is in reality illusive, highly deceptive, and doesn't guarantee any individual his existence on earth within the next second. Yet, with all of our wits and intelligence, our pride, coupled with our arrogance, tends to exacerbate our ego, emotions, and greed, which acts as a bath that intoxicates our souls which yearns for evil to succumb to the path of wrongful and immoral behaviors which are outwardly manifested in physical manner as a form of sin or transgression against our fellow human beings. The Quran drew our attention to man's existence on earth when it contends:

Set forth to them (mankind) the similitude of the life of this world: it is like the rain which we send down from the skies: The earth's vegetation absorbs it, but soon it becomes dry stubble, which the winds do scatter: it is (only) Allah who prevails over all things. (Sura al-Kahf 18:45)

The similitude of the above-stated reality is an example of the vulnerability of our existence on planet Earth if we divert our attentions to the love of this *dunyah* instead of submitting to the will of Allah as the main purpose of life. Henceforth, man is only left to carry with him to the grave the deeds of his lifetime, be it good, bad, or evil. Moreover, spiritual reminders of this nature are difficult to grasp for some people for it deals with both the *nafs* (desires of the soul) and the hereafter. But it is vital to emphasize the fact that Allah does guide whom He wills, and whomever Allah guided will be endowed with relevant understanding and wisdom to distinguish right from wrong in order not to go astray.

Following the narrative of these discussions, the Muslim who fears Allah and submits to His will must strive to comply with the teachings of both the Quran and the Sunnah of the Prophet Muhammad (saw) in order to stay on the straight path and be righteous in his deeds. However, Muslims of this category may have the intention to always engage in righteous deeds but if their love for Allah is at a low ebb and their deeds are not for the sake of Allah, they may one day fall into the trap of Satan and falter.

In order to try and bring to light the various categories of Muslims that prevail within the domain of Islam, we will make efforts to summarize each of the four categories of Muslims and/or believers in relation to Islamic principles and practices in their efforts to seek Allah's rewards. These categories of Muslims are different from the two types that were discussed in the preceding chapter. Because of this, we will now proceed to explain these categories based on the standard Islamic nomenclature.

First among these types is a Muslim who is a believer and acts upon the pillars of Islam but at the same time is neglectful of many commands such as to abstain from alcohol, smoking, lying, backbiting, and definitely is not committing any acts from *shirk*. *The second type* is a *mu'min*: a believer who is aware that Allah is watching and does everything for fear of punishment. He strives to abstain from all kinds of sin for the sake of being saved from hellfire. *The third type* is a *muttagi*, a believer who does everything for the sake of satisfying Allah. That is, this type of believer has crossed the level of a *mu'min* and now follows Islam not just for the fear of Allah but to satisfy Allah. *The fourth type* is a *muhsin*: the highest level of believer, who does everything for the Love of Allah. He not just follows Islam for fear or only to satisfy the principles and conditions attached, but has become a pure lover of Allah. However, it is worthy of note that apart from these four types of Muslims there also exist those special favored class of Muslims referred to as *muqarribun* (those nearest to Allah).

We have discussed in this chapter why the Muslim should submit to the will of God, fear Him as He is the all-knowing and seeing, and venture to do good at all times and refrain from sinful, evil, and wrong deeds. Furthermore, the Muslim should venture to be among the category of the *muhsin* or those of the *muqarribun* (those close to Allah). In order to attain any of these two levels just for the fear and love of Allah, the Muslim needs to understand that the ultimate purpose of life is to be among those righteous souls whom God will be well pleased to welcome to His haven. The validity of this argument is manifested in the Quran as a reminder to mankind when in the Day of Judgment God reveals:

> To the righteous soul will be said: "O (thou) soul, in (complete) rest and satisfaction! Come back thou to thy Lord. Well pleased (thyself), and well-pleasing unto Him! Enter thou, then, among my devotees! Yes, enter thou my heaven." (Sura al-Fajr 35: 27-30)

On the contrary, the evildoers, those who followed the pleasures of their *nafs* (soul) and the life of this world in sins and transgressions beyond bounds, without repentance, and failed to cleanse their souls while they were alive will now regret and wish they could be sent back to earth to rectify their wrongs, but to no avail. The Quran does explain how gracious and merciful God is, and how He gave those who transgress a chance to repent for the forgiveness of their sins. In relation to this fact, the Quran reveals that "God is the one that accepts repentance from His servants and forgives sins: And He knows all that you do" (Sura Ash-Shura 42:25).

However, those who failed to repent for their transgressions, evil deeds, and sins until death approaches them will then have to account for their wrongful deeds. In this regard, the Quran testifies: "And if any do evil, their faces will be thrown headlong into the Fire: 'Do ye receive a reward other than which ye have earned by your deeds' (Sura an-Nami 27: 90)?"

The abovementioned verse should serve as a stern reminder for mankind to take heed of the punishment that awaits the evildoers and to understand that each will be judged and rewarded or punished according to his/her own deeds in this life. As for the Muslim, his success in this life is based on submitting to the will of Allah, following the guidance of the Sunnah of the Prophet Muhammad (saw), doing good deeds, staying righteous in order that he may have the mercy and reward of Allah both in this world and the hereafter. The bone of contention in trying to attain a model concept that will keep the Muslim out of mischief and other temptation of this life is not an easy task, and could be fraught with difficulties. However, based on the teachings of my beloved Sheikh Harun Fye Al-Faqir of Senegal, us as his students should try and adhere to the simple triangle model based on home, work, and *masjid* (mosque) in order to keep out of mischief. The adherence of this model would imply that first the Muslim will be devoted to spending time with his family and to sharing with them their individual concerns, assisting in the household chores each according to his assigned responsibilities. It should be the responsibility of the head of the family to inculcate the adherence of the social and ethical norms and values of Islam such as learning the Quran and the Sunnah and other related issues. Second, the Muslim should learn to be a productive member of society and must not be complacent to depending on food stamps. Attitude that invites laziness must be avoided and not tolerated, for it is an invitation to the dependency syndrome which will have very serious social and financial consequences for self and family. The Muslim must also strive to attain the best education in order to be among the professional category of the workforce. Also, when at work, he should give out the best of his skills, knowledge, and attitude. As regards attitude toward work, he must respect the agreed upon employer/employee contract based on labor laws of the state or country he is in. He must not develop the bad habit of killing or wasting time such as staying long periods of time in the restrooms. Finally, he must be responsible for completing his given assignments on time. The third relates to the Muslim's relationship with the *masjid* (mosque) he belongs to or the one closest to his residence or that of his choice. His first obligation is to ensure that he performs all of his five daily prayers at the mosque, ranging from *fajr* (early morning), *zoor* (noon), *asr* (late evening), *maghrib* (sunset), and *isha* (late evening) prayers. However, he should try by all means not to miss the *fajr*, *maghrib*, and *Jumma* (Friday) prayers. He also needs to be fully responsive to the needs of the mosque, as well as that of the community.

Based on the author's personal observation of prevailing live circumstances of society in general, we can give an example of some of those neglected victims of drug and/or alcohol abuse who might be good people in nature but may lack the right kind of guidance or willpower to combat their own lust and desires of this *dunyah* (world). Other influences are sometimes due to bad peer-group influences or being carried away by the temptations of the whispers of Satan. However, a way for such people to combat and abstain from their wrongful deeds, bad peer-group influences, and the whispers of Satan is for them to instill the fear of Allah in their hearts, seek spiritual guidance, knowledge, and wisdom that will eradicate their addictive habits and make them find sanctuary in a well-balanced social and moral spiritual way of life. The spiritual way of life to Islam is a choice that the individual needs to rationalize and ponder upon in order to voluntarily embrace it as a religion. Actually, Islam has the capacity and/ or potential to positively change the individual from his old and bad practices (of wrongful deeds) and make him cling on to a new way of spiritual life (of righteousness) that will bring him closer to Allah. In other words, what is implied here is that man should endeavor to refrain from those kinds of wrongful deeds and temptations that could lead him to instances where he will be carried away by the lust of this *dunyah* (world) to an extent that he becomes inept to seeking knowledge and/or wisdom that will lead him closer to Allah and His creations. The fact of the matter is based on the premise that man's close connection and/or affinity with Allah will purify his heart from the temptations of Satan and his lust and evil desires of this *dunyah* (world).

The Muslim also needs to acknowledge the reality that knowledge seeking, especially spiritual knowledge, is a prerequisite of the believer whose intention is to attain the affinity and love of Allah. The basis of this reality is revealed in the book of truth, guidance, and wisdom, as was God's advice to the Prophet when the suras of the Quran were being gradually revealed to him through Angel Gabriel. This advice was necessary due to the fact that it is part of man's nature that he was created in haste, which is adequately addressed in the Quran, which states: "High above all is Allah, the King, and the Truth! Be not in haste with the Quran before its revelation to thee is completed, but say, my Lord! Advance me in knowledge" (Sura Ta-Ha 20:114).

Another indication that does point to man's quest to attain spiritual knowledge is according to Dr. Ali Mohammed M. As-Sallaabee (2010), who explained the following:

> The Messenger of Allah used to make the undermentioned supplications. "O Allah, I seek refuge in you from knowledge that does not benefit, from a heart that is not fearful (of you), from a soul that does not become full (or satisfied but instead continuous always to chase after its desires), and from a supplication that is not answered."

It is in view of the abovementioned facts that the commentary notes of the Quran for Sura Ta-Ha verse 114 above, C3639, elaborated on the issue of knowledge that God is above every human event or desire. His purpose is universal. But He is the truth, the absolute truth, and His kingdom is the true kingdom that can carry out its will. That truth unfolds itself gradually, as it did in the gradual revelation of the Quran to the Holy Apostle. But even after it was completed in a volume, its true meaning and purpose only gradually unfolded themselves to any given individual or nation. No one should be impatient about it. On the contrary, we should always pray for increase in our own knowledge, which can never, at any given moment, be complete.

Furthermore, the Muslim should acknowledge the fact that spiritual knowledge supported by fear of Allah remains among those very strong foundations to strengthen faith, as ignorance is a vehicle to disbelief. The nature of this fact should be a vital tool to divulge the Muslim in accepting the reality that understanding the difference between knowledge and disbelief lies the foundation of wisdom. Relative to this fact is for the Muslim to also comprehend the reality that knowledge and disbelief are opposites in that knowledge accompanies faith, just as ignorance accompanies disbelief. It is crucial, therefore, for the Muslim to endeavor to acquire some knowledge and basic concept of understanding of the Quran depending on how much he can absorb out of this divine book of God when he says, "Say! Are those who know equal to those who know not? It is only men of understanding who will remember (i.e., get a lesson from Allah's signs and verses)" (Sura az-Zumar 39:9).

However, when it comes to the clarification about knowledge and the tendency for part of it to be rendered blameworthy, Imam Al-Gazzali (Ra), (2008) contends that "could a thing be knowledge and at the same time be blameworthy?" Be advised then that knowledge is not held to be blameworthy in itself. It is only regarded as such in the eyes of men for the following reasons, such as when it leads to any harm that should befall its practicer or someone else besides, for which reason the science of magic and talismans is held blameworthy. Relative to this argument which might be a controversial issue, should not restrict the Muslim to adhere to the Quranic explanation that "your Guardian Lord is Allah, who created the heavens and the earth in six days, and is firmly established on the throne (of authority); He draweth the night as veil over the day, each seeking the other in rapid succession. He created the sun, the moon, and the stars, (all) governed by laws under

OMAR NJIE

His command. Is it not His to create and to govern? Blessed be Allah, the Cherisher and Sustainer of the Worlds (Sura A'raf 7:54)!"

Complementary to these references, it is vital for the Muslim to *first* acknowledge some of these basic underlying facts from both suras Rahman and A'rafthat the laws governing the rotations of the sun, moon, and stars are computed subject to their reckoning under the commandment of God the Almighty. Secondly, he needs to understand the notion that part of astrology is purely guesswork, and in the opinion of the average man the influence of the stars is not determined either with certainty or even with probability.

The third validating factor in this regard is for the Muslim to realize the fact that in the pursuit of knowledge there are various branches, and for those kinds that may be pronounced blameworthy is when the pursuit of that kind of knowledge does not give the practicer any real scientific advantage; consequently, such knowledge is intrinsically blameworthy.

In view of the foregoing discussion, it is imperative to remind mankind of these kinds of scientific and technological rat race or rivalry that has bred jealousy, envy, greed, ignorance due to brainwashing or ill-informed and hatred all of which are diseases of the heart and could be cured through spiritual healing of the soul and/or *nafs*. In relation to this material rivalry, the Quran contends:

> *The mutual rivalry for piling up (the good things of this world) diverts you (from the more serious things); until you visit the graves. (Sura at-Takathur 102:1-2)*

In view of the foregoing, we have discussed how God has promised to reward those who believe, submit to His will, and practice good deeds by letting them enter His paradise. On the contrary, we have also explained how God, with His infinite grace and mercy, allows those who transgress and commit sins to repent and seek His forgiveness, and for which failure to do so they will be punished in the hellfire. It is these crucial aspects of good deeds and bad deeds accompanied by their respective and appropriate rewards that will lead us to discuss in chapter 5 the wisdom, merits, and blessings associated with repentance (*tawbah*).

CHAPTER 5.0

The Wisdom of Tawbah (Repentance), Its Merits and Blessings

ACCORDING TO THE Random House Webster's School and Office Dictionary (2001), the meaning of *repent* is explained as follows:

> *Firstly, the individual should have a feeling of contrite regret. Secondly, the individual needs to be penitent and determined to change for the better.*

The former implies that the individual has to show a sincere remorse or regret for the wrong he committed. In the case of the latter, the individual has to manifest a feeling of sorrow for the sin or wrongdoing and should be disposed to atonement. According to zawaf.com:

> *Tawbah is an Arabic word derived from the origin "Taaba," meaning returned back. Tawbah thus means turning back in repentance. It also means showing regret for the error and sin that the individual has got himself involved in.*

As for the Muslim who transgress and commits a sin, he must psychologically acknowledge that by doing wrong he has wronged his own soul and his act is displeasing to Allah (God). He must then show sincere remorse, a feeling of sorrow, and an intention to atone for the sin that he committed. He should then cast his mind back that as a Muslim he did vow to submit to the will of Allah, venture to have an adequate understanding of the Quran, follow the Sunnah of the Prophet, followed by the prescribed five daily prayers, among other factors. He should then reaffirm his faith in God and acknowledge the fact that those who do wrong are among the victims of Satan, for Allah dislikes those who manifest anger, impatience, transgression, do wrong or evil. Even when the Muslim finds himself under any of these kinds of circumstances, his moral duty is to continually ask for Allah's guidance and protection from the temptations of Satan. For instance, God reminds us in the Quran about Prophet Jonah who was sent to the people of Nineveh in the land of Mosul. He called them to the way of Allah but they rejected his call and disbelieved him. After a long time passed, he fled from among them and threatened them with divine punishment after three days. However, Ibn Kathir (2003) explained that "after Jonah fled from his people in anger and rage, they became certain that the punishment was imminent, to be inflicted upon them at any time, so they repented from their sins and showed their regret about the way they dealt with their Prophet." In fact, the Quran has also manifested this statement when it says:

> Why was there not a single township (among those we warned) which believed so its faith should have profited it except the people of Jonah? When they believed, we removed from them the penalty of ignominy in the life of the present, and permitted them to enjoy (their life) for a while. (Sura Yunus 10:98)

As regards "it was when Jonah fled to the laden ship that he (agreed to) cast lots and he was of the losers. Then the whale swallowed him, and he was blameworthy. Had he not been of those who glorify God, he would certainly have stayed in its belly until the Day of Resurrection" (Sura as-Saffat verses 142–144). Actually, the case of Jonah and his people confirms our statement above that the believing Muslim, after acknowledging the fact that he has transgressed, done wrong, or committed a sin, then it is his duty to repent and seek Allah's forgiveness. We have seen how both Jonah and his people repented for their wrongs and benefitted from the mercy and forgiveness of Allah. In the case of

Jonah, God reminded us in the abovementioned Sura (Saffat: 37:142 to 144) that first he was blameworthy and after he realized it he glorified God and sought His mercy and forgiveness. Apparently, the manner in which Jonah glorified his Lord is explained in the Quran when it states:

> And remember Zun-Nun (Jonah) when he departed in anger (wrath): He imagined that we had no power over him! But he called out through the depths of darkness, "There is no god (worthy of worship) but you; Glory be to you! I was indeed wrong (Sura-Anbya 21: 87-88)!"

The Muslim is reminded by God in numerous suras and verses of the Quran to try and reflect on and understand its messages so that he may derive wisdom from it. In this regard the Quran states that "ALA-these are the symbols (or verses) of the perspicuous Book. We have sent it down as an Arabic Quran, in order that ye may learn wisdom" (Sura Yusuf 12: 1-2).

The wisdom in the Quran which teaches the Muslim to turn to God when he is in distress due to his own transgression, wrongdoings and sins, just like the way Jonah turned to God for repentance, which was immediately accepted. Another example of this kind happened to Prophet Job when the Quran revealed the following:

> And (remember) Job, when he cried to his Lord, 'truly distress has seized me,' but thou art the most merciful of those that are merciful.' So we listened to him; we removed the distress that was on him, and we restored his people to him and doubled their number as a grace from ourselves and a thing for commemoration for all who serve us. (Suraal-Anbya 21: 83-84)

These two examples of Jonah and Job are marvelous testimonies of the fact that when the believing Muslim is in distress or has transgressed and sincerely seeks repentance from Allah, He does listen to him and responds appropriately. Indeed, the Quran explicitly reminds us of this fact when Allah says: "When My servants ask thee concerning me, I am indeed close (to them). I listen to the prayer of every supplicant when he calls on me. Let them also, with a will, listen to my call and believe in me that they may walk in the right way" (Sura Al-Baqarah 2:186).

This verse of the Quran is a powerful reminder and a reaffirmation of one of Allah's modes of communication with His servants. It also reinforces the fact that He is the ultimate who hears, sees, and knows everything that prevails both on earth and in the universe. Moreover, God is sending a reminder to His servants that He answers to all of their prayers and supplications. Apparently, on top of all of these modes of communication between God and His servants, interestingly enough He is also appealing for His servants to listen to His call with a will and to believe in Him so that they may stay on the course of the straight path. In fact, as Muslims, if we ponder for a while and seriously reflect on these communication modes and facts between Allah and His servants, it does leaves us with an indelible legacy of appreciation and submission with regards the infinite amount of mercy, love, and guidance that He possesses for His servants that are righteous and believe in Him. What a unique manifestation and testimony of how much God likes to see His servants achieve their ultimate success in this divine two-way communication between Him and those who believe and submit to His will and do good deeds! In relation to this two-way communication vis-à-vis man's innate tendency to falter, do wrong, transgress, or *sin*, Yasir Fasaqa in his lecture of the six C's contends that "sin is that which pricks in the heart."

He further explains that before man engages in an act of sin, there is a divine latent voice from God which draws attention to his inner moral (conscience) self to warn him of his desires of the *nafs* (soul), and to reflect, refrain, and desist from the wrongful act that he intends to commit. Instantaneously will follow a second latent voice which is Satan, who tricks the individual, plays with the desires of his *nafs* (soul), and makes him believe that the act he intends to commit is rightful and will benefit him beyond all reasonable doubt. It is only after the wrongful or evil act is committed by the individual that Satan will remove his veil of deception, thereby enabling the individual to face up to the sinful, devastating, or wrongful act that he just committed.

Relative to this fact, the Quran also reminds us of the deceptive nature of Satan against man when it states:

> And the Satan shall say after the affair is decided: "Surely Allah promised you the promise of truth, and I too gave you promises, but I failed in my promise to you. I had no authority over you except to call you, but you listened to me, then reproach not me but your own souls. I cannot listen to your cries, nor can you listen to mine. I reject your former act in associating me with Allah. For wrongdoers there must be a grievous penalty." (Sura Ibrahim 14:22)

The mere fact that God created man with a freewill does reflect the fact that under normal circumstances he has the ability to discern on matters that he is confronted with, and to choose between its right and wrong. This being the manner in which we were created, then it is man himself who is following the inclinations of his heart, lust and desires of the *nafs* (soul), which if not controlled has the affinity to yearn for evil. The irony regarding this issue lies in the fact that despite God's divine warnings in those books (Tawrat, Zabur and Injeel, and Torah) that were sent to Jesus and Moses then followed by the Quran, which God revealed to Prophet Muhammad (saw) through Angel Gabriel. The Quran attests to this fact when it states the following:

> Say yes: We believe in Allah and the revelation given to us, and to Abraham, Ismail, Isaac, Jacob, and the Tribes, and that given to Moses and Jesus and that given to (all) prophets from their Lord: We make no difference between one and another of them and we bow to Allah (in Islam). (Sura Al-Baqarah 2:136).

Despite the fact that all of these books came as a guide to man and to make them believe in the oneness of God, still up to now exist some men who choose to be among the category of wrongdoers, sinners, and unbelievers. Furthermore, even among the believers there are those who are enslaved by their *nafs* (soul) and the fake material illusions of this dunyah (world) which makes them fail to adhere to Allah's guidelines in the Quran and the Sunnah of the prophet. It is these categories of people who are susceptible to falling easy prey and victim to Satan. Man has to empathically learn how to fight (*jihad*) with both his *nafs* (his own soul) and Satan, and to face up to the reality and understanding that the life of this world is full of trials and tribulations forming part of our spiritual existence in life. Part of this *jihad* is to discipline his desires of the heart and soul and not to succumb to the call and/or the invitations of Satan to engage in wrongful or evil deeds.

Another notion of this jihad is to train one's heart and mind to always acknowledge the fact that we are responsible for programming the destinations of the GPS of our lives, and must not always shift the blame to Satan. The reason being that Satan has no ability to force man to indulge in wrong or evil deeds; all he does is invite, incite, and create an environment that will be conducive to your heart, *nafs*, and desires. In fact, we can say that based on both the Bible and the Quran it was such kind deception tactics that Satan used to get Adam and Eve out of the Garden. The validity of this statement is revealed in the Quran when God says:

We said: "O Adam! Dwell you and your wife in the Garden, and eat of the bountiful things therein as (where and when) you will, but approach not this tree or you run into harm and transgression." Then did Satan make them slip from the (Garden) and get them out of the state (of felicity) in which they had been. We said: "Get you down, all (you people) with enmity between yourselves, on earth will be your dwelling place and your means of livelihood for a time." (Sura Al-Baqarah 2:35-36)

Actually, when God said, "Get you down, all of you people," this implies Adam, Eve, and Satan. Therefore, it will be true to say that Adam and Eve were the first of men to transgress against the instruction of God when they were deceived by Satan. Since then, Adam, Eve, and their children have become the enemy of each other and that of Satan the devil.

The Muslim must also acknowledge the fact that irrespective of these underlying factors mentioned above he should also strive to effectively utilize his thoughts, motives, emotions, and conscience in an efficient manner that is commensurate to the practices of Islam wherever possible. The mere fact that he is using wisdom to nurture his mind and conscience in this manner is an effort to purify his body and soul from the temptations of this world (*dunyah*) and that of Satan the outcast. It is imperative, therefore, for the Muslim to understand that when he falters, transgresses, or faces adversities or calamities to apply *wisdom* and return his mind to Allah, submit to His will in repentance, ask for forgiveness, and change his wrongdoings with the intention of not repeating it again so that he can return to the right path. The Quran reminds us of the fact that whoever believes in Allah and does good will receive good and guidance from him to stay in the right path. In Sura Al-Baqarah, Allah reminded the prophet of this fact when He said:

> *It is not required of you (O Apostle), to set them (the disbelievers) on the right path, but Allah sets on the right path that he pleaseth. Whatever of good you give benefits your own souls, and you shall only do so seeking the "face of Allah." Whatever good you give shall be rendered back to you, and you shall not be dealt with unjustly. (Sura Al-Baqarah 2:272)*

In view of the above stipulated verse, it is imperative for the Muslim to note that following his reaffirmation in the faith of Islam, whatever good he does in this world will be rewarded back by Allah. This statement is further manifested in the Quran when it states that

> *nay, whoever submits His whole self (Wajh) to Allah and is a doer of good, he will get rewarded by his Lord; on such shall be no fear, nor shall they grieve. (Sura Al-Baqarah 2: 112)*

It is evident from these two verses (272 and 112) of Sura Al-Baqarah as stipulated above that if the Muslim fully submits himself to the will of Allah, does good deeds, then he is assured of being rewarded, and above all, will have protection from his Lord to an extent that he shouldn't fear nor grieve. Furthermore, it also reinforces the fact that such a Muslim is paving his way to success in the sense that he is desisting from doing wrong and fighting in the way of *jihad* with his *nafs* (soul). There is ample evidence in the Quran which manifest a strong correlation between *tawbah* (repentance) and the individual's success in this life and the hereafter. It is in this regard that we will proceed to discuss next the correlation between *tawbah* and the individual's success in this life and of the hereafter. Relative to these statements, it is important to shed light on the benefits and blessings of repentance (*tawbah*) as discussed in subsection 5.1.

5.1 The Wisdom of Tawbah (Repentance) to Facilitate Success

The Muslim who transgresses or commits a sin must not be neglectful or complacent in asking Allah for forgiveness. *Tawbah*, if done with sincerity and remorse, could facilitate the way toward success if the individual constantly vows to refrain from committing the same sin and ventures to adhere to the principles and guidelines revealed by Allah in the Quran and the Sunnah of the Prophet. Complementary to this vow, the Muslim should pray for Allah's mercy and His associate benefits, rewards, protection, and help. The fact of the matter, as discussed above, is to sincerely repent and advocate for Allah's help in his prevailing life undertakings that will lead to success in this life and the hereafter. Allah reminds the Muslim of such a success when he says in the Quran:

> And beg Allah to forgive you all, O believers, that you may be successful. (Sura An-Nur 24:31).

In this regard, it is important to shed light on the benefits and blessings of repentance (Tawbah). At this juncture, it is imperative to reiterate the point that in Islam true success is to fulfill the main purpose of life, which is to acknowledge the oneness of God, believe in his creations, submit to His will, work righteously under the set guidelines of both the Quran and the Sunnah of the Prophet in order to acquire His pleasures and rewards to enter His paradise. However, success has a multifaceted dimension which includes *tawbah* (repentance). The validity of this statement is supported by iqrasense.com, which states the following:

> *Tawbah refers to asking repentance from Allah for sins that we commit. Making sincere repentance or Tawbah raises a Muslim's stature with Allah because the process of making Tawbah involves the following three steps: first and foremost, recognizing one's mistakes and sin; secondly, feeling ashamed of violating Allah's trust; and thirdly, making a promise never to repeat such behavior. Moreover, Tawbah paves the way for success by choosing to stay the course prohibited by Allah; we consciously forego Allah's mercy and associated benefits and rewards, His protection and help. However, the moment we sincerely repent, we can be assured of Allah's help in our lives that in turn is a precursor to success in this life and the hereafter.*

5.2 The Wisdom of *Tawbah* (Repentance) to Alleviate Hardships, Trials, and Tribulations

Apart from the Muslim performing *tawbah* (repentance) to attain the ultimate success in life, he can also do tawbah as a means of dealing with trials, tribulations, and their related hardships. In the case of the latter, it is imperative for the Muslim to understand that the sins he commits can haunt him in this life and the hereafter. Actually, the more sins the individual commits, the more likely it is that he will be detached from and/or deprived of God's blessings, and the more trials and challenges he could be put through. The Quran reminds us relative to this type of scenario when Prophet Hood told his people:

> *And O my people ask for forgiveness of your Lord and then repent to Him. He will send you from the sky abundant rain, and add strength to your strength, so do not turn away as mujrimoon (criminals, evildoers, etc.). (Sura Hud 11:52)*

Repentance, therefore, can provide us a way out of our miseries and troubles of this *dunyah* (world). To this end Allah reminds us in the Quran when He says:

> *See them not that they are put in trial once or twice every year (with different types of calamities, disease, and famine) yet they turn not in repentance, nor do they learn a lesson from it.* (Sura Al-Tawbah 9:126)

In view of the foregoing discussion, it is vital for the Muslim to acknowledge the fact that when he is faced with adversities, calamities, trials, and other forms of hardships to apply wisdom and seek for repentance and forgiveness from Allah. He should do it with sincerity to dispose of his bad ways or wrong deeds and to vow never to have them repeated. Once he does this, then he should have faith in Allah, and to acknowledge the fact that He knows what is best for him and must not doubt His favors and blessings at any given time. Moreover, once the Muslim has undergone the process of repentance, he needs to have the *imaan* that Allah tries man both by prosperity and adversity. In the former, he should show humility and kindness, and for the latter patience and faith. In other words, the Muslim has to have the *imaan* to always praise and thank Allah for whatever befalls him, both prosperity and adversity, thereby strengthening his trust and love of Allah, who knows what is always best for him. This kind of relationship, attitude, and behavior that the Muslim displays intrinsically and extrinsically will serve as an endorsement of the favors (during trials and rewards) he receives from Allah at all times. Relative to the abovementioned characteristics and behaviors of the Muslim, he must also at all times refrain and/or try to control his pride, impatience, arrogance, anger, and other associated negativity for self and the people he interacts with on a daily basis. As regards the Muslim's daily interaction with believers and other brothers in faith, he should be vigilant and careful in selecting his friends and associates by striving to ensure that they fear Allah, are righteous and trustworthy. In this regard, Dr. Ali Muhammad M. As-Sallaabee (2010) pointed out that

Umar ibn Al-Kattab explained the true meaning of brotherhood and friendship in Islam when he said: "Seek out truthful brothers, brothers that you know will care for you [and look out for your best interest]. In times of comfort, such [sincere and caring] friends are like decoration pieces [in your gatherings] in that one is pleased to look at them, and is happy to know that they are by one's side; and in times of hardship, they are like tools [in that they are always willing to help and be of use]."

The abovementioned explanation by Umar could serve as a guide for the Muslim when selecting his choices of friends so as to avoid associating with the wrong types of people who are not God-fearing, evil, deceitful, untrustworthy, arrogant, and operates under the dictates of Satan and loves best the life of this *dunyah* (world). In fact, the Muslim should also take heed of the reality that it was as a result of arrogance, jealousy, envy, pride, impatience, lack of faith, and wisdom that led Satan to refuse to bow down to Adam as was commanded by Allah. The Quran gives us the clarity of this situation when Allah says:

Did I not tell you that I know the secrets of the heavens and earth, and I know what you reveal and what you conceal? And behold, we said to the angels, 'Bow down to Adam' and they bowed down. Not so Iblis (Satan): he refused and was haughty. He was of those who rejected faith. (Sura Al-Baqarah 2:33–34)

Having discussed how the Muslim could turn to *tawbah* as a means of repentance and seeking forgiveness from Allah so that he will alleviate his hardships, trials, and tribulations, and guide him toward righteousness. We will discuss next in subsection 5.3 the relationship of *tawbah* vis-à-vis how it can help clear man's conscience.

5.3 The Wisdom of *Tawbah* (Repentance) to Facilitate Man to Clear His Conscience

We can see that part of Satan's problem as revealed in the abovementioned Sura Al-Baqarah verses 33–34 was due to his lack of faith in Allah when he was tested during and after the creation of Adam. Therefore, the Muslim must acknowledge the fact that having faith in Allah constitutes a fundamental aspect of Islam which teaches us those essential values related to *tawbah* such as being regretful and remorseful of our wrong and evil deeds, and purifying the *nafs* (soul) to attain Allah's mercy and blessings, both in this life and the hereafter. If tawbah teaches the Muslim to exercise regret and remorse in relation to his sins, evil, and wrong deeds, then reciprocally it is vital for the Muslim to clear his conscience in order to have that inner peace of purifying self and his soul with sincere intention of not repeating the same.

This process of self and soul cleansing is of paramount importance for the Muslim, as a way of fulfilling his main purpose of life. This process of self and soul cleansing is to enable the Muslim to acknowledge the fact that any sin that he commits is always associated with an accompanying sense of guilt that gets lodged in his heart. It is in this regard that we refer to Yasir Fasaqa's lecture on the Six C's in chapter five above that "sin is that which pricks in the heart." Too often it is man's neglectful nature to try and turn a blind eye to those guilty feelings. We know from experience that such guilt is responsible for gradually eroding our happiness and putting us in a miserable and/or depressed state of mind. *Tawbah*, then, as a process of atonement and by its very nature, eradicates that guilt and fills our heart with happiness.

In order for the Muslim to fill his heart with happiness, not only must he learn how to repent and be remorseful to those whom he offend wrongfully, and sincerely request their forgiveness and that of Allah depending on the prevailing circumstances. However, on the same vein, the Muslim must also learn how to deal in a very responsible manner with those who trespass against him, and on a daily basis forgive them for the sake of Allah in order to purify himself and his own soul. The reason for this dual approach to forgiveness is to have a clear conscience that as a Muslim he doesn't harbor any bad feelings and or grudge against those whom he offended and those who also transgressed against him. The importance of this dual approach of *tawbah* (repentance) and forgiveness is to try and attain the ultimate purification of the soul and success in this life and hereafter. Furthermore, it is imperative for the

Muslim to have the understanding that Allah as the sole creator is pure, and so is His creation, including His haven, which we all yearn for to be our final resting place and to dwell therein forever. According to the daily *hadith* on abuaminaelias.com, Anas ibn Malik reported:

> *We were sitting with the Messenger of Allah, peace and blessing be upon him, and he said, "Coming upon you now is a man from the people of paradise." Then came a man from the Ansar whose beard was disheveled by the water of ablution and he was carrying both of his shoes with his left hand. The Prophet repeated the same message for three days and the same man appeared . . . Abdullah ibn Amar requested from the man to stay with him for three days . . . As he was to return home, the man said to him, "I am as you have seen, except that I do not find dishonesty in my soul toward the Muslims (implying forgiving all those who trespass against me before I go to sleep). Moreover, I do not envy anyone because of the good that Allah has given them." Abdullah said, "This is what you have achieved and it is something we have not accomplished." (Musnad Ahmad 12286, and Sahih, authentic, according to Ibn Kathir)*

According to the above *hadith*, we can see those good qualities and values which make the man that the Prophet referred to as the man of paradise that it was not because of his prayers that made him earn this position of the *nafsmutmainnah* (the soul at rest), but due to his nature and compassion to forgive all those who trespass against him before he goes to bed each day. The nature of this reality that is associated with a Muslim of this caliber such as the *mutmainnah* type whose soul is at rest has been described in the Quran when it states:

> *O soul at rest that found comfort in Allah, return to thy Lord, thou well pleased with him and he well pleased with thee. Now join my servants and enter my garden. (Sura Fajr 35: 27-30)*

In view of the abovementioned discussion, it is vital for the Muslim to advocate and pray for Allah's guidance so that he will move away from the *nafsal-ammara bissu,* which means the self that incites to evil,

OMAR NJIE

or in order words the animal state of man, and pass the *nafslawwama* or the reproving self (*see Sura al-Qiyamah 75:2*). The Muslim must not aim to stay at this station of *nafslawwama*—also known as the moral state of man—but must strive to seek further guidance from Allah so that *he could find comfort and sanctuary in the nafsmutmainnah* or the soul at rest, of which the man of paradise whom the Prophet mentioned said, *"I do not find dishonesty in my soul toward Muslims nor any form of envy toward them."* The amazing thing about this man is the fact that while he was still living on earth he wasn't aware that he had already been ranked among the people of paradise until when it was revealed by the Prophet (saw). Moreover, as a Muslim, he is worth emulating for he has taught us a way of attaining the ultimate success of life by performing just regular prayers, not envying others, being content with what he has, praising Allah at night, forgiving his enemies, and saying only good things so that he doesn't have a dishonest soul before going to bed.

Having discussed how the wisdom of *tawbah* can help clear man's conscience, we will now proceed to discuss how *tawbah* pleases Allah.

5.4 The Wisdom of *Tawbah* (Repentance) to Please Allah

The Muslim should endeavor to bear in mind that *tawbah* is a way of turning to Allah and asking for His forgiveness. Repentance, therefore, paves the way for Allah's grace in this life and the hereafter. Among some of Allah's grace to man in this world can be attributed to wealth, children, and increased blessings, among other things. In this regard, the Quran states:

> *Seek the forgiveness of your Lord and turn to Him in repentance that He may grant you good enjoyment for a term appointed, and bestow His abounding grace to every owner of grace. But if you turn away, then I fear for you the torment of a great day (i.e., the Day of Resurrection). (Sura Hud 11:3)*

The Muslim who performs *tawbah* with absolute sincerity to please Allah attains his mercy and forgiveness for his sins, and alleviates his hardships, trials, tribulations, including the wrong deeds for which he has regretted and shown remorse. Actually, Allah will be pleased with this kind of Muslim so long as he adheres to his pledge to abstain from repeating the same sin and/or wrongful deed. Once the Muslim remains constant to his pledge, continues to be righteous, and henceforth works according to the guidelines of the Quran and the Sunnah of the Prophet, these are among the best ways to earn him the love and happiness of Allah.

But what are the signs that Allah is in love with His servant? Answers to this question are numerous both in the Quran and *hadith* of the Prophet. However, we will venture to give few examples as follows:

First: The Quran sheds some light in this regard when it states:

> *Say, if you do love Allah follow me: Allah will love you, and*
> *forgive you your sins, for Allah is oft forgiving, most merciful.*
> *(Sura AliImran 3:31)*

As regards the above stipulated verse, we can easily manifest that a servant's devotion and love for Allah is reciprocated by Him to forgive the servants his sins through His infinite mercy.

Second: Refers to a situation whereby Allah chooses to love a particular servant and/or a true Muslim for Himself. Under such circumstances AbdurRahman.org cited Abu Hurairah (may Allah be pleased with him) who reported that the Prophet (*sallallaahu alayhi wa sallam*) said:

> *When Allah loves a slave and/or a servant, calls out Jibril and*
> *says: "I love so-and-so, love him!" Then (Jibril) announces to*
> *the inhabitants of heavens that Allah loves so-and-so, so love*
> *him; and the inhabitants of the heavens (the angels) also love*
> *him and then make people on earth love him.*

Third: Deals with a servant who is righteous, performs regular and voluntary prayers, including other religious obligations according to Islamic rules and principles. Relative to this statement, sabir.com explains the point that

> when a true Muslim acquires nearness and love of Allah by means of performing religious obligations, supererogatory and voluntary prayers, Allah then becomes his special helper and protects his limbs and organs and does not let them work for his disobedience. Then he does not use any part of his body for things which are disliked by him.

In view of the foregoing, it is imperative for the Muslim to acknowledge the fact that turning to Allah in repentance greatly pleases Him because it is the most beloved act of worship to Him. The validity of this statement goes with the fact that when the Muslim, having acknowledged his wrongdoing, repents and exercises remorse to join the ranks of those who repent, will also earn him Allah's love. However, further validation of the abovementioned statement is revealed in the Quran when it states:

> Truly, Allah loves those who turn unto Him in repentance and loves those who purify themselves. (Sura Al-Baqarah 2:222)

We will now recapitulate on our discussion regarding Allah's love for those of His servants who perform sincere *tawbah* (repentance) and use it as a reminder to the Muslim that while he is engaged in the process of *tawbah* it is best not to neglect any one of the three steps described below:

Firstly, the believer and/or the Muslim needs to recognize his wrongdoing and/or sin that he committed. Secondly, he needs to feel ashamed of violating Allah's trust and guidelines based on the Quran and the Sunnah of the Prophet. Thirdly, he has to make a promise never to repeat such wrongful behavior. Iqrasense.com reiterated the point that

> according to many studies, if one of these three is missing, then the repentance is not sincere.

Although the subject matter pertaining to *tawbah* (repentance) is very interesting, nonetheless we have to acknowledge its multifaceted nature regarding God's dealings with man, which on the one hand leads to mercy, whereas on the other hand deals justice and punishment of sin when all grace is resisted.

We will now proceed to discuss the wisdom of *tawbah* and its significance as a life-transformational process for the Muslim and his *duas*.

5.5 The Wisdom of *Tawbah* to Transform the Life of the Muslim and His Duas

The Muslim should acknowledge the fact that Islam as a way of life is about positively shaping both his intrinsic and extrinsic outlooks in life and so too is *tawbah* (repentance). Both are dynamic, synonymous, and have the potential to propagate his spiritual and moral growth and transformation, including that of his family and community depending on the conduciveness of his environment vis-à-vis Islam. The nature of this transformation is to enable him to strengthen both his moral and spiritual development with a positive inclination that will take him closer and closer to Allah each day. His efforts to nurture this transformation should be supported with prayers to seek affinity and refuge with Allah so that he will be able to safeguard those positive trends of life which he has already developed and not to allow them to deteriorate or reverse to a negative pattern of disobedience, transgression, or wrongful deeds. The Muslim commitment of good deeds and righteousness is a manifestation of part of what shapes his character and the affinity for people around him to love and admire his way of life. Relative to these viewpoints, a publication of bewleyvirtualave.net contends the following:

> When someone becomes Muslim, they change. The change can be seen in their faces, their lives are transformed. This is absolutely inevitable, and if it does not happen, it means that they have not really become Muslims, their Islam was not "taken."

The above stipulated statement by bewleyvirtualave.net gave us an insight into the positive spiritual and physical transformation of these changes on someone who becomes a Muslim. In the same token, the statement further indicated that when all of these spiritual and physical transformations don't occur to the one who becomes a Muslim, then it implies that their Islam was not taken (i.e., that something is deficient in their Islam). The nature of this narrative is a testimony to indicate the spiritual powers and blessings that are intrinsic to a true believer when he enters the religion of Islam. In order to shed more light on someone who becomes a Muslim, it is imperative for him to always endeavor with sincere intention to do good, pray for Allah's forgiveness and mercy so that He will help him purify his heart and soul, and to enjoin him among His righteous servants, both in this world and the hereafter. In view of this noble intention by someone who becomes a Muslim, the Quran reminds us of Prophet Solomon who prays to submit to the will of God so that He will join him among those servants that are righteous. We are reminded of this fact in the Quran when it states:

> My Lord! Inspire and bestow upon me the power and ability that I may be grateful for your favors which you have bestowed on me and my parents, and that I may do righteous good deeds that will please you, and admit me by your mercy among your righteous slaves. (Sura An-Naml 27:19)

The Muslim should also acknowledge the fact that the bounties and favors of Allah upon mankind are numerous, such as His gift of good health, wealth, and children, among other things. These acknowledgments by the Muslim should serve as a way of expressing his sincere gratitude for the enormous number of blessings and gifts that Allah gave him and his family, among other things. Notwithstanding these acknowledgments and expressions of gratitude, the Muslim should by all means make it a point of duty to regularly perform his mandatory prayers, makes duas, and thank Allah for all of the favors that He bestowed on him and his parents, and to ask for His forgiveness and that of his parents even after they departed from this world (*dunyah*). The Quran explains the following:

You are kind to your parents and lower to them the wing of
humility, and say: "My Lord! Bestow on them thy mercy even
as they cherished me in childhood." (Sura Bani Israil 17:24)

The bone of contention here is to note the fact that Allah has asked us to honor our parents and lower to them the wing of humility at all times. To this end, we should acknowledge the reality that parental love should not be seen as that of a paternal, maternal, moral obligation, but because of the divine duty attached to it through this revelation of the Quran that makes it a relationship of love, dedication, and care till eternity. Therefore, we cannot expect Allah's forgiveness if we are rude or unkind to those who unselfishly brought us up, for if we do then it is a form of transgression. Notwithstanding the very nature and imperfection of who we are as human beings, if in the event such kind of transgression occurs then it is incumbent to the person concerned to request for forgiveness (*tawbah*) from his parents, for Allah likes those who perform *tawbah*. Moreover, as we have mentioned in the preceding paragraphs of this chapter, the Muslim should take the issue of *tawbah* (repentance) very seriously. This is because *tawbah* has the potential to make our prayers and *duas* worthier of response. This being the case, it is of paramount importance that the Muslim should endeavor to give top priority to his obligatory prayers and *duas* in order to spiritually connect to Allah and seek his mercy, guidance, and forgiveness.

The bone of contention here is for the Muslim to take heed of the reality that *tawbah* (repentance)will make his *duas* worthier of response, especially if done during his state of prostration(*sujood*) in performing prayers. This statement according to *iqrasense.com* is in line with so many of the Prophet's *hadith* that

> *Allah is more responsive to the duas and calls of those who*
> *are oppressed, travelers, the ones who ask Allah in a state of*
> *prostration, the ones who are fasting, and the like.*

The reason for Allah's responsiveness to the *duas* of the kind stated above is attributed to the nature, position, and state of prayer that they are in which brings out humility and humbleness in their hearts. Moreover, *tawbah* also brings forth humility and humbleness in a person's heart; therefore, at such a state the *duas* of this kind of a believer is more likely to be heard and answered by Allah due to the state and mode of prayer that they are performing. The believer must also take cognizance of the fact that even when he is in a state of distress, despair, anguish, pain, and the like Allah does not lay upon him a burden more than he can bear. The Quran reminds us of this fact when it states:

> *On no soul doth Allah place a burden greater than it can bear. It gets every good that it earns, and it suffers every ill that it's earned. (Sura Al-Baqarah 2:286)*

Finally, the believer should always take his repentance with sincerity and seriousness knowing that Allah's doors for accepting repentance are always open. Relative to this statement, the Quran further reminds us of the reality when it states:

> *Verily, Allah is the one who forgives (accepts repentance), the most merciful. (Sura Al-Baqarah 2:37)*

In order to recapitulate on this chapter, we need to reiterate the fact that those servants who repent sincerely to Allah, acknowledging their sins and committing not to return again to those sins, will have their sins forgiven. Therefore, the Muslim should constantly seek Allah's guidance and forgiveness throughout his short journey of this life (*dunyah*) so that with His mercy he could be among the chosen people of paradise. Actually, to be chosen to join the people of paradise can be regarded as the "true success of life" that a believer should yearn for, and to wish the same for his fellow Muslims.

Now that we have concluded this chapter with Allah's reward of paradise to His believing servants, a favor and fact that He promised to them of which the unbelievers are in denial. In view of this statement, we will venture to discuss the relationship between predestination and how it affects the individual's belief in Allah.

CHAPTER 6.0

The Wisdom to Believe in Al-Qadar(Predestination) to Strengthen One's Al-Birr (the Quality of the Individual's Belief in Allah)

IT IS IMPORTANT before we embark on the distinction between *al-qadar* (predestination) and al-birr (the quality of one's belief in Allah) that we establish the fact that Allah created man with a free will to be able to discern and distinguish right from wrong. The nature of this reality is manifested in the Quran when it states, "(With profit) to whomever among you wills to go straight; But you shall not will except as Allah wills, the Cherisher of the Worlds" (Sura at-Takwir 81:28-29).

The above stipulated verses as explained in the footnotes of the Quran revealed that God is the Cherisher of the Worlds, Lord of Grace and Mercy, and *"His guidance is open to all who have the will to profit by it."* But that will must be exercised in conformity with God's will, as stated in the above verse. The nature of such conformity is Islam, which is solely guided by both the Quran and the Sunnah of the Prophet (saw).

The first part of the verse points to the individual's free will and responsibility, whereas the latter aspect of the verse points to its limitations. Both extremes, for example, which solidify the determinants of the idea of chaotic free will are condemned.

Now that we have given an overview of man's free will, we will proceed to throw some light on the Islamic view of the divine will and decree of God. In islamqa.info/en/49-published 03/30/2010, it is explained the following:

> The word al-qada (the divine will) is certain belief that everything that happens in this universe happens by the will and decree of Allah. The word qada means perfection and completion, and the word qadar means evaluating and planning.

Efforts to try and find out if there exists a difference between *al-qada* and *al-qadar* led some of the scholars to have the notion that there was a difference between them. Recently, scholars have agreed that the most correct view is that there is no difference in meaning between *al-qada* and *al-qadar*, and each of them points to the meaning of the other. For instance, to believe in *al-qadar* (the divine decree) is the sixth pillar of faith, and no one's faith is complete without it. *Qadar* means Allah's decree of all things from eternity, and His knowledge that they will come to pass at the times that are known to Him and in the specific manner that He has decreed and willed. Allah's decrees will always materialize the way they are meant to and the way they are created. Furthermore, there is no clear evidence in the Quran or Sunnah to indicate that there is a difference between them. In this regard, the scholars are in agreement that the one may be applied to the other, yet be mindful of the fact that the word *qadar* is mostly used in the texts of the Quran and the Sunnah, which indicates that the Muslim must believe in this pillar and acknowledge the fact that Allah knows best.

It is imperative for the Muslim to note that *al-qadar* is Allah's plan for his creation. This statement is reflected in the Quran when it states:

> Verily, we have created all things with Qadar (divine preordainments of all things before their creation as written in the Book of Decrees Al-Lawh-Mahfooz). (Sura al-Qamar 54:49)

It is also vital for the Muslim to understand that whatever Allah has shown his servant of *al-qadar* he will know and has to believe in it, and those things that are latent and/or hidden from him should also be accepted and believed in as part of his faith. The Muslim must not have doubt and/or dispute with Allah concerning His actions and rulings due to his limited understanding of his mind and comprehension of His creations. Rather, the Muslim must always believe in Allah's complete justice and wisdom, and he must try and refrain from being doubtful about what He does except to glorify and praise Him at all times.

Furthermore, we need to acknowledge the fact that Allah's justice is strict but in favor of man. However, irrespective of this fact and reality of man's life experiences, many of which he is in despair and can't find solutions for, should serve as an awakening factor to shift him from this loss state to the spiritual state of enlightenment. The reality of this spiritual state of Enlightment is facilitated by man's submission to the Will of Allah, in order to face up with the reality of his existence and purpose of life. The nature of this spiritual shift and submission to Allah has the propensity to facilitate this spiritual shift so as to enable man to reject and/or desist to operate from his insular, insincere, and ungrateful tendencies of which he is neglectful toward his creator.

The analytical perspective of our foregoing discussion has enabled us to accept the fact that for the Muslim to believe in *al-qadar* equates to his belief in the divine decree of Allah which constitutes his sixth pillar of faith in Islam. This being the case, there is the need, therefore, to briefly explain the six fundamental pillars of Islam (*Al-Aqidah Al Islamiyyah*) as a prerequisite requirement of understanding for this chapter. In order to shed light on this issue, we will refer to Sheikh Muhammad ibn Saleh Al Uthaymin when he contends that

> *Al-Aqidah AlIslamiyyah's (the Islamic creed) basis are the Belief in Allah, his angels, his books, his messengers, the last day, and Al-Qadar, it's good and bad.*

Sheikh Al Uthaymin further elaborated that *al-qadar* is the ability with which He (Allah) knew, wrote, willed, and created all things in

OMAR NJIE

predestined proportions and precise measures. *Al-qadar* is different from *al-birr*, which is the quality of the one who believes in Allah, the last day, the angels, the Book, and the prophets. It is imperative to appreciate and note the degree of wisdom that is embedded in the Quran to guide those servants of Allah who believe in Him, remain righteous, and perform good deeds. These categories of righteous and believing servants are different from the disbelievers who lack truth and wisdom of *al-birr*, hence their lack of faith in Allah. However, as for the disbeliever, that is his way of viewing the world, but nonetheless, none have the right to seduce or compel him to succumb to Islam, for Islam propagates the noncompulsion in religion as a way of respect for the individual's right to worship, and for the promotion of a peaceful coexistence among men. Contrary to the disbeliever, the believer is one who submits to the will of Allah, has faith in Him during the periods of adversities and of rewards given to him by Allah. Relative to this statement between the disbeliever and the believer, the Quran does shed some light on issues of this nature when it states:

> *Let there be no compulsion in religion; truth stands out clear from error: whoever rejects evil and believes in Allah hath grasped the most trustworthy handhold that never breaks. And Allah heareth and knoweth all things. (Sura Al-Baqarah 2:256)*

The preceding paragraphs stipulated the five pillars of Islam which are the fundamental framework of the Muslim's life. This framework constitutes for the Muslim the testimony of faith, prayer, giving *zakat* (assisting the poor and the needy), fasting during the month of Ramadan, and performing *Hajj* (pilgrimage) to Mecca (Makkah) once in the lifetime of the Muslim if he could afford it. We will proceed to elaborate briefly on each of these five pillars of Islam as follows.

First is the testimony of Faith: The essential factor as regards the testimony of faith is for the Muslim and/or the individual to say with conviction, "La ilaha illallah, Muhammadur Rasulullah," which simply connotes that "There is no true god (deity) but God (Allah), and

Mohammed is the Messenger (Prophet) of God." The first part is for the individual to attest and/or testify that Allah is the only one and true God, and none have the right to be worshipped but him alone. It also connotes the fact that God has neither partner nor son. This testimony of faith which is the most vital pillar of Islam is called the *Shahada*. The *Shahada* is a simple method which should be said by an individual who wants to embrace Islam.

Second, is the performance of Prayer: It is an obligatory requirement for the Muslim to perform the five daily prayers as prescribed in Islam, and as a duty toward Allah. These five daily prayers are performed at *fajr* (dawn), *dhuhr* (noon), *asr* (midday), *maghrib* (sunset), and *isha* (night). These prayers are preferably performed in a mosque or in any other clean place within his environment, such as at home, in the fields, and even when traveling so long as it conforms with the prescribed or recommended conditions of prayer. However, it is important to note that the Muslim, after the performance of prayer, especially the midday *Jumaah* prayer, should proceed with his other daily chores for his survival. The Quran explains this further when it states:

> And when the prayer is finished, then may you disperse through the land and seek the Bounty of Allah and celebrate the praises of Allah often (and without stint) that you may prosper. (Sura al-Jumu'ah 62:10)

Prayer in Islam establishes a direct spiritual link between the worshipper and God, thus allowing no intermediaries between the worshippers and God. Prayer also reinforces and nurtures the individual's belief in Allah, raises his inspiration to a higher morality, purifies the heart, and prevents him from the temptations of wrongdoings and evil deeds.

Third, to give zakat *(that which purifies):* Zakat al-mal or *zakat* on wealth or *zakat* denotes a mode of almsgiving treated in Islam as a religious obligation or tax, the importance of which, by Quranic ranking, is next after *salah* (prayer). The Muslim is obligated to pay out *zakat* on an annual basis of 2.5 percent of his net savings as a religious duty and purifying amount to be spent on the poorer sections of the community. This concept of *zakat* is based on the fact that all things belong to Allah, and wealth is therefore given to mankind from him as a trust. Giving *zakat*, therefore, implies giving a specific percentage on certain properties to certain classes of needy people. The percentage which is due on the total amount of gold, silver, and cash funds equal to about 85 grams of gold and held in possession for one lunar year is 2.5 percent. The reason for the inclusion of possessions is based on the premise that they are purified by setting aside a small portion for the poor and the needy.

Fourth, fasting in the Month of Ramadan: It is ordained by Allah as an obligatory duty for Muslims to fast every year in the month of Ramadan. It implies fasting from dawn until sunset, abstaining from food, drink, sexual relations, and all forms of evil intentions and desires. It is beneficial to health and spiritual self-purification.

Fifth, the pilgrimage to Makkah: Muslims are urged to perform the annual pilgrimage (*Hajj*) to Makkah as an obligation once in a lifetime depending on whether they can afford it financially and are physically fit to conduct all the necessary rituals ascribed for this purpose. The annual *Hajj* is performed in the twelfth month of the Islamic lunar calendar.

In view of the foregoing discussion, we will use the example of Prophet Abraham to demonstrate on the one hand the effects and impact of *al-qadar* in which Allah decreed by choosing him to be the father of the Abrahamic faiths (i.e., Judaism, Christianity, and Islam). To this end, John L. Esposito (1988) contends that

> *Islam stands in a long line of Semitic, prophetic religious traditions that share an uncompromising monotheism and belief in God's revelation, His prophets, ethical responsibility and accountability, and the Day of Judgment. Indeed, Muslims, like Christians and Jews, are the children of Abraham since all trace their communities back to him. Islam's historic religious and political relationship to Christendom and Judaism has remained strong throughout history. This interaction has been the source of mutual benefit and borrowing as well as misunderstanding and conflict.*

Despite Abraham being the father of these three faiths, he was a Muslim, hence his call to the disbelievers to reject worshipping their idols and believe in Allah. On the other hand, Abraham distinctively and equivocally demonstrated the *al-birr* (the quality of) his belief in Allah, including the other five pillars of Islam. Furthermore, his strong conviction led to the immaculate and unique testimony and experiences that he encountered as a prophet of Allah. Abraham's *al-birr* as a prophet played a crucial factor in strengthening his conviction to build the Holy Kabba together with his son Ishmael, including his experience when the idol worshippers threw him in the fire. We have briefly explained in subsection 3.5 above why the idol worshippers chose to put Prophet Abraham in the fire. In this chapter, we will briefly highlight how Prophet Abraham's *al-birr* and his belief in Allah's decree (*al-qadar*) led him and his son Ishmael to lay the foundation of the Kabba until it reached its completion, which was followed by a prayer to Allah. The testimony of this statement is revealed in the Quran when it states:

> *And remember Abraham and Ishmael rose the foundations of the House (with this prayer): "Our Lord! Accept (this service) from us: for thou art the All-Hearing, the All Knowing. Our Lord! Make of us Muslims, bowing to thy (will), and of our progeny a people Muslim, bowing to thy (will), and show us our places for the celebration of (due) rites and turn unto us (in mercy), for Thou art the All-Hearing, the All-Knowing. (Sura Al-Baqarah 2: 127-128)*

We can acknowledge the fact that Prophet Abraham's will and ability to build the Kabba did not prevail outside the *al-qadar* (will and decree of Allah), who is the one who has given him the ability, first, to be able to distinguish the fact that the disbelievers' worship of idols was wrong, and for him submitting to the will of Allah was the right thing to do. In other words, it was Allah who gave him the ability to distinguish between good and evil, which led to the choice for him to build the Kabba as a house for Muslims to use as a sacred place to worship Allah. The fact of the matter is that like Prophet Abraham who made both the choice and decision in dealing with the challenges he faced, this ability is innate in every normal human being, which is known as freewill. Relative to the individual's notion to will for something can only materialize if Allah wills and decrees it to be.

Relative to the foregoing discussion, it is also important for the Muslim to acknowledge the fact that generally will is the belief that everything that happens in this universe and all that is therein happens by the will of Allah. The reason is based on the fact that whatever Allah wills must occur, and whatever He does not will does not happen. In other words, nothing happens outside His will. It is because of this fact that the Muslim must, when planning to do something, start with *Bismilahi ar-Rahmanar-Rahim* (in the name of Allah, the most gracious, the most merciful) and support it with *inshallah* (if it pleases Allah), particularly if it is to deal with the unknown, such as tomorrow or planning for the future.

However, the fundamental aspect of belief for the Muslim in *al-qadar* is to pray for Allah's guidance and mercy to enable him do that which pleases Him, because his belief in *al-qadar* is incomplete if he doesn't truly believe in the undermentioned Islamic principles:

Firstly, for the Muslim to acknowledge the fact and to believe that the *knowledge of Allah* encompasses all things in the universe and all that exist therein. Therefore, it will imply that not a minute and/or an iota of atom in the heavens or on earth fall outside His knowledge. Secondly, Allah knew the nature of all of His creation before He created them. Remember, in the process of the creation of Adam, Allah said to the angels:

> *"I will create a vicegerent on earth." They said, "Will thou place therein one who will make mischief therein and shed blood whilst we do celebrate thy praises and glorify thy holy (name)?" He said: "I know what ye know not." (Sura Al-Baqarah 2:30)*

The above stated verse confirms Allah's knowledge of His creation even before He created them. Furthermore, because His knowledge encompasses everything, this implies that He is well acquainted with what they would do by means of His ancient and eternal knowledge. Apart from this solid acquaintance that prevails in the minds of those believing Muslims, there is also the reality that they constantly reaffirm the fact that He is Allah (God) and that none have the right to be worshipped except Him alone, the knower of the unseen and the visible.

A statement to back his knowledge of the unseen and/or the unknown including the visible is manifested in the Quran regarding Prophet Abraham's prayer stipulated below, when he prayed to God and said: "Our Lord! Send amongst the man apostle of their own, who shall rehearse your signs to them and instruct them in Scripture and wisdom, and sanctify them: For you are the exalted in might, the wise" (Sura Al-Baqarah 2:129).

There is a mystery of the unknown as regards this prayer, because the people then were not yet aware at that time that this apostle was to be among the progeny of Abraham (the Arabs of the Ishmaelites). However, the correlation in connecting this jigsaw puzzle was also manifested in the NIV (New International Version) Study Bible, which raised issues that were similar and/or related to Abraham's prayer for an apostle among his progeny. The nature of this similarity is expressed in Barker, Kenneth, *et al.*, (1985), when in this Bible Moses stated: God told him: "I will raise a prophet like you from among their brothers; I will put my words in his mouth, and he will tell them everything I command him. If anyone does not listen to my words that the prophet speaks in my name, I myself will call him to account" (Deuteronomy 18:18–19).

In the same vein, the Quran states that "Your mission, O Muhammad! Is to deliver Quran while it is we who will call them to account" (Sura ar-Ra'd verse 40). In view of the foregoing discussion, it is imperative for the Muslim to appreciate the fact that Islam, which is based on the revelations of the Holy Quran through Prophet Muhammad and the origin of the religious practices via Prophet Abraham, and both were further perfected through the teachings and living examples and practices of the Messenger (may the blessings and mercy of Allah always be with him).

Furthermore, even the Jews and the Christians were ordained by God to observe the *salah* prayers. This fact is in the Quran, which states: "O children of Israel! You shall observe the *salah* (prayers) and *zakat* (charity); and that you shall bow down with those who bow" (Sura Al-Baqarah 2:43). Similarly, Mary, mother of Prophet Jesus, received instructions to pray as revealed in the Quran: "O Mary, you shall obey your Lord, and you shall prostrate and bow down with those who bow down" (Sura AliImran verse 43). Likewise, Jesus, son of Mary, said: "God has made me blessed wherever I go, and commanded me to observe the *salah* (prayers) and *zakat* (charity) for as long as I live" (Sura Maryam verse 31). But the Jews and the Christians then lost the *salah* (prayers). The reason for this is due to the fact that "after them, there followed a posterity who missed prayers and followed after lust; soon then will they face destruction" (Sura Maryam 19:59).

Having explained in the preceding paragraphs how Allah's knowledge of His creation even before He created them, including unknown events to man such as the case of Abraham who after raising the foundation of the Kaaba with his son Ishmael relied on his prayer to God and waited for its outcome. However, God answered his prayer and manifested it in reality, which past generations as well as our generation have become witnesses to this testimony. Now, we will proceed to explain the similarities that both the Christians and the Muslims share as regards (Deuteronomy 18:18–19).

The similarities here are threefold: the first characteristic is that the apostle and/or the *prophet will be like Moses*. The likeness of the two prophets Moses and Muhammad was rare in prophethood. However, both were given a comprehensive law and code of life. Both had encounters with their enemies and came out to be victorious in miraculous ways. Both were accepted as prophets and messengers. Regarding them being messengers is due to the fact that they each had a book. The Tawrat (Old Testament) was given to Moses by God, and the Quran, also from God through Angel Gabriel, to Muhammad. Both migrated due to conspiracies and attempts by their enemies to assassinate them. Furthermore, their difference with prophet Essa (Jesus) is that they both were born through natural birth, had a family life, and natural death. Although Jesus was the last of the Israelite prophets, he informed them of the coming of the last of all prophets with clear signs, as explained in the preceding paragraphs.

The second characteristic revolves around the statement that the prophet will be from the brothers of the Israelites. It is a biblical fact that Prophet Abraham had two sons, Ishmael and Isaac (Genesis 21). Over time, Ishmael became the grandfather of the Arab nation, and likewise Isaac became the grandfather of the Jewish nation. The bone of contention here is that when Prophet Abraham and his son Ishmael raised the foundation of the Holy Kabba in Mecca they prayed for their progeny and said: "Our Lord! Accept this duty from us; you are the hearer, the knower of all things. O Lord! And make us Muslims to you, and from our descendants let there be a nation of Muslims to you; and teach us how to practice our religious duties and redeem us, you are the redeemer, the merciful" (Sura Al-Baqarah 2: 127-128). In this regard, Prophet Muhammad is from the progeny of Abraham; i.e., the Ishmaelites, and therefore Prophet Essa (Jesus) cannot be the prophet mentioned in (Deuteronomy 18:18–19) because he is from among the nation of the Jews.

The fact of the matter is that the prophets and messengers prior to Abraham were not given any religious practices. At that time human society was so primitive, hence the emphasis was based on the teachings of *tawheed* (Islamic monotheism) for the benefit of their salvation. Based on the ignorant and/or crude nature of early Arabian society, their quest for God made Abraham and Ishmael implore Him to teach them the religious practices of Islam, as mentioned above. The abovementioned prayer from Abraham was possible due to the fact that he was neither Jewish nor Christian. He was a monotheist and never an idol worshipper. In this regard, Muslims believe in this evidence in the Quran that Abraham is the founder of Islam, because he contributed to its religious practices such as *salah*, *zakat*, fasting, and *Hajj*, as was revealed to him by God. This testimony in the Quran states, "It is Allah who has named you Muslims, both before and in this (Revelations) that the Apostle may be a witness for you, and you be witnesses for mankind! So establish regular prayer, give regular charity, and hold fast to Allah!

He is your protector—the best to protect and the best to help" (Quran Sura Hajj 22:79).

The third characteristic solidifies the correlation of both this biblical evidence in (Deuteronomy 18:18–19) and the very strong evidence in the Quran that although Prophet Muhammad was not literate in Arabic the first words of the Quran that he received from God through Angel Gabriel were: *"Proclaim (or read) in the name of your Lord and cherisher who created" (Quran Sura Al-Alaq 96:1).*

This is solid proof that Prophet Muhammad received the Quran from God and transmitted its messages to his people, the Ishmaelites. This solid evidence matches the biblical evidence in which God said:

> *I Will put my words in his mouth, and he will tell them everything I command him. (Deuteronomy 18:18–19)*

First and foremost, as believing Muslims it is vital that we acknowledge the fact that Allah's knowledge encompasses all things and is also infinite. Furthermore, Allah is He who created seven firmaments, and of the earth a similar number. Amidst them (all) descends His commands so that those who believe in Him will know and appreciate that "He is the sole creator and has power over all things, and that Allah surrounds all things in (His) knowledge" (Sura at-Talaq 65:12)

Secondly, it is important for the Muslim to believe that Allah has decreed all of His creations. This will imply that "He has written the decrees pertaining to all created beings in Al-Lawh Al-Mahfuz (Divine Book) and this is easy for Allah" (Sura Hajj 22:70).

In view of the abovementioned statement, it is vital for the Muslim to understand that Allah is omniscient and knows what has happened with His creations and is happening and what is yet to come. Allah also knows what each believer and disbeliever is doing, and the nature of their fate in the hereafter.

Thirdly, it is vital for the Muslim to believe, as explained above in the preceding paragraphs of this chapter, that whatever occurs and/or takes place in this earth, the heavens, and the entire universe happens by the will of Allah.

Fourth, the Muslim needs to have the firm belief that Allah is the sole creator of all things, and whomsoever He guided will not go astray; and whosoever is misguided, follow evil, and wrongful deeds none can guide. Moreover, he who has Allah's guidance is with the best of guidance, but he who is misguided will go astray due to the enjoyment of his own desires and a slave who follows his own lust, devoid of guidance from Allah. "For Allah guides not people who submit to wrongdoing" (Sura al-Qasas verse 50).

The Muslim should also be mindful of the fact that true guidance is that which leads to the truth and the right path. It will imply, therefore, that true guidance to the truth lies with Allah, and no human being has any share in that. In order to comprehend this statement from a spiritual point of view, we will refer to the Quran when it says:

> *Verily you (O Muhammad) guide not whom you like, but Allah guides whom He wills. And He knows best those who are the guided. (Sura al-Qasas 28:56)*

Actually, the main essence of this verse does draw our attention in relation to our earlier discussions in this chapter where it is cited in Sura ar-Ra'd verse 40 that the main mission of the Prophet is to deliver the Quran, and Allah will call to account those who didn't listen and adhere to His message that He gave to the Prophet for the benefit of mankind. Therefore, from a spiritual perspective it is Allah and His message contained in the Quran that guides to the truth and the straight path. Also based on this evidence from the Quran, we can echo the fact that the Messenger (peace and blessings of Allah be upon him) explained and conveyed the message that he received to his people, and in some instances to the disbelievers, the Jews, Christians, and mankind in general. In this regard, messengers did show their people the way to the truth through spiritual guidance but they cannot force them to follow it.

In order to conclude this chapter, it is of great importance for the Muslim to know and remember Allah by His beautiful names, His sublime attributes, submit to His commands with peace of mind, and to trust in Him at all times.

We will now proceed to discuss the correlation between spiritual inspiration and faith in Allah.

6:1 The Wisdom in Spiritual Inspiration and Faith in Allah

It is a fact of life that since the Dark Ages up to the prevailing times among mankind there are those who have failed to put their belief and trust in Allah for him to guide them along the straight path and reward them for their righteousness and good deeds both in this *dunyah* (world) and in the hereafter (Day of Judgment). The effects of this kind of attitude among mankind is responsible for his egocentric tendencies and naivety to believe in himself to an extent that he relates all of his achievements in terms of wealth, power, and prestige to be his own making, thereby negating the fact that it is Allah who gives all of these provisions to whom He wills. The Quran reminds us of this statement when it states:

> *Know they not that Allah enlarges the provision or restricts it for any He pleases? Verily, in this are signs for those who believe. (Sura az-Zumar 39 52)*

The stipulated verse above is a reminder to mankind that Allah is He who is responsible for our provision on earth irrespective of your faith or belief in Him. However, as regards the Muslim, he should venture to attain spiritual wisdom, inspiration, and faith in Allah in order to develop the understanding that wealth, power, and prestige are factors that are given to man due to the permission and blessings of Allah who distributes it to whom He wills irrespective of his belief status. This is because Allah's mercy, which is one of His attributes, is spread all over His creations. However, due to the arrogant nature of man, we may believe that we can take care of ourselves, but the question that still remains is for how long and to what extent? Nevertheless, these gifts to man from Allah, such as wealth, power, and prestige, are nothing but to test him in order to see how righteous he will be with respect to their utilization. For example, Shekh Abu Ammar Yasir al-Qadhi confirms this statement concerning wealth when he contends that

> wealth, while one of the greatest blessings that mankind has been given, is at the same time one of the greatest trials and temptations.

In fact, the yearning for wealth accumulation among mankind has been a vital factor in the escalation of greed, corruption, hostility, hatred, and enmity which prevails in today's families, communities, societies, and nations globally. Notwithstanding, the Quran states:

> And know you that your possessions and your progeny are but a trial; and that it is Allah with whom lies your highest reward. (Sura al-Anfal 8: 28)

In view of the above stipulated verses, it is imperative for the Muslim to learn and master that the best way to deal with those individuals, family members, and loved ones who have wronged or transgressed against him is to exercise patience, tolerance, and forgiveness for the sake of Allah.

Moreover, because of the intrinsic value of wealth, it has virtually become a temptation for those who love the life of this *dunyah* (world) to an extent that they failed to acknowledge the hereafter (Judgment Day). The issue of wealth is relative, especially in the building of personal relations with family members, loved ones, and individuals in society. Its utilization has the propensity to generate love, hate, greed, jealousy, and other related issues. The effective utilization of wealth could be a vital factor to benefit and earn the reward of Allah, both in this world and the hereafter. The nature of this utilization by the individual could be done by spending toward good ventures such as helping the poor, needy, refugees, community projects (such as the building and/or development of a mosque and hospital). In this regard, the Quran reminds us of the fact that "those who spend (freely), whether in prosperity or in adversity, who restrain anger and pardon (all) men, for Allah loves those who do good deeds" (Sura AliImran 3:134).

While Allah loves those who spend their wealth on good deeds, He also censures those who hoard wealth and fail to take heed of His messages and to believe in His revelations and books sent down to some of the prophets. As regards those who hoard wealth, Allah says: "Woe to every slanderer and backbiter who has gathered wealth and counted it. He presumes that his money will make him everlasting" (Sura al-Humazah 104:1-3).

Furthermore, Allah has taught us in the Quran to try and maintain the straight path, implying the middle path. Similarly, when it comes to wealth earning and its distribution, we are aware of the *zakat* that the Muslim has to pay annually, which is obligatory as one of the fundamental pillars of Islam. However, our main concern here is about wealth being given out by the Muslim at his own accord depending on prevailing circumstances and/or need. To this end, the Quran explains the nature of this balance when it states:

> *Make not your hand tied (like a niggard's) to thy neck, nor stretch it forth to its utmost reach so that thou become blameworthy and destitute. Verily, your Lord does provide sustenance in abundances for those whom He pleases, and He provides it in a just measure: For He knows and regards all His servants. (Sura Bani Israil 17:29-30)*

As much as man loves to spend to show his status, the Quran warns us not to be wasteful when it states that "O children of Adam! Wear your beautiful apparel at every time and place of prayer: eat and drink, but waste not by excess, for Allah loveth not wasters" (Sura al-A'raf 7:31).

Relative to the abovementioned verses, it is imperative for the Muslim to endeavor to seek this balance to give from his wealth in a moderate manner, and not to follow his lust and desire for these worldly temptations until it leads him to a state of destitution. The former is desirable, whereas the temptations of the latter, which may intentionally lead to a state of destitution, might be seen as an act of excess or transgression.

As regards those who disbelieve in Allah and his revelations to mankind, they are misled by the love of this *dunyah* (world), forgetting the fact that they are doing so at their own peril.

In view of the foregoing discussion, it is imperative for the Muslim to take heed of the fact that some of mankind have failed to put their trust in Allah for Him to solve both their earthly problems and reward them for their righteous and good deeds both in this *dunyah* (world) and that of the hereafter (Day of Judgment). Based on my experience, it is factual nowadays for some men to put their trust in men of riches, power, and prestige to solve their earthly problems for them, disregarding the reality that it is Allah who is in control of the distribution of wealth to mankind.

Notwithstanding this fact, man must not be complacent or stay aloof without making any effort and/or productive measure to facilitate his survival and that of his family and/or dependents. However, based on experience, we have seen this kind of scenario, especially in some third-world countries such as in Africa, where one or two people in a family will work to support the rest of the family who make no effort whatsoever to find gainful labor (either formal/informal). This kind of negative dependency syndrome dominates and has become a reality and a social way of life based on the *mashlaa* (compromise to appease others) tradition of living, contrary to that in Europe or America, where the individual's productivity is paramount to his survival and that of the prosperity of his family, community, and country, among other factors.

The nature of horrific scenes of human disaster, sufferings, and callousness on the either side of the spectrum is disheartening, and it is painful to watch such scenes of loss of young lives that remain unaddressed by our world leaders, and in particular the African Union, who should have been the first to spearhead ways to alleviate both the brain drain and back-way issues of our human resources wastage. The latest of these ugly scenes has been escalated by the most recent exploitations, barbaric, inhumane, and undignified ways of capturing and selling migrant West Africans transiting to Europe via Libya as slaves.

Apart from the African Union and the United Nations doing something about these prevailing human catastrophic crises, first they could make efforts to arrest the prevailing situation and then bring the perpetrators responsible to justice. Second, they could come up with intervention strategies and programs to raise educational, economic, and political awareness that will enable such young people to venture to be part of their productive societies and effectively and efficiently contribute toward their respective national developments. Such development strategies could be aided by their financial institutions such as the IMF, World Bank, ILO, EEC, and the like. Similarly, the Islamic World should also be part of this framework, using their financial organization such as the Islamic Development Bank (IDB), to adopt skills training and entrepreneurship development programs that are linked to job creation and employment programs both in the private and nonformal sectors of industry. In this regard, the Islamic countries that are affected by the Libyan crises, such as Senegal and the Gambia, could liaise with organization such as the Islamic Bank who could assist them in their quest to address this unfortunate epidemic situation of young people dying in vain.

But how do we seek a balance to eradicate this unproductive way of life in some African countries and get their governments to promote policies of gainful employment both in the formal and informal sectors that will facilitate job opportunities for their youths? This approach to gainfully engage our young people to earn a decent wage for their livelihood and that of their families and/or dependents is by far better and more productive than seeing our young people die and/or perish at sea through the so-called back way to Europe or America.

Actually, those Muslims in these affected countries in West Africa who have adequate knowledge and experience of Europe and America can be of advisory help to such inexperienced young people intending to take the back way to these countries. They can explain to them the harsh realities of the way of life in these countries where assistance from the extended family doesn't prevail, and your survival as an individual will wholly depend on your productivity and earnings. Alternatively, the affected countries could establish an indigenous business advisory bureau (IBAS) to adopt the following: first an advisory role, second a support role to finance feasible business projects, and third a monitoring role and/or function that will help alleviate prevailing constraints and assist incumbent project owners in their marketing strategies to grow.

Complementary to the abovementioned strategies, what are the rich Islamic states doing to reach out and assist those poorer countries in Africa with Muslims who are dying of poverty, malnutrition, poor health, and unsanitary conditions and infrastructure, not to mention their poor economies and labor market conditions? All of these social phenomena that affects mainly the poor are evident as severe socioeconomic and sociopolitical conditions of inequalities between rich and poor, and contradict the very spirit and dignity of Islamic brotherhood. Although we shouldn't downplay some of the current efforts being made by Islamic organizations such as the Islamic Development Bank and the Islamic Trade Finance Corporation, who are helping some of the poor countries in Africa meet some of their financial and developmental needs in sectors such as energy and agriculture, among others. Perhaps, more of this kind of bilateral and/or multilateral agreement needs to be encouraged to assist youths obtain gainful employment in the sub-Saharan African regions.

In view of the foregoing discussion, the Muslim must not be complacent to allow either internal or external personal or social influences make him to engage in negative situations such as the back-way phenomenon to Europe and America. This kind of thinking among some young people could also be attributed to factors such as their level of faith in God, arrogance, self-conceited attitude, greed, and succumbing to the lust and desires of the material nature and temptations of this illusive world. This ignorance about God is also propagated by their failure to sincerely acknowledge His powers and that He is in control of our sustenance and destiny. In this regard, we can make reference to the apostles and the companions of the Prophet who were very different in so many ways from men of today. Actually, they were men who devoted their lives mainly for their belief and faith in Allah. Their commitment to Islam and love of Allah were different from that of the men of today who don't fear Allah, struggle daily for the accumulation of material gains used as a symbol to demonstrate prestige and power, among other factors.

The bone of contention here is for the Muslim as well as mankind to try and desist from evil deeds that the soul yearns for, which we have discussed earlier in this book and referred to it as the animal state of man or the *nafsal-ammarabissu* (or the self that incites to evil). The fact of the matter is that man needs to make a positive shift away from the worldly temptations of the *nafs* and to try and adopt a spiritual path that leads to truth and righteousness at all levels of society. The nature of this spiritual shift needs to take all of the three Abrahamic faiths on board with an open mind that will enable them to find a solution to world peace, with a spiritual and moral agenda that will make the world a better place for all of mankind. The nature of such an agenda should be carried out without any form of discrimination such as religious, political, and prevailing negative national and international crises. The reason for such a need for a global agenda is due to the fact that both prevailing political and economic issues at national and international levels are fraught with endless problems and crises, such as the prevailing case in Libya. The irony of such major crises is sometimes exacerbated initially due to politics or economic factors, and ending up as a religious crises propagated either by egocentric tendencies of governments or radical activist groups hiding under the pretext of Islam such as ISIS and in Christianity such as the KKK. Our world leaders should be able to work out positive socioeconomic and sociopolitical frameworks and strategies that will alleviate some of the prevailing crises that impinge on mankind in both developed and developing countries so as to make the world a better place for mankind.

In the past, when man was at a loss and evil became rampant, God's promise was to grant man (through the age's apostles) to warn and explain to them His oneness so that their hearts will yearn for good deeds rather than evil. Associated with this promise lies the fact that Allah, through His infinite mercy and guidance, uses the prophets to propagate and instill the knowledge and spirit of *tawheed* (the oneness of Allah) to men of wisdom, understanding, and faith in order that they and their communities can maintain righteousness and refrain from wrongdoings and evil deeds. The justification of these statements can be traced in the Quran when it contends:

> *Behold Allah took covenant of the prophets saying: "I gave you a Book and wisdom, then comes to you an apostle confirming what is with you. Do you believe him and render him help?" Allah said: "Do you agree and take this my covenant as binding on you?" They said: "We agree." He Said: "You bear witness, and I am with you among the witnesses." (Sura Ali Imran 3:81)*

Relative to the foregoing discussion, it is imperative for the Muslim to note that the nature of this covenant that Allah took was initially pertinent to the prophets until he gave them a book followed by an apostle to confirm what it entails. He then made it binding on them so that they too will bear testimony to it as witnesses. The above stipulated verse reminds us that when Allah took the covenant of the prophets there were among them those who didn't have a book given to them, therefore making them only have the honor of prophethood.

At this juncture, it is vital that we to try and explain the basic difference between a prophet and a messenger. On the one hand, a messenger (*rasool*) is someone to whom a law is revealed, and he is commanded to convey it. This implies, therefore, that every messenger is a prophet, but not every prophet is a messenger. Whereas, on the other hand, a prophet is one to whom a law is revealed but he is not commanded to convey it. Furthermore, a prophet is also commanded to call people, convey the message, and judge among the people. In this regard, a prophet is someone whom Allah communicates with, and a messenger is one that He communicates with and sends to disbelieving people. Another point is that the messenger will speak the language of his people. In addition, the messenger will remain with his people until they accept the message or Allah will destroy them. Another point of concern is that the legislation given to the messengers is different, and the prophets follow the legislation of the messengers. A related testimony to this statement is revealed in the Quran when Allah took the covenant of the prophets and said: "Take whatever I gave you from the Book and Hikmah (understanding of the laws of Allah, etc.) as a covenant to you, and afterward there will come to you an apostle confirming what is with you; it is incumbent on you to believe in him and assist him." Allah said: "Do you agree (to it) and will you take up my covenant (which I conclude with you) as binding?" They said: "We agree." He said: "Then bear witness, and I am with you among the witnesses (for this)" (Sura Ali Imran 3:81).

And most of the prophets sent to Bani'I Israel followed the legislation of Musa (Moses). The first messenger sent to mankind was Nuh (Noah). In Islam, as believing Muslims, we acknowledge the fact that Allah sent to mankind, based on an authentic *hadith* by Ahmed (5/265), who contends that the messenger of Allah revealed that 124, 000 prophets were sent to mankind, and from that number 315 were messengers. Allah communicated to Prophet Muhammad by means of Angel Gabriel and communicated directly to Prophet Musa (Moses). There were five prophets who had divine books and independent teachings. They are referred to as Nuh (Noah), Ibrahim (Abraham), Musa (Moses), Esa (Jesus), and Muhammad (saw).

Apart from the covenant among Allah, the apostles, and the angels, there is further evidence in the Book of Wisdom (the Quran) that the apostles were also used to spread the message of Allah, including His warnings to mankind. The testimony of this mode of spiritual communication and/or inspiration link between Allah and the apostle(s), His Messenger(s) are stipulated here as examples when Allah says:

> *O mankind! The Apostle hath come to you in truth from Allah.*
> *Believe in Him: it is best for you. (Sura an-Nisa 4:170)*

As regards Allah's inspiration to His messengers, the Quran contends that "we have sent thee inspiration, as we sent it to Noah and the messengers after him. We sent Inspiration to Abraham, Ismail,

Isaac, Jacob and the tribes, to Jesus, Job, Jonah, Aaron, and Solomon. And to David we gave the Psalms" (Suraan-Nisa 4:163).

However, there is further evidence in the Quran which also reveals the fact that some apostles were told about the stories of others, and to some they were to reveal good news as well as warnings to their communities, nations, and/or mankind. To this end, the Quran states:

> Of some apostles we have already told them the story; of others, we have not; and to Moses Allah spoke directly. There were apostles who gave good news as well as warnings that mankind, after the coming of the apostles, should have no plea against Allah: for Allah is exalted in power, wise. (Sura an-Nisa 4:164-165)

Another example in relation to Allah's messages regarding the apostles lays in the fact that that were instances when the apostles were sent by Allah only to give good news and to warn "so those who believe and mend (their lives), upon them shall be no fear nor shall they grieve" (Sura al-An'am 6:48). In this verse, Allah is reminding the believers to adhere to the glad tidings as well as the warnings of the apostles in order that we will be able to mend our lives in a manner that is righteous and pleasing to Allah. Moreover, their affirmation that such believers, including those that are righteous, will receive a gratifying reward from him so long as they adhere to the messages of the apostles, and for them shall be no fear nor shall they grieve.

Based on the foregoing discussion, there is a clear manifestation of the fact that God's inspiration was sent to many messengers, and the inspiration was of the same kind as that sent to the Apostle Muhammad, for God's Messenger is one. In this regard, it is imperative for the Muslim to note that the words that are spoken here are inspiration and not necessarily a book. In addition to the foregoing statements reaffirming the spiritual inspiration and/or communication link that prevailed between Allah and His apostles should be a stringent reminder in motivating the Muslim to strengthen his faith in Allah, and to reaffirm his trust and allegiance in Him as the true God to be worshipped.

Having discussed some aspects of spiritual inspiration and faith in Allah, we will now proceed to discuss the notion of spiritual inspiration and hidden knowledge.

6.2 The Wisdom in Spiritual Inspiration and Hidden Knowledge

Muslims bear testimony to belief in the Five Pillars of Islam, one of which is to believe in what Allah has made visible to mankind, including the unseen (the hidden). To this end is the reality that "Allah (alone) knows the unseen, and He doesn't make anyone acquainted with His mysteries" (Sura al-Jinn 72:26).

However, in the Quran there many testimonies related to Allah's acquaintance with the mysteries of His creation. The logical question to ask is "Should Allah not know, He that created? And He is the one that understands the finest mysteries (and) is well acquainted (with them)" (Sura al-Mulk verse 14). The bone of contention here is for the believing Muslim to acknowledge the fact that absolute knowledge belongs to Allah alone, and He gives it to whom He wills. A case in point is that of our beloved Prophet Muhammad (saw) and his knowledge regarding the unseen (*ilm-ghaib*), of prophets, and relevant Quranic verses/*ahadees* proving this category of knowledge. In relation to this fact, there is various evidence in the Quran, some of which we will venture to tabulate as follows:

(a) *And this prophet is not miserly upon the hidden. (Allah gave the knowledge of the hidden to the Holy Prophet, peace and blessings be upon him. (Sura at-Takwir 81:24)*

(b) *There are the tidings of the unseen that we reveal to you in secret. (Sura AliImran 3:44)*

(c) *The Knower of Unseen reveals not His secret to anyone except to His chosen Messengers. (Sura Al-Jinn72:26)*

(d) *Nor will he disclose to you the secrets of the unseen. But He chooses of His apostles for the purpose. (Sura AliImran 3:179)*

Similarly, the powers of hidden knowledge was also given to the Prophet Jesus (Sayyiduna Esa, peace be upon him). Allah taught him the Book and wisdom, the Law, and the Gospel, and appointed him an apostle to the children of Israel. Thereafter, when he addressed his *ummah* (nation) he contended the following:

> *I have come to you with a sign from your Lord, in that I make for you out of clay, as it were, the figure of a bird and breathe into it, and it become a bird by Allah's leave. And I heal those born blind and the lepers, and I quicken the dead by Allah's leave. Surely, therein is a sign for you if ye did believe. (Sura AliImran 3: 48-49)*

However, as we venture to briefly discuss about the knowledge of the unseen, it is vital that we highlight the fact that there is also the term *ghayb*, meaning something only known to Allah; i.e., that which is concealed. Notwithstanding, the knowledge of *ilm al ghayb* (the knowledge of the unseen) is different from the knowledge of the Book (*ilm al-kitab*). The crux of the matter is for the Muslim to appreciate and acknowledge the reality that "with Allah are the keys of the unseen (*ghayb*), the treasures that none knoweth but He. He knoweth whatever there is on earth and in the sea. Not a leaf doth fall but with His knowledge. There is not a grain in the darkness or depths of the earth, nor anything fresh or dry (green or withered) but is (inscribed) in a record clear (to those who can read)" (Sura al-An'am 6:59).

Relative to the foregoing discussion, it is also imperative for the Muslim to understand that Allah's powers are infinite and beyond man's comprehension. For instance, it is easy for us to just take some of the bounties that Allah gave us for granted, yet neglecting the fact that every grain in the darkness and/or depth of the earth, including any fresh or dry green that withered, are inscribed in a record. *This is the mystic record*, the archetypal plan, the eternal law according to which everything seen and unseen is ordered and regulated. The simplest things in nature are subject to Allah's law. The fresh and the withered, the living and the lifeless—nothing is outside the plan of His creation.

As regards the knowledge of the unseen (*ghayb*), it is latent, and there is evidence in the Quran when Allah instructed Prophet Muhammad to tell people that he has no knowledge of the unseen when he says: "Say, O Muhammad! 'I do not say to you that I have the treasures of Allah or that I know the unseen (*ghayb*). And I do not say to you that I am an angel. I only follow what is revealed to me.' Say, O Mohammed! 'Are the blind and the seeing equal? Do you not think (Sura al-An'am 6:50)?'"

In spite of all of the above stated facts about knowledge of the unseen, the Muslim should be mindful of those individuals who use fortunetelling, magic, hypnotism, brainwashing, and the like to promote innovations that are contrary to the principles and morals of Islam. In this regard, the Muslim should also be mindful of other forms of knowledge which fall under the category of innovations and made-up novelties.

There is also in the Book of Truth, Knowledge, and Wisdom verses which are of basic and/or fundamental meaning constituting its foundation. In relation to these basic fundamental virtues are verses of allegory, which are narratives of characters representing abstracts ideas or moral principles to guide man to attain piety, hidden knowledge, and wisdom. For example, some of the signs of Allah may be visible to man, but in reality there is always a fine or thin line which is latent to us as human beings. Among these examples lies the hidden knowledge of Allah which forms a barrier between ocean water and that of a river or between two different oceans' waters as explained in chapter 4. The mystery behind the convergence of these different waters and oceans around the globe is the fact that we can visually observe their barriers forming on the surface, yet it is very difficult for us to ascertain the forces preventing them from amalgamating their differing constituencies. This mystery and/or hidden secret is only known to Allah, and up to this day there is no scientific justification for it.

Similarly, we are aware of the fact that night and day changes without the control of man, for in reality we don't have the power nor the capability, capacity, knowledge, and wisdom to do so. Relative to this statement, there is ample evidence in the Quran explaining to man, especially those who believe and have the reflection and understanding of God's infinite creations of the heavens and the earth. In this regard, there is ample evidence in the Quran to substantiate these arguments. Among this evidence lies the explanation that "Allah is the light of the heavens and the earth. The parable of His Light is as if there were a niche and within it a lamp. The lamp enclosed in glass. The glass, as it was, a brilliant star" (Sura An-Nur 24:35).

Complementary to the abovementioned statement is the reality that Allah is a light which mankind doesn't have the capacity to contain. Notwithstanding, as believing Muslims we do acknowledge the fact that it is through his mercy that He has manifested His creations as a reflection of His signs. For instance, among His signs is His creation of night and day, the sun and the moon. Moreover, all the celestial bodies swim around, each in its rounded course. The manifestation of this reality is backed up by the fact that it is explained in the preceding paragraph, coupled with the powers and might of how he made the sun to be a shining glory and the moon a light of beauty, and measured out stages so that we can know the number of years and the count of time. In addition to these benefits to man, the sun helps man in the growth of our vegetation and plants on earth. Moreover, the sun and the wind also drive the ocean's oscillations, but it is the moon's gravitational tug that is responsible for the lion's share of the predictable tidal flux.

The crux of the matter will therefore depend on those categories of believing servants who appreciate His signs and some of their benefits and blessings to mankind. The irony lies in the fact that mankind benefits from all of these wondrous bounties that Allah provides for us, but it tends to make us take it for granted without much appreciation. This kind of attitude is typical among us humans, as was the case with Prophet Musa, who with all of the divine powers that Allah gave him still wanted more and requested to see Him physically. This evidence is manifested in the Quran where it is revealed that Allah had chosen Moses above all people of his era for His messages and to speak with Him. Furthermore, Allah said to Moses, "So take what I have given you and be grateful. We have inscribed for you on the tablets the admonitions and explanation of all things, and gave you instructions to take them with strong will and to command your people to follow it according to their best sense" (Sura al-A'raf 7:144-145).

In Islam, it was during the tenth of Dhul-Hijjah (month of pilgrimage), in the Muslim Festival of Sacrifice, when Allah spoke to Moses. And it was the same day when Allah completed the religion of Islam, perfected it for his Prophet Muhammed (saw), and accomplished His favors. We can obviously derive from Moses enthusiasm and a craving to get more divine blessings from Allah as the dominant factor that led to his appointment to see his creator. But the fact of the matter is that when the Lord manifested Himself on the mount it was crushed to a fine dust, and Moses fell down in shock. When he regained consciousness, he said: "Glory is to you! I repent to you, and I am the first of the believers."

The nature of this kind of curiosity is inherent in man and must be acknowledged and understood by His believing servants. Consequently, as believing servants we need to send an abundance of glory to Allah, who created in pairs all things that the earth produces, as well as their own (human) kind and (other) things of which we have no knowledge about. And to comprehend that among His signs is the alternating of night and day. Actually, it is He who withdraws the day, and behold man is then plunged in darkness. And the sun runs his course for a period determined by Him, that is decreed by Him, the exalted in might, the all knowing. And the moon, under the guidance and control of Allah, is not permitted to catch up with the sun and vice versa, nor can the night outstrip the day. Each just swims along in its own orbit according to law.

In view of the foregoing stated examples, Allah is reminding mankind that He is the light of the heavens and the earth; the one who created humankind, night and day, and the sun and the moon, including the galaxies and all that prevails in His creations. Therefore, Allah is the one to be glorified, for He has also created things that we have no knowledge about. However, through His infinite mercy and blessings He created all things in pairs, including mankind. He made the sun to be shining with its beneficial effects to us, including the vegetation among other things, and for the moon a light of beauty with also its beneficial effects to man and in controlling the sea tides, among other factors. In this regard, the Quran endorsed this statement when it states that "Allah is He who is firmly established on the throne of authority, regulating and governing all things" (Sura Yunus 10:3).

As a reminder, we have also mentioned in the preceding paragraph that among Allah's regulating powers includes His latent mode of governing the rotation and path of both the sun and moon and to facilitate mankind to be aware of the number of years and count the time. Complementary to these facts lies the indisputable reality that the pair of eyes that Allah gave mankind has the capacity to discern the moon which is 238,900 miles, the sun 92.96million miles, and the stars 100,000 light years away, a manifestation of the magnitude of His creation and love for mankind. Irrespective of the enormous distance of the moon, sun, and stars from planet Earth, there exists the hidden mystery of man's inability to comprehend that changing moment when the night fades away and the start of a new dawn. This changing moment happens so fast that it remains a mystery to man. The nature of this mystery which deals with verses which manifest characters of allegory (representations of abstract concepts, the symbols employed in such literature, including any symbolic representations) in the Book of Wisdom are reflected in the Quran when it states:

> Allah it is who has sent down to thee the Book: In it are verses basic or fundamental (of established meanings). They are the foundation of the Book: others are allegorical. But those in whose hearts is perversity follow the part thereof that is allegorical, seeking discord, and searching for its hidden meanings. But no one knows its hidden meanings except Allah and those who are firmly grounded in knowledge say: we believe in the Book; the whole of it is from our Lord: and none will grasp the message except men of understanding. (Sura AliImran 3:7)

The fact of the matter is for the Muslim to strive hard in order to attain a spiritual and/or divine level of understanding commensurate to that which is intended in the above verse in Sura AliImran. The attainment of this kind of understanding from a Muslim requires major sacrifices such as the rejection of the temptations and desires of this *dunyah* (world), striving to perfect oneself spiritually and morally, seeking knowledge, wisdom pertaining to the guidance and principles of both the Quran and the practices of the Prophet Muhammad (saw). In other words, there exist some people who are categorized by Allah as belonging to the wise. For instance, one of the reminders pertaining to such category of people is reflected in the Quran when Allah said that "in His signs indeed are signs for people that are wise" (Sura Al-Baqarah 2:164).

In today's world, man's quest for knowledge is geared toward money and related material gains. It is a world that is driven by how man can accumulate wealth, for those who have it in abundance are either tempted to utilize it wisely as ordained in the Quran or wrongly to fulfill their *nafs* (desires) and/or desires of this world. The nature of this ego and/or lust for many has resulted to greed among men to an extent in which he no longer has trust or faith in what he consumes, including the health hazards generated by his environment. This fear and lack of trust are reflected in the food we eat, some of which have traces of toxins and/or cancerous agents. Moreover, the air we breathe is given to us by Allah in a pure and natural state, and nowadays, our so-called development masked by financial greed has affected the ozone layer of the Earth's atmosphere to an extent that the air we breathe is considered to be polluted in some major cities and even in rural settings where chemical industries are established. The nature of this pollution is exacerbated by hazardous carbon monoxide gases and/or fumes and toxic waste, among other factors.

Allah's blessings, mercy, and gifts to mankind are always pure and beneficial to our survival. For instance, the nature of man's greed has reached an epidemic level where even some of the food we consume is genetically engineered and produced in order to maximize profit for the rich. Even in some countries like China, rice is now being manufactured from plastic and exported to Africa as their dumping ground. These are among the few examples of man's failure to utilize the natural ways of growing the food we consume, but persistently bent on his lust and greed for money and consistently jeopardizing the health of their poor consumers. Apparently, due to this unfortunate situation the affluent food consumers are aware of these health risks, hence their choice to buy food products grown naturally, which agents refer to as "organic" type of food, which is healthy but expensive for both the poor and underprivileged consumers, especially in developed societies. In this regard, the lack of moral aspect by food investors to protect the health of their consumers is no longer a primary concern but a secondary matter, and this leaves much to be desired.

Another example of man's disregard for the health, safety, and wellbeing of his fellow human being, especially if they are from a different nation, tribe, race, and/or religion, remains a serious social and moral concern. Relative to this issue is the proliferation of atomic and nuclear long-range missiles by some of the advanced nations whose ambition is related to national and international power control and dominance for weaker nations to succumb to their sociopolitical and socioeconomic doctrines. Notwithstanding, such advanced nations are aware of the dangers and threat of nuclear weapons to the extent that they are bargaining for their reduction.

The crux of the matter and a question that remains unanswered is why can't they get rid of these nuclear weapons and introduce a policy to have them banned on the surface of planet Earth? All of these factors have become a universal social and health concern for mankind. A case in point is the continuous testing of nuclear long-range missiles by North Korea. Even in West Africa, one of its small and poor countries has allowed a Chinese manufacturing company to dump its chemical waste in its riverbanks, killing and eroding the fish supply and other marine lives, which if consumed by its citizens could have devastating health risks and consequences relating to their lives. However, it is imperative for man to come to terms with the reality of his own greed and self-destructive intentions, motives, and agendas in developing these weapons of mass destruction that are detrimental to the survival of the human species on planet Earth.

But the hidden mystery is the superweapons possessed by Allah (such as meteorites), which scientists and astronomers now fear could one day destroy our planet Earth. This prediction by man remains one of Allah's mysteries that man will not know until it comes as a surprise when the world will be in darkness, the sun and the moon joined together depicting the Day of Resurrection. On that day mankind is reminded in Suraat-Takwir 81: 1-15 that "the Sun (with its spacious light) will be folded up; the stars will fall, losing their luster and the mountains will vanish (like a mirage) . . . and the scrolls laid open, the hellfire is kindled, and the Garden is brought near; then shall each soul know what it has brought forward and put back."

Actually, if only man was to ponder and reflect on both the trauma of this day when no soul will be in a position to avail each other. The reason being that each individual will be focused on how to account for his own deeds, not knowing what his reward or punishment will be.

In view of the foregoing discussion, there is ample evidence for mankind to take heed of the infinite powers of Allah and His hidden knowledge which is beyond our comprehension. For instance, there is stern evidence in Sura Al-Baqarah 2:117 that "to Allah is due the primal origin of the heavens and the earth: when he decreeth a matter he said to it 'Be,' and 'it is.'"

However, for the Muslim, it is imperative for him to note the reversal manner in which Allah draws the attention of mankind in Sura Al-Baqarah verse 117 in which He emphasizes his hidden powers of creating the heavens and the Earth, and in Sura at-Takwir verses 1 to 3 he warns mankind of a day when he will end and/or wrap-up this same creation of the heavens (planets and related galaxies) and the earth. These hidden powers of Allah to bring to an end the existence of the entire solar system and mankind should serve as a warning for man to relinquish his greed for power and wealth, remembering that day when the souls are sorted out, the scrolls laid open for each individual to account for his deeds.

Why is man so arrogant and not doing good deeds in readiness for this day of certainty (Judgment Day)? Relative to the prevailing discussion, we can clearly see that the emphasis for knowledge is out of balance, focusing more on science and technology innovations, believing it will propagate the development and wellbeing of mankind. To this end, man has overlooked the significant importance of the moral and spiritual development of the human mind, creating and fostering healthier and more balanced communities, societies, and nations where mankind will be able to coexist in peace, harmony, understanding, and prosperity.

Be it Jew, Christian, or Muslim, it is imperative for mankind to propagate good moral values that will accept the fact that all men are created equal and put these indelible words of reality into practice for our children and generations yet unborn to emulate. In order to effectively propagate this peaceful coexistence among mankind, there has to be the spiritual teachings and understanding of the oneness of God (*tawheed*) to be backed by each of the Abrahamic faith respecting each another's faith (i.e., the exercise of the right and freedom of worship, for Islam is against the compulsion of religion). Relative to this statement, the Quran reminds us the following:

> *Say! O ye that reject faith: I worship not that which ye worship; nor will ye worship that which I worship, and I will not worship that which ye worship, nor will ye worship that which I worship, to you be your (way) religion, and to me mine. (Sura al-Kafirun 109:1–6)*

In the preceding discussion under subsection 6.2 we have stated the fact that there are some among mankind who will challenge the existence of Allah, create innovations without much knowledge or evidence to back their statements and/or arguments. The crux of the matter lies in the reality that without faith (belief in the oneness of God), spiritual guidance, the practice of righteous deeds accompanied by patience and tolerance, a society is doomed to fail in its effort to establish a moral and just social coexistence for its citizens. We are now witnessing a world that is disintegrating socially, morally, and spiritually due to man's failure to atone spiritually in order to have true guidance to be righteous in our everyday dealings with each other. Actually, this is the kind of period we are living and it is sad and pathetic to witness the moral degeneration of man at an unprecedented scale. Moreover, this social degeneration of man is exacerbated by evidence of mass killings due to either political or religious factors, including crimes such as homicide in families, schools, workplace, social gatherings and the abuse of authority by law enforcement officials due to racism and other related factors such as anti-immigrants to name a few. These patterns of behavior is prevalent as a norm across the globe at the individual and national levels in both developed and developing countries. It is ironical to point to the fact that such race hate groups and so called religious radical extremist are victims of brainwashing and wrong kind of indoctrination which makes them lack the moral principles, teachings and understanding of faith in God. As we wrote the text of this paragraph, the news from MSMBC News came, which was also confirmed by the guardian newspaper of May 23,2017:

> *Sources said the initial theory was that a suicide bomber was behind the suspected terrorist attack at the Manchester Arena, United Kingdom, which caused havoc, and casualties of about 19 deaths and more than 50 injured in an explosion. (Source: The Guardian, by Vikram Dodd, Helen Pidd and Kevin Rawlinson, 2017)*

The timely occurrence of such a callous and irresponsible killings of innocent civilians (men, women children) is a cowardly act of hatred and cannot be attributed to any of the teachings of the Abrahamic faiths mentioned in the preceding paragraph. We need to take cognizance of the fact that such groups are out to terrorize people, they are out to kill indiscriminately be it Jews, Christians or Muslims, and by any measurable moral and social standards, their acts of brutality is unacceptable. For the justification for this argument lays the fact that none of the Abrahamic faiths (i.e.,Judaism, Christianity, and Islam will teach any of their followers to deliberately kill people of any of these faiths including the massacre of innocent civilians such as women, children, the elderly, and refugees in some instances.

The crux of the matter lies in the fact that there is the ideal world dictated by our own perceptions of how we discern and interpret those matters of concern that impinges on our daily lives. Actually, this notion of viewing the world is deceiving and not pragmatic. Notwithstanding, we need come to terms that the world out there depicting its harsh realities is palpable with its wretchedness, inhumane and immoral practices that makes the so-called "Breaking News" of the Day. In the real world we live in, it is so ironical to see that man no longer have the love, mercy, sympathy, empathy, respect and consideration for each other. Frankly, speaking, this is irony and misery of an era, where the degeneration of some men have led to mass killings, terrorism and genocide at an unprecedented scale, and slavery as the case is in Libya, of which ultimately future generations will undoubtedly question. Yet still, as intelligent and advanced man have attained academically as well as in science and technology, we have no answers and/or resolutions to these cowardly, brutal, callous and irresponsible behaviors of the few in our societies.

As we now live in a world that is corrupted by egocentric political, religious, and racial biases, it is imperative for the Muslim to stay impartial as regards issues pertaining to these three factors, including their residual effects nationally and internationally. But how can the Muslim remain impartial yet not aloof in a diverse world of traditional, religious, and educational doctrines and beliefs. This divergent reality has in some circles turned man into a wild animal (like a beast), and in other circles, man has remained intoxicated with power, greed, and materialism. The resultant effects of all of these factors has turned the world into a wretched place of survival of the fittest. However, in developed countries, while all of these kinds of negative activities are taking place, such as mass killings and genocide, some families are left morally, physically, and psychologically devastated, thereby leaving their survivors and their immediate families to undergo daily traumatic circumstances of poverty, malnutrition, starvation, and unplanned refugees, among other factors. Likewise, in developing countries such as in Africa, similar things are happening and are attributed to factors such as poor governance, tribalism, nepotism, religious discrimination, poverty, illiteracy, and the poor state of the economy, among other factors. For instance, according to dosomething.org, it is stated that *nearly half of the world population, more than 3 billion, live on less than $2.50 a day; more than 1.3 billion live in extreme poverty, less than $1.25 a day. One billion children worldwide are living in poverty. According to UNICEF, 22,000 children die each day due to poverty. 805 million people worldwide do not have enough food to eat. More than 750 million people lack adequate access to clean drinking water.*

However, this evidence of worldwide poverty, coupled with brutality, callousness, and irresponsible behavior is unacceptable for any of the Abrahamic faiths and therefore points to man's lack of understanding and intolerance, which also existed throughout the ages. This lack of understanding among mankind is reflected in Sura Al-Asr 103: 1-3, in which the Quran draws our attention: "By (the token of) time (through the ages), verily man is in loss, except such as have faith, and do righteous deeds, and (join together) in the mutual teaching of truth, and of patience and constancy."

The above stipulated verse from Sura Al-Asr can't be disputed by men of faith, understanding who reflect and fear Allah. The amazing reality of this verse is the manner in which it proclaims that throughout the ages up to the present time man is at a loss, but there prevails an exception during all of these periods. The encouraging and gratifying aspect of this exception refers to those who have faith in Allah, perform righteous deeds, and join together in the mutual teaching of truth, patience, and constancy. It is these men of faith who are the exceptions and/or the few in society, and their sacrifices to propagate these noble moral virtues have remained a test and challenge for the rest of mankind to emulate in order to attain piety.

The crux of the matter is how can we attain piety at the home, school, community, national, and international levels? We will probe with another question in an effort to find answers. In reality, are we behaving spiritually and righteously as human beings, or have we degenerated to the lowest of our existence (such as the animal state) as human being, thereby making us vulnerable toward the manner in which we rationalize in solving our problems? The magnitude of this lack of spiritual and moral guidance has eroded the social fabrics of societies to an extent that it is reflecting on the style and apex of national leadership, breeding dictatorship, autocracy, and corruption, among other factors. The manifestation of these factors in modern-day leadership, be it in developing or developed nations, renders us to live in a period of time where greed, egocentric tendencies, failure to adhere to the democratic principles of justice and fair play.

Furthermore, their inability to promote the mutual teaching of truth, patience, and constancy in the execution of their duties are eroding the moral trust of the people that they govern. The prevalence of this kind of society leaves much to be desired, thereby depicting the lack of good leadership and guidance. However, acknowledging the wretchedness of the world that we live in, it is of moral concern that the Muslim must take a leading role in standing out for justice in order to help alleviate some of these negative prevailing socioeconomic and its corresponding sociopolitical constraints that are impinging on the progress and peaceful coexistence of mankind. It would require a proactive approach that will bring about a positive change toward peace and prosperity to all of mankind irrespective of their political, religious, racial, or ethnic backgrounds or affiliations.

Also, with the Muslim being someone who believes in God, he should venture to nurture a spirit of civic and moral duty to learn and understand his rights and duties toward Allah, his nation, his community, and to people that he interacts with and others within the society. For instance, he needs to know how the internal and external socioeconomic and sociopolitical forces and constraints are impinging on his daily life as well as his religion. He needs to know the duties of political leaders toward his communities, those of judges, those of children toward their parents, likewise parents toward their children, spouses toward each other, relatives, and other such matters with which those who enjoin good and forbid evil should be well acquainted. In this regard, the Quran addresses the issue of justice when it states:

O you who believe: Stand out firmly for justice as witness to Allah, even as against yourselves, or your parents, or your kin, and whether it is (against) rich or poor: for Allah can best protect both. Follow not the lust of your hearts least you swerve, and if you distort justice or decline to do justice, verily Allah is well-acquainted with all that you do. (Sura An-Nisa 4:135)

However, the best of guidance is that which is from Allah. The reason being that Allah's guidance to man is a gift blessed with His infinite mercy and wisdom. Furthermore, His gift to man is for a purpose in which he is given the freewill to acknowledge, rationalize, and utilize it in a positive way showing his gratefulness, or a negative manner to manifest his ungratefulness. The former acknowledgment by man is an indication of appreciation, whereas the latter depicts a sign of loss, pride, and arrogance, forgetting the fact that there was a time when he was nothing and there will also come a time when he will exit this world and be nothing. In order to put this statement within the context of the Quran, Sura Al-Dahr 76: 1-3 contend that "has there not been over man a long period of time when he was nothing, not even mentioned? Verily we created man from a drop of mingled sperm in order to try him, so we gave him the gifts of hearing and sight; we showed him the way; whether he be grateful or ungrateful rest on his will."

The rationality of man, therefore, is guided by the free will that Allah endowed us with, as mentioned in the above verse. The irony of man's pompousness, arrogance, and ungratefulness is often triggered by factors such as status, power, wealth, and knowledge, among other factors. For it is a reality that when Allah tests him with any of these gifts, he verily assumes that he is the one who made it happen, forgetting the fact that the allocation of knowledge, power, and wealth to man is a hidden gift from Allah. This fact is also manifested in the Quran, Sura At-Taghabun 64:15, when Allah says: "Your wealth and your children are only a trial (*fitnah*)." However, it is up to the individual to appreciate and understand the fact that in the course of such a trial it can either be temporal or permanent, depending on Allah's wishes.

In relation to this fact, it is crucial for the believing Muslim to maintain a strong level of *imaan* (faith) in God during such periods of trials, both in adversity and in prosperity. We are being reminded in the Quran, Sura al-Fajr 35:15-16 of this kind of situation which can befall us at any given circumstance when it states that "now, as for man, when his Lord trieth him, giving him honor and gifts, then saith he (puffed up), 'My Lord hath honored me.' But when he trieth him, restricting his subsistence for him, then saith he (in despair), 'My Lord hath humiliated me!'"

If we reflect on the first verse of Sura Ad-Dahr stated above, then man can apparently come to terms with himself to acknowledge the fact that even there was a period of time when he was nothing to be mentioned or considered. In this reality lies another hidden sign of Allah as the sole creator. Another reality is that our grandfather Adam was created out of dust and we (his children) are created from the drop of a mingled sperm. The fact of the matter is that both of these elements and/or substances are not always pleasant things to touch or handle, which does compel us to wash our hands or body when in contact with any of these elements. These are undisputable facts which should remind mankind of the kind of substance he originated from and to choose to be humble rather than to be arrogant because of the gifts that Allah endowed him with as a test.

Another reality in relation to our creation is that when we come to this world the first thing is to clean the residue of fluids on the baby that are from the womb of the mother. In this regard, let us not be naive or misguided not to highly appreciate this gift of creation which enables man to multiply on earth, and to acknowledge the fact that God is pure and anything attached to His creation comes in a purified state of being. Hence the fact that man came to this world in a pure state, implying that we were created sinless, innocent, and ignorant of what we are to face in this world. These are hard realities depicting the fact that all knowledge, including that of the future (hidden knowledge), belongs to Allah alone. Hence in the preceding paragraph we have highlighted this reality in Sura Ad-Dahr 76:1-3 that Allah gave man the gifts of hearing and sight and showed him the way, and his gratefulness or ungratefulness rest on his will. This is a very powerful statement from Allah that after He showed us the way it is incumbent on man to be able to utilize these gifts efficiently and effectively to facilitate him in his acquisition of knowledge in order to enable him to use his free will to discern right from wrong through his ultimate journey to submit to the will of Allah.

As for the Muslim, the nature of this submission to the will of Allah must be accompanied by the vim, vigor, determination, and sacrifices to leave behind the temptations of this *dunyah* (world) and adopt a distinct path of righteousness that will enable him to know the way of Allah which He revealed in Sura Ad-Dahr verses 1-3 above. Submitting to the will of Allah enables the Muslim to have greater trust and affinity for Him, and in connecting and seeking His help. An example pertaining to Allah's help among the believers is in the Quran, Sura Al-Imran 3:160, which contends that "If Allah helps you, none can overcome you. If He forsakes you, who is there after that, that can help you? In Allah, then, let believers put their trust."

The Muslim, therefore, must desist to behave like the people who received earlier revelations and confined themselves to partial truths, and in their pride shut their eyes to the whole of the Book of God (the Quran). This statement does make us ask the question who are the people that are righteous and God-fearing? In response to this question, we will venture to provide the reader with some brief explanation concerning righteousness and draw few examples from the Quran.

In relation to the foregoing statements, it is of valuable essence for the Muslim to understand the fact that his purpose in life on earth is to worship Allah and Him alone. The nature of his worship must be marked with devotion, commitment, and sincerity just for the sake of Allah. Once these virtues are spiritually and physically manifested as part of his daily life endeavors, it will automatically transform his body and soul to tame his lower *nafs* (the animal state of man that yearns for evil), also known as *nafsal-ammara bissu*.

In this subsection we are discussing the body and soul within the context of spiritual inspiration and hidden knowledge to help man attain righteousness. Discussion pertaining to the body and disciplining the soul are explained in detail in chapter 7 below.

The *nafsal-ammarabissu*is the self that incites evil and is hidden. It is when the animalistic behavior of man is outwardly and/or physically manifested that we sometimes see the brute nature of man, which is an impediment to righteousness. This implies that it is a characteristic of the human self to incite evil as opposed to his efforts to attain perfection which will lead to his moral state to distinguish right from wrong. In Islam, the attainment of the moral state by man is also regarded as the self that reproves itself for every vice and intemperance. It will imply, therefore, that the reproving self is the second source of human state from which the moral state is generated as a vehicle to the journey of righteousness. Though at this stage man, in his search and struggle to attain righteousness in respect of vices, is still not adequately effective and efficient in practicing virtue and occasionally is circumvented and/or dominated by natural emotions, when it stumbles and falters, trying to overcome those constraints, weaknesses, and huddles that impede him from the attainment of righteousness.

The nature of this weakness in man in his moral state does make him feel remorseful over his infirmity. In other words, it tends to put man in a mode of frustration while he is making efforts to reach success and righteousness of his *nafs* (soul). Consequently, it is a moral state where man seeks to comprehend within it high moral qualities and is frustrated with obstacles of disobedience, and realizes that still it is difficult for him to achieve success and righteousness. However, it is when the soul is at the beginning of the spiritual state of man, also known as the *nafsmutmainnah*, implying the soul at rest, can man then be able to find comfort in Allah. The nature of this kind of comfort is regarded as the stage when the soul of a believing servant is deterred from all weakness and filled with spiritual powers. It is such spiritual powers that will facilitate a believing servant to fully establish a lasting relationship with Allah the Almighty without whose assistance it can't prevail.

Righteousness can also be attributed with the measure of certain moral and spiritual characteristics which starts with the individual's belief and fear in Allah and being truthful, among other factors. These moral and spiritual characteristics are also mentioned in Sura Al-Baqarah

2:177, which states that "it is not righteousness that you turn your faces toward east or west, but it is righteousness to believe in Allah and the Last Day, and the angels, and the Book, and the messengers; To spend of your substance, out of love for him, for your kin, orphans, the needy, the wayfarer, those who ask, and for the ransom of slaves. To be steadfast in prayer and practice regular charity. To fulfill the contracts which you have made. And to be firm and patient in pain (or suffering) and adversity, and throughout all periods of panic. Such are the people of truth, the God-fearing."

Furthermore, pertinent to righteousness, we will give two qualities that are mentioned in the Quran which if attained by a believing Muslim can enable him to come closer to the path of righteousness. First among these two qualities is to forgive when being offended or wronged by others. In order to support our line of argument, in Sura Al-Baqarah 2:237 Allah says: "To forego and/or forgive is nearer to righteousness (*taqwa*)." As regards the second quality, He says: "Deal justly, for that is nearer to righteousness (*taqwa*)." The emphasis pertaining to these two examples is on forgiving and acting justly, qualities that require a great deal of sacrifice regarding the individual's ego, such as arrogance to begin with. At this point, it is vital to remind the reader that it was as a result of sacrificing one's ego relating to the creation of Adam by Allah that caused *Ibliss* (Satan) to be cursed and brought down to earth.

Actually, the lessons to be drawn out these two explanations in the above paragraph is the fact that a good deed does not automatically equate or translate to righteousness, but has the propensity to bring the individual closer to it. In more explicit terms, we can say that what has been derived from this explanation is the understanding that good deeds lead to righteousness. The bone of contention here is that if good deeds are factors that facilitate our efforts to righteousness, then it must be such that there is a hidden and/or spiritual factor that has the capacity to make us attain our aim to righteousness. In fact, this aim translates to an intention by the individual to forgive and act justly. The nature of his intention must therefore come from the heart. Righteousness, therefore, is measured based on the heart and its commitment and willingness to forgive, yet at the same time enabling the individual to be just and impartial.

In order to sum this chapter up, we will refer to the Arabic word for righteousness, *birr*, which connotes various levels of meaning. Firstly, it has been used to mean righteousness, piety, virtue, and charity. Secondly, *birr* encompasses the inner satisfaction, pleasure, and happiness a person feels when he does the right thing, when everything feels correct and at peace with itself and the surroundings. Therefore, from an Islamic perspective, when a Muslim does the right thing, obeys Allah and worships Him correctly, he feels satisfied, have that sense of gratification, security, and happiness within him. In this regard, *birr* denotes righteousness, and it prepares and facilitates the individual to act in a way that invokes this inner peace. It is a rigid set of beliefs (as stipulated in the above Sura Al-Baqarah 2: 177) and actions that will enable the individual to maintain a well-balanced and safe life.

We will now proceed to discuss the relationship between disciplining the soul and the body in chapter 7 below.

CHAPTER 7.0

The Wisdom in Disciplining the Soul and the Body

THE MUSLIM, IN his quest to adhere to Islam as the religion of truth, should also venture and acknowledge the fact that the revelation of the Quran has multidimensional spheres, guidelines, and effects to purify him and his soul. Likewise, the Sunnah of the Prophet, known as *hadith*, should be a guideline for him to emulate the noble traits and character of the Messenger of Allah. These two divine characteristics of both the Quran and the Sunnah are factors that tend to make Islam a religion which is perfected with divine guidelines and revelations to help shape man's moral and spiritual traits and characteristics in his quest and journey to submit to the will of Allah. The nature of this guidance is discussed in chapter 6 of this book, which reiterated the fact that the servant and/or believer who submits to the will and love of Allah remains righteous, does good deeds, and refrains from evil. He also performs regular prayers, pays *zakat*, and assists the poor and the needy in paving his way to Allah so that he will surely be guided in the right path through His infinite mercy and blessings. In fact, the Muslim must consider himself to be very lucky to be among those believers who choose to read the Quran that is revealed by Allah through Angel Gabriel to Prophet Muhammad. In fact, Allah did guarantee that it is a Book that is assuredly guided and protected by Him against any form of corruption by man.

To this end, there is no other divine book like the Quran, which was revealed about 1,400 years ago, and the evidence and accuracy of its contents of reality and the nature of its uniqueness remain undisputable even with modern scientific discoveries which occurred beginning in the nineteenth century. Relative to these factors, the Quran reminds us of the divine messages contained therein and how God associates Himself with it when He says in Sura Al-Hijr 15:9 that "We have, without doubt sent down the message, and we will assuredly guard it from corruption." However, further authenticity of the revelations of the Quran is mentioned in Sura An-Nisa 4: 82, which contends "Do they not consider the Quran with care? Had it been from other than Allah they would surely have found therein much discrepancy."

As regards issues relating to the Quran and modern science, we have briefly discussed it in chapter 4.0. Usually, science conflicts with religion, but such is not the case with the Quran, for it brought adequate evidence that is in conformity with modern science. Because of these harsh realities, many a scientist has now embraced Islam as the religion of truth and became practicing Muslims after their careful analysis and consideration of the facts available at their disposal.

A typical case in point is that of Dr. Maurice Bucaulle, a French doctor and scientist who was born a Christian, and during his assignment to investigate the mummification of Pharaoh was convinced that the revelation of the Quran pertaining to the preservation of Pharaoh's body as a sign to mankind made him accept the fact that Prophet Muhammad, a man who could not read or write, knew such detailed facts about modern science, which made scientists agree then that the Quran is a book which was revealed by God. Because of Dr. Maurice Bucaulle's acceptance of this reality, he became a Muslim.

But what is this reality that the Quran teaches mankind? It is a reality of total submission and love for Allah so that the believer and/or His servant who stays righteous and humble will refrain from the arrogance which made nations and men in the past perish due to their persistent denial and unjust behavior. We have discussed in previous chapters of this book how men like Pharaoh, Thamud, and their like who oppressed their people and transgressed beyond bounds received the wrath of Allah and perished. Inevitably, their destruction as a punishment from Allah was but a foretaste of their doom to come in the hereafter, when all creation will be on a new plane and true values will be fully established for each individual to account for his own deeds. On this day, the righteous will be blessed and the evil punished.

Actually, Islam teaches mankind to refrain from all kinds of evil thoughts and deeds against his fellow human beings, including Allah's creations, among other things. The Quran gave an example of men who choose to do evil when God says:

> And we have sent thee as an apostle to instruct mankind, and enough is Allah for a witness. (Sura An-Nisa 4:79)

We can derive from the abovementioned verse that all good deeds of man are from Allah, but it is his soul which yearns for evil (*nafsal-ammara bissu*) that needs to be discipline in a way that he will venture to refrain from evil and wrongful deeds and to submit to the will of Allah. It is this divine submission, reinforced by his sincerity to practice Islam as a religion of truth, which will become a vital ingredient to assist and guide him to be righteous and toward his endeavor to adhere to the straight path and succumb to a life of good deeds.

We have discussed in some detail about the *nafs* in subsection 5.3 and the various stages and influences it could have on the individual and his efforts to attain the station of a soul that is at rest (*nafs mutmainna*), which predominates due to his good deeds in this *dunyah* (world). Notably, good deeds are rewarded by Allah, whereas evil deeds have the tendency to corrupt the individual; his environment and society at large will not prevail without Allah's recompense.

The resultant effects of man's efforts to stay righteous and to submit to the will of Allah is in earnest one of the main functions of Islam, whose effort is to purify the soul (*nafs*), which when unweaned is constantly enjoining evil. In order to throw more light on issues relating to the *nafs*, we will refer to Al-Ghazali (1995), who pointed out that "The evil (*nafs al-ammara bissu*) is the subtle, unfixable abode of *hawa*, the condition of desire, and of *shahwa*, the desire itself."

Relative to Al-Ghazali's point, it is imperative to note that the soul (*nafs*) which yearns and/or craves evil needs to be spiritually disciplined for its cravings. However, some of these cravings of the *nafs* are multifarious and untiring for wealth, fame, power, and physical gratification, among other factors. The crux of the matter is that these factors do have the tendency and/or affinity to sway man away from God and succumb him to the lower engagements of the human condition. The crucial factor here is for man to refrain from all of the desires of the soul (*nafs*) and move toward its purification, which also requires a high degree of spiritual and material sacrifices.

As for the Muslim, these sacrifices would require him to nurture a profound degree of detachment from this world, which could materialize through the solid test of self-discipline (*riyada*). The self-discipline of the soul is better attained when the believer conforms to God's will, which will facilitate the soul which constantly enjoins evil to be tamed and over time grow enfeebled. This weakness of which the soul yearns for evil, by Allah's permission, will be unseated from its dominant place in the heart and give way to the soul which blames (*nafs al-lawwama*). The *nafs al-lawwama* denotes the active conscience stricken by guilt and self-reproach when God's commands are violated and the lower soul wins a skirmish with the rational mind. At this stage, it is vital for the Muslim to continually and persistently strive for the inward labor and purification of himself in order to attain the *nafs mutmainna* (the soul at peace), which should then predominate. The soul which dominates is the soul at rest, implying a high degree of spiritual attainment which has the propensity to draw man closer to God. The Quran substantiates this fact when it says:

> To the righteous soul will be said, O thou soul in complete rest and satisfaction, come back thou to thy Lord well pleased with thyself, and well pleasing unto him! Enter thou, then, among my devotees! Yes, enter thou my heaven. (Sura Fajr: 35:27-30)

In view of the foregoing discussion, it is worthy to recapitulate on our earlier explanation of the three characteristics of man regarding his relationship with his soul. These we have stipulated as the physical, moral, and spiritual states of man.

First is the physical (*nafsal-ammara bissu*), which is the source of all-natural states of man (the self) that incites evil. This stage of the *nafs* is a characteristic of the human self which urges or incites man to do evil. It sways him to a direction opposed to his struggle in attaining perfection of his moral state, and urges him toward undesirable and evil ways. Therefore, the temptation and propensity toward evil and intemperance is a human state which predominates over the mind of a person before he embarks upon the moral state. The animal state of man is his natural state so long as he is not guided by cognitive reasoning and understanding but follows his natural desires and conditions of eating, drinking, sleeping, walking, anger and provocation, similar to the animals. In fact, man can move away or distance himself from these kinds of desires or lust when he is guided by cognitive reasoning and understanding to enable him to bring his natural state under control and regulate it in a proper manner, so he ceases to remain in such a state and enters into a moral state of man (*nafsal-lawwama*). The state of this kind of *nafs* is mentioned in the Quran in Sura al-Qiyamah verse 2 when God says: "And I do call witness the self-reproaching spirit eschew evil."

This is the state of the *nafs* which feels conscious of evil and resists it, asks for God's grace and pardon after repentance, and tries to amend in order to reach salvation. In order words, God is calling to witness the reproving self, for he loves the self that is righteous and reproves itself for every vice and intemperance. Furthermore, *the reproving self is regarded as the second source of human state* from which the moral state of man is generated. The gratifying aspect of this stage reinforces the fact that man ceases to resemble the animals.

Calling to witness is for the purpose of honor by God's permission in which man advances from the state of the self that is prone to evil and arriving at the state of the reproving self, which has now become worthy of honor from a divine point of view. Though it reproves itself in respect to vices, yet it is not completely effective in practicing virtue due to the fact that it can occasionally be dominated by natural emotions when it falters, stumbles, and falls. The nature of this fall does manifest the weakness of man to falter and stumble, which he can balance again through his remorsefulness over his physical and/or moral weakness (infirmity). At the stage of the reproving self is the state of man when he struggles with his soul in an effort to seek and/or comprehend within its inner self to attain high moral qualities, and is disgusted by disobedience and lack of overall success.

At this stage of our discussion, we can proceed to *the third stage of the development of the soul, implying the soul at rest (nafsal-mutmainnah)*, which we mentioned earlier in the preceding section of this chapter and also in subsection 5.3. We have mentioned how the soul at rest will return to His Lord well pleased with Him, and in return Allah pleased with it, thereby instructing, "Now join my chosen servants and enter my paradise."

During this stage of development of the soul at rest, the individual is being delivered from all weaknesses, filled with spiritual powers, establishing a relationship with God without whose support and guidance such a relationship cannot exist. Furthermore, it is important to note that the soul at rest will always have the affinity to reach toward God. The nature of this kind of spiritual affinity will imply the soul that has found comfort in God and to return to Him well pleasing. It will also have the ability to undergo a great transformation in this life, and yet still is bestowed a paradise while still in this world. The nature of such transformation does resonate the explanation of Mirza Ghulam Ahmad of Qadian (1979) when he said that "In its direction for such a soul to return to its lord, it is nourished by its lord and its love of God becomes its nurture and it drinks at this fountain of life and is thus delivered from death."

In relation to the abovementioned statement concerning the soul, the Quran also pointed out the following:

> *By the soul, and the proportion and order given to it, and its enlightenment as to its wrong and right, truly, he succeeds that purifies it, and he fails that corrupts it. (Sura ash-Shams 91:7-10)*

However, there are other factors which may have influence over the soul. For example, the nature of relationships that prevail between the three levels of existence of the soul. In this regard, the natural state of man has a very strong relationship with his moral and spiritual states, so much so that even a person's manner of eating and drinking affects his moral and spiritual states. Furthermore, experience also revealed the fact that different types of food affect the intellect and the mind in different ways. This is reinforced by the evidence of divine law of nature that the herbivorous animals do not possess the same degree of courage as do carnivorous ones.

Also, wearing your best clothes at the time of prayer can influence the state of mind of the individual by propagating joy, happiness, and spirituality. We will refer to the Quran in Sura al-A'raaf 7:31, when Allah says: "O children of Adam! Wear your beautiful apparel at every time and place of prayer: eat and drink, but waste not by excess, for Allah loveth not wasters."

Actually, we have explained in the latter part of subsection 6:2 above that Allah created man with a free will and showed him the way. The manners that are required for eating and drinking are a case in point where Allah is guiding mankind to eat and drink moderately and try not to be wasteful, for all of these factors could influence man's moral and/or spiritual state. Thus, it could imply, for instance, that man may choose to eat meat and other foods, but when done in excess his moral state could be adversely affected and consequently his health might suffer. Another example is that if the natural state of man is subjected to the control of the directions of divine law it becomes his moral state and deeply affects his spiritually. Based on my personal experience, I have gone through that intuitive feeling that physical prostration in prayer induces humility in the soul. In fact, it is at this position in prayer that man comes closer to his creator. The supporting evidence is in the Quran, which contends the following:

> *Nay, heed him not but bow down in adoration, and bring yourself the closer to Allah. (Sura Al-AIaq 96:19)*

Moreover, if say we accept that a person's natural state is subjected to the control of the directions of divine law, it becomes his moral state and deeply affects his spiritually. Similarly, man's moral conditions are not entirely distinct from his spiritual conditions. When moral conditions develop absolute devotion to God and complete purification of self and cutting asunder from the world, turning wholly to God, and to perfect love and complete devotion and full serenity and satisfaction and complete accord with the divine will, they become a spiritual condition. Relative to this statement is the fact that as the soul is affected by the physical conduct, in the same way sometimes the soul affects the body. For example, during moments when man experiences sorrow his eyes may become wet, and on instances when man feels happy he smiles.

Another example of how the soul and body are interdependent is if a certain part of the brain is injured severely it could lead to memory loss. If an injury also occurred on the other side of the brain, it could lead to unconsciousness. In this regard, it does imply that physical injuries in certain parts of our body do manifest the fact that there is a mysterious relationship between the two (body and soul) which is beyond the comprehension of man. In this kind of reflection, there is affirmation that the body is the mother of the soul. Added to this point, the Quran 23:12-17 convey the fact that the soul becomes manifest from the framework that is prepared in the womb from the sperm when it states that "man we did create from a quintessence of clay, then we placed him as a drop of sperm in a place of rest firmly fixed; then we made the sperm into a cloth of congealed blood; then of that cloth, we made a (fetus) lump; then we made out of that lump bones and clothed the bones with flesh; then we developed out of it another creature. So blessed be Allah, the best to create!"

Relative to the above-stipulated verse, we have also learned that while these frameworks of actions are being developed the soul with which they are charged begins to shine, and when that framework becomes complete the soul inside it shines forth in its full manifestation and discloses its spiritual aspect. At that stage, those actions become fully alive. According to Mirza Ghulam Ahmad of Qadian (1996), "The claim of becoming fully alive denotes that when the framework of actions is complete something comes forth from it suddenly, like a flash of lightning is manifested." Complementary to this statement, the Quran 15: 29 reveals the fact that "When I fashioned him in due proportion and breathed into him my Spirit, fall you down in obeisance unto him.

These stipulated verses from the Quran reaffirm the fact that the soul is a fine light developed inside the body which is nurtured in the womb. We have extensively discussed about the soul, and will now proceed to the summary and conclusions of this book in chapter 8.0 below.

CHAPTER 8.0

Summary and Conclusions

IN VIEW OF the foregoing discussion, we have attempted to explain briefly how Islam as a religion of truth, guidance, and wisdom has established a solid foundation of good social, moral, ethical values and discipline for believing Muslims who fear Allah. Besides, not only does the believing Muslim fear Allah, he also acknowledges those guidelines and warnings He set for mankind in order to help him positively shape his life and destiny.

Among these guiding principles and values are the belief in Allah and submitting totally to his will; perform regularly the five daily prayers; fasting in the month of Ramadan; giving out *zakat* and assisting the poor and the needy; and performing *Hajj* at least once in the individual's lifetime when affordable. We have explained that these five guiding principles form the basic fundamental principles and pillars of Islam.

Having explained these five fundamental guiding principles of Islam, we will now recapitulate our earlier discussion in chapter 1, where we tried to explain and define the word *wisdom* and its correlation to both man and the Quran.

It has been explained that man's quest for wisdom can be correlated to the quality of being wise, exhibiting a scholarly knowledge of learning, and/or manifesting a wise act. The nature of this kind of wisdom has the tendency to be able to equip man with a sense of acknowledgment, appreciation, and belief that God is the creator of the heavens and the earth and all that they encompass.

Man's wisdom should also venture to appreciate the reality that both the physical and the spiritual worlds existed before his creation of man. The evidence of this statement goes with the narrative when the

Quran in Sura Al-Baqarah verse 30 states, "'Behold,' thy lord said to the angels, 'I will create a vicegerent on earth.' They said, 'Wilst thou place therein one who will make mischief therein and shed bloodwhilst we do celebrate thy praises and glorify thy Holy Name?' He said, 'I know what you know not.'"

In fact, a variety of lessons can be derived from the hidden knowledge that Allah taught Adam, of which the angels didn't know. This is a manifestation of the reality that all knowledge belongs to Allah and he gives it to whom he wills. Adam's lesson taught us that for man to have adequate knowledge and understanding of his environment, he must have the desire and willingness to obey the instructions of his mentor. This transfer of hidden knowledge could materialize in many different ways, such as divine, spiritual, or cognitive means through either a teacher and/or sheikh to facilitate the learning exercise for the individual being taught.

It is through learning that man should be able to develop his cognitive skills through the acquisition of the relevant knowledge and skills that are to be pursued for a given discipline and/or domain pertaining to the environment that he inhabits. In relation to this factor, it is of significant importance that man tries to seek knowledge to understand more about the physical and spiritual worlds that constitute part of his environment.

In the case of the former, such as in the domain of science and technology, there are principles, procedures, and ethical guidelines which are binding and must be understood and adhered to in order to be able to obtain the desired outcomes. As for the latter, there are men like Jesus (Prophet Isa) and Prophet Solomon (Sulayman) and Prophet Muhammad (saw) whose possession of divine spiritual knowledge was a gift from God. The nature of such divine spiritual power was behind the hidden knowledge that they possessed and utilized each in a different way. For instance, in the case of Jesus, because of the divine spiritual power that God gave him, he was able to heal lepers, make blind people see, and give back life to the dead. As for Prophet Solomon, we have explained in chapter 4.0 the divine powers that Allah gave him to be able to communicate with the birds and understand their language, and also to have heard what one of the ants communicated to the rest of the ants as Prophet Solomon passed by together with his host of men, jinns, and birds.

Relative to Prophet Muhammad's divine powers was his ability to receive messages of the Holy Quran, which were revealed to him through Angel Gabriel at intervals. Moreover, his night of ascension from Masjid al-Haram (in Mecca) to Masjidal-Aqsa (in Jerusalem), where he led all the other prophets in prayer and then proceeded with the guidance of Angel Alburah through the seven heavens to meet up with his Lord at the Lote Tree, where he saw the greatest signs of his creator.

In order to throw more light of this statement about the Prophet, the Quran reveals this fact in Sura Bani Israil 17:1, which states: "Exalted is he who took his servant (Prophet Muhammad) by night from al Masjid al-Haram to al-Masjid-al- Aqsa, whose surroundings we have blessed, to show him of our signs. Indeed, he is the Hearing, the Seeing."

The fact of the matter is that man's understanding of such divine and spiritual powers from God are very limited due to the nature of their complexities (i.e., some are manifested physically, spiritually, and others are hidden and unknown). The complexities associated with these kinds of divine and spiritual powers are among the signs of Allah and are sometimes difficult to comprehend by man. Actually, they are in very special circumstances understood by those whom Allah has favored with these kinds of knowledge and understanding as a gift to them.

In order to shed more light on the issue of divine revelation, we will refer to Mohammad Ali Shomali, who wrote in al-islam.org that "In Arabic, the term *wahy* literally means giving a message quickly and secretly, whether by gesture, in a written form or by inspiration." Complementary to this statement, the issue of inspiration is also attested in Sura al-Ankabut 29:45 when Allah says: "Recite what is sent to the Book by inspiration to thee, and establish regular prayer: for prayer restrains from shameful and unjust deeds; and remembrance of Allah is the greatest thing in life without doubt. And Allah knows the (deeds) that you do."

In the abovementioned verse where Allah says, "Recite what is sent to the Book by inspiration to thee," connotes the fact that the Prophet was inspired by Allah to recite what was in the Book (the Quran) without any form of fault or crookedness. The evidence of this statement is revealed in Sura al-Kahf 18:1, which states: "Praise is to Allah, who hath sent to his servant (the Prophet) the Book, and hath allowed no crookedness."

Furthermore, there is also evidence of this inspiration in the Quran when Allah revealed it in gradual succession to Prophet Muhammad (saw) and made it easy for him to remember. As regard this statement, there is also evidence of *wahy* as explained in the preceding paragraph related to Sura al-Ankabut verse 45 of the preceding paragraphs above, and Sura al-Ala verses 6–7 stipulated above. Despite these facts, it is worthy to note that there are instances when God suggests certain ideas or courses of action to some people who are not necessarily prophets. For instance, Imam Imaduddin Abdul-Fida Ismail Ibn Kathir Ad-Dimashqi (2003) explained the following:

> When Awhayna gave birth to Moses, it was inspired to her that she should make a chest and tie it with a long rope, with the other end tied to her house. As her house was on the bank of the Nile, she would feed him, and whenever she had fear she should place him in the chest and let the rope lose so it could hide in the reeds in the Nile River.

The abovementioned explanation is also confirmed in the Quran 28:7 when Allah says: "So we sent this inspiration to the mother of Moses: 'Suckle (thy child), but when thou hast fears about him cast him into the river, but fear not nor grieve, for we shall restore him to thee, and we shall make him one of our apostles.'" "This inspiration that was given to Moses's mother from God was direct and didn't pass through an angel. The evidence of this mode of inspiration is a reminder that God does whatever He wills, making it factual, therefore, that there exists also a fundamental gift that is related to our functionality to see, hear, communicate through differing languages, and to use our mouth and tongue to consume food, all of which are inspired to perform their various functions through the aid and command of Allah.

The Quran has reminded us of this fact, when it states: "Have we not made for man a pair of eyes, and a tongue and pair of lips: and shown him the two highways(Sura al-Balad 90:8-10)?" Generally, all of these various functional parts of the human body are gifts from God. To make mankind have two eyes as a faculty of seeing may be taken in both the literal and the metaphorical sense. Similarly, the tongue gives us the faculty of tasting in both senses. Complementary with the lips, it also enables man to speak by the permission of God, to request for information and seek guidance, and to celebrate the praises of his creator.

Now that we have given few examples of *wahy* and established the fact that it is not restricted to the prophets but i also used generally to refer to different sorts of guidance given by God to His creatures, and since divine guidance is all inclusive, his *wahy* is extended to all forms of creations.

In view of the prevailing discussion, the first form of divine guidance is that intuitive ability that is embedded in an inner and instinctive instruction which is innate in all beings. Therefore, it is through the grace and mercy of Allah that each created thing derived its form and nature, including such free will and power as that of man. But on a similar token, He has granted everything, all the means and opportunities of development according to his guidance. The divine nature of His creation and guidance is further revealed in the Quran, Sura al-Ala 87: 1-3, which point out: "Glorify the name of thy Guardian Lord Most High who hath created and further given order and proportion; who hath ordained laws, and granted guidance."

The mere fact that Allah's guidance prevails in all of His creations reflects His might and mercy over His creations. In fact, we have discussed in subsection 6.2 about His hidden knowledge and later about His powers to create the sun and the moon, including the heavens and the earth. To this end, we can refer to our earlier discussion where by Allah's command the rotation of the earth, sun, and the moon is a perfect example of how they are ordained by His law to obey and follow their given paths through His guidance. This mode of guidance is different from the second type of divine guidance in which God sends the prophets and divine books to facilitate man to learn the purpose of his creation and to be able to pursue and attain his true potential. In this regard, Mohamad Ali Shamali, who wrote in al-islam.org, explained that "Human beings enjoy two sorts of guidance: the general guidance (*al-hidayat al-amah*), which is shared by all creatures, and the special guidance (*al-hidayat al khassah*), which is exclusive to those beings that have reason freewill."

The issues of divine *wahy* relative to the Quran are classified, based on the mode of messages, into these categories: (a) natural instinct, which does reveal the wonder, complexities, and amazing way of life, and admiration of insects such as bees, ants, spiders, and butterflies among others; (b) inspiration, as discussed in the preceding paragraphs where God suggests certain ideas or courses of action to some people, as with the mother of Moses; (c) prophetic revelation, which is exclusive to the prophets, such as the Quran revealed to Prophet Muhammad (saw), and other divine books, such as the Torah, the Gospel, and the Psalm of Prophet David.

However, it is apparent that prophets are fully aware of divine communication to them. In this regard, the reception of *wahy* is of the kind that the prophets never doubt the veracity of what has been revealed to them. Such was the incident with Prophet Lot and the angels who came to warn him before God's destruction of the city of Sodom, as discussed in chapter 3.6 of this book. In the same token we have discussed the story of Abraham and the idol worshippers who placed him on a catapult, shackled in chains, and then thrown in the fire. Imam Imaduddin Abul-Fida Isma'il Ibn Kathir (2003) explained that "It is narrated that when Abraham was thrown and was still in the air, Gabriel approached him and said to him: 'Abraham, do you need any help?' He replied: 'If from you, then no.'" The Quran 21: 69 further revealed: "We said, O Fire! Be thou cool, and a means of safety for Abraham."

As Muslims, we need to acknowledge the fact that our acquisition and/or attainment of knowledge, understanding, and wisdom are all gifts from Allah. Therefore, as a sign of gratitude, we are obligated to perform our duty and conviction to him who created us and gave us all of the bounties that we enjoy in life. The prime factor regarding such a conviction is to always remember that our existence on earth will be meaningless without adhering to the pledge we made in entering Islam as Muslims, submitting to His will and loving and fearing Him at all times.

The fear of Allah on a constant basis could serve as a valuable reminder to engage in doing good deeds, remain righteous so as to be rewarded both in this world and the hereafter (Judgment Day). In fact, Allah has reminded mankind of such a day in Sura Luqman 31: (4) 33, when He says: "O mankind! Do your duty to your Lord, and fear the coming of a day when no father can avail aught for his son, nor could a son avail aught for his father. Verily, the promise of Allah is true. Let not then the present life deceive you, nor let the chief deceiver deceive you about Allah."

Furthermore, the Muslim should take cognizance of the fact that the fear of Allah can be a good deterrent in controlling our *nafs* (soul) and its *hawa*, which is the cause of *dallal* (going astray). But from an Islamic perspective, what is the fear of Allah? For the Muslim, *taqwa* is the fear of Allah, and it is an action that is coming from the heart. Therefore, it is vital for the Muslim to have a good heart and endeavor to purify it at all times so that it will not be corrupted by his evil desires that are associated with the life of this *dunyah* (world).

This reality, although ancient, has remained a vital message in Islam until now. For example, crmosque.com, in one of their *imam's* messages, stated the fact that "Allah (swt) informs us in the Quran through the words of His Khaleel Prophet Ibraheem that on the Day of Judgment the whole of mankind will be in loss 'except' he who brings to Allah a sound heart (*al-qalb-e-saleem*)." Related to this statement is the fact that the human heart is considered to be the most important organ in the body. Therefore, what appears to be an ordinary organ is actually the seat of human feelings, desires, aspirations, intuitions, and belief. To this end, the Prophet (saw) said: "Surely, in the body there is a small piece of flesh, if it is good, the whole body is good, and if it is corrupted, the whole body is corrupted, and that is surely the heart" (*Bukhari*).

We have explained in the preceding paragraph that *taqwa* is the fear of Allah and is attributed with an action coming directly from the heart. *Taqwa*, therefore, also connotes piety, truthfulness, doing good deeds, and remaining righteous. But the crux of the matter is that for man to remain righteous, he needs to have *ihsan* (perfection in worship). In Islam, *ihsan* is the Muslim responsibility to obtain perfection or excellence in worship, such that he tries to worship God as if he sees Him. Despite the fact that he cannot see God, he undoubtedly believes that He is constantly watching over him. In this regard, the Muslim has to have adequate faith in Allah and to fear Him at all times so that he will live and die as a believer. The degree of his faith and/or trust in Allah (i.e., have *tawakkul* on Allah) constitutes a corresponding foundation of his *ihsan*, which also impinges on both his level of commitment in his *deen* (Islam) as well as his *iman*. It is of great importance, therefore, for the Muslim to endeavor to nurture these three I's (iman, ihsan, and Islam) to enable him to be among those of the *muttaqeen*, pious and righteous. The Quran highlights in Sura al-Anfal 8: 2-4 five qualities of a true believer of Islam (a Muslim) when it states: "For, believers are those who, when Allah is mentioned, feel a tremor in their hearts, and when they hear His signs rehearsed, find their faith strengthened, and put all their trust in their Lord. They are also those who establish regular prayers and spend freely out of the gifts we have given them for sustenance. Such in truth are the believers, for them are graces of dignity with their Lord, and forgiveness and generous sustenance."

The Muslim, therefore, is one who ventures to take heed of these verses and assesses the state of his heart in any given circumstance in order to gain *taqwa*. For instance, if a believer is thinking of and/or about to commit an act of injustice or a sin but abstains from doing so when he is reminded by his fellow Muslim brother "have *taqwa* in Allah, "he desists because his heart becomes fearful that he is being watched by his creator. Such a believer will be among those who will earn grades of dignity with their Lord and of generous sustenance in paradise.

Another example of show of *taqwa* by the Muslim is during the month of Ramadan when he is fasting. He is definitely aware of the fact that while fasting he can hide and eat or drink and nobody will know, but because he understood the reality that irrespective of people's inability to find out the truth Allah is constantly watching over him. In this regard, the act of fasting is regarded in Islam as an element of *taqwa*. It is imperative, therefore, for the Muslim to try and have adequate knowledge of Allah by learning about what He revealed in the Quran and the Sunnah of Prophet Muhammad (saw). This is based on the logical factor that man should endeavor to seek and have knowledge of things before he acts on them. It does imply, therefore, that we may be able to have the best resultant outcome of things we are trying to pursue if we have prior knowledge of their advantages and disadvantages before we act. In the same vein, it is vital for the Muslim to try and acquire knowledge about Allah first, then embark on the path to worship Him. In this way, the Muslim will have a true balance of knowing what Islam is about, and moreover, worship Allah with *taqwa, imaan,* and *ihsaan* in order to purify his heart and soul to join the company of the *muttaqeen*.

Relative to these factors, we have discussed in chapter 6. 0the five qualities of a true believer in Islam, which we will recapitulate as follows. The first factor relates to the fact that the believer, whenever he hears Allah being mentioned, feels the fear of Him in his heart. The second factor is associated with the reality that their faith increases every time they hear and/or ponder over Quran verses. The third factor is that he puts his trust in Allah, meaning that he has *tawakkul* in Allah. The fourth factor is based on his faith in Islam (as a believer) to regularly perform his five daily prayers. And the fifth factor is that he spends for charity in the path of Allah. In fact, the path of Allah is the straight path, and as Muslims we are constantly asking Him in the opening sura (Al-Fatiha) of each of our five daily prayers to show us the straight path, strengthen our belief, faith, consistency to worship Him alone, and to be righteous in deeds at all times.

Allah has reminded Muslims that they are the ummah *(nation) of the middle path.* The statement connotes that Islam teaches us to be moderate and balanced in all aspects of life. The nature of this moderation impinges on many shepherds of our daily lives, such as in religion, worship, relationships, ideas, among other factors. Principled moderation is one of the defining characteristics of good character in Islam. The Quran reminds us of these factors when Allah says:

> Thus have we made of you as "ummat" justly balanced that you might be witness over the nations, and the Apostle a witness over you." (Sura al-Baqarah 2: 145)

The term *justly balanced* could be interpreted as *equilibrium* (in Arabic, the justly balanced is *wasat*), *the middle*, or *of moderation*. Moderation is the center point between two extremes. In this regard, as Muslims, we are constantly requesting and/or making a plea to Allah in the beginning of each of our five daily prayers to be guided to the straight path at least seventeen times a day. The beginning of this prayer is Sura Al-Fatihah (the first or opening chapter) of the Quran. In this opening chapter of the Quran we are making a plea for His mercy to guide us (*ihdina*) to the straight path. In Arabic, the word *hidayah* does not simply mean guidance but also denotes to guide gently. Moreover, we need to acknowledge the fact that religious guidance is the greatest gift that a person can possess. In addition, it is something that is beyond our control or ownership, but rather it is bestowed upon us in an act of infinite mercy and grace of Allah the Almighty.

The nature of this *hidayah* from Allah of four different types. The first type of *hidayah* is general and is given to all of Allah's creations. For example, it is the nature of this guidance that is present in animals, plants, and even inanimate objects for them to fulfill the purpose for which they were created. Also, present in this gift is the general intellect, wits, and inherent intuitive knowledge that Allah gave to responsible beings, irrespective of their faith, color, or creed.

The second type of *hidayah* is related to explanation and/or knowledge of things, as was the case with Adam after his creation, when he had to give the names of things which the angels and the *jinns* couldn't, because God taught only Adam those names. This will lead us to education, which is also a vital aspect of this *hidayah*. However, the main focus of such type of education is to enable man to discern and be able to distinguish the two paths of good and evil.

From an Islamic point of view, it is as when someone guides you and explains that which is good and warns you of that which is evil. A case in point is in the Quran when it states that "We have made the Quran a light wherewith we guide such of our servants as we will, and verily, O Muhammad! You guide men to the straight path" (Sura Ash-Shuraa 42:52).

The mere fact that the Quran is a light, Muslims have a divided concept as regards the statement that the Prophet Muhammad (saw) is also endowed with a spiritual light that existed prior to his creation and that of the origin of the first man Adam. However, before we proceed to explain the light(noor) that is attributed to the Prophet, let us address first the light associated with the Holy Quran. When we talk about the light associated with the Prophet (saw), it is important that we first clarify the point that Allah the Almighty clearly declares in the Quran that He created the angels from noor (light) and He created human beings, commencing with Adam, out of clay. This being the case, there is no doubt that Prophet Muhammad (saw) was created as a human being and one of the sons of Adam. The Quran testifies to this fact when Allah says:

> Say, O Mohammed: "I am only a man like you. It has been revealed to me that your 'Illah (God) is one 'Illah (God, implying Allah)." (Sura al-Kahf18: 110)

However, the bone of contention regarding this issue is the reality that although Prophet Muhammad was a human being, he was special because he was chosen by Allah to deliver perfectly the message of Islam.

Complementary to this statement which confirms the fact that Prophet Muhammad was a human being, now we can proceed to explain the meaning of noor, an Arabic word which denotes light. In this regard, the Quran made reference to the nature of this light when it stated:

> O people of the Scripture, there has come to you our messenger making clear to you much of what you used to conceal of the

Scripture and overlooking much. There has come to you from Allah
a light of Guidance and a clear Book. (Sura Al-Maidah 5:15)

The bone of contention here is to note that as much as this light is put within the context of guidance, some renowned Islamic scholars like Imam Tabari in his Tasfir Tabani Tassir Fathul Qadeer pointed out that *noor* means that the Prophet is the light of guidance for entire humanity. It therefore signifies the he was guidance for the whole of mankind. Therefore, he was both noor (light) and human.

The third type of *hidayah* from Allah is related to *tawfiq*, which connotes a specific type of divine guidance and inspiration (*ilham*). It is imperative to note that the nature of this *hidayah* is to be guided to that which leads to the truth of *iman* (faith), *Islam* (submission), and similar virtues. In this regard, Muslims strongly believe that which is in the Quran, that Allah guides whom He wills, and whoever He leads astray none can guide, and He does what He wills. For this reason, we have explained in chapter 6 that Allah's justice is strict but in favor of man.

The fourth type of *hidayah* is that of the hereafter, the next life of man. However, it is important to note that each type of the abovementioned *hidayah* has a sequential connection and relationship. This is mainly due to the fact that without the first level of guidance man will not have the capacity to attain the second, and without the second he will not be able to attain the third and fourth levels.

In relation to the foregoing discussion, it is of paramount importance and significance for the believing Muslim to acknowledge the reality that the Quran is a book of light and guidance to the truth, and will benefit those who adhere to its revelations, both in this world and in the hereafter. The manifestation of this reality is stated in the Quran, which contends the following:

> *And we have sent down to you the Book (the Quran) as an*
> *exposition of everything, a guidance, a mercy, and glad tidings*
> *for those who have submitted themselves to Allah as Muslims.*
> *(Sura An-Nahl 16:89)*

As Muslims, efforts to try and understand the Quran mean seeking ways to understand Islam, and venturing to understand Islam implies seeking a balanced way to stay on the straight path. In other words, the benefits of adhering to the straight path will lead the Muslim to attain spiritual truth as well righteousness, perform good deeds that are rewarding both in this world and the hereafter. Adherence to the straight path will also require sacrifices to seek a spiritual as well as a moral balance that puts the believer in a condition to start relinquishing the temptations of this *dunyah* (world) and to work relentlessly toward the positive benefits and rewards of the righteous and inheritors of paradise in the hereafter. In other words, the aim here is for the Muslim to strive for moderation in his life's endeavors so that he will not falter to any of the extremes on either side. His goal, therefore, should be to adhere to that center and always return back to it when he moves away from it or falter.

Efforts on the part of the Muslim to maintain a steady balance on the straight path is to work and build on his spiritually. He should endeavor to learn and to also acknowledge the fact that God's creations are always in good and perfect balance and in harmony with their environment of existence. The paramount factor here is for man to appreciate God's creations on earth, and to understand that we are the supreme custodian of the planet Earth that we inhabit. Therefore, as Muslims, we should exhibit both the necessary spiritual and moral virtues and characteristics that manifest a high degree of good behavior and moral responsibility for others in the community to emulate.

This goodness should also aim for perfection to nurture, protect, and preserve His creations which can be viewed from various dimensions. For example, in His creation there is immense beauty, goodness, adaptation, proportionality, functionality to serve their various purposes, including the process of rejuvenation and/or reproduction, as the case may be. Also, there is no evil or disorder in it, implying a well-balanced creation.

Let us take a look at the earth that we inherited, how it is structured and laid out with rivers, seas, fresh water, including their beneficial material and health effects on mankind. Yet, still based on man's greed for wealth, we have polluted some of these rivers and seas with toxic materials and plastic waste, among other factors. Perhaps, with the aid of spiritual teachings based on good deeds and morality, with the intention to raise awareness that will help bring about the desired positive changes that will revert some of the negative damages already impacted on our planet.

We have seen this balance and harmony in the prevalence of the sun, moon, the stars, including His creation of the planets such as Jupiter and Mars. God has also reminded mankind of this fact when He first created the universe as one and later separated it and made a balance between the heavens and the earth, including all that they contained. Presently, due to industrialization, the greed and lust that we have for money are affecting our environment, resulting in pollution in our major cities, causing the current global warming phenomenon, river pollution due to chemical waste products and residues that are toxic, among other factors.

In relation to what each of these creations (heavens and earth) contained, they are enormous, and man knows only a few number of them. For instance, if we take planet Earth we can feel the air and the winds that blow, and can navigate through the oceans, seas, and rivers and yet still benefit from the resources that they contain.

As for some of that which is in the heavens, tracks that are of hidden knowledge known to Allah facilitate the control paths of motion in which the planets orbit. It is He, Allah, who also made the clouds to gather and transform into rain to benefit mankind. The validity of these statements is revealed in many parts of the Quran, such as Sura adh-Dhuha 93:7 and 3; Sura an-Naba 78:37; and Sura As-Sajdah 32:4, all of which explain what is between the heavens and the earth. In this regard, we will therefore refer to these examples the control of the hidden track which facilitate the motion and orbit of the planets, and the supply of rain from the sky, both of which are revealed in the Quran when it states the following:

> *And we have made, above you, seven tracks, and we are never*
> *unmindful of our creation. And we send down water from the*
> *sky according to due measure, and we cause it to soak in the*

soil. And we certainly are able to drain it off with ease. (Sura al-Mu'minun 23:17-18)

Also, Allah did remind mankind that what He created between the heavens and the earth is not done like the display of an idle sport, but rather to benefit mankind through His infinite mercy and blessings. What we can derive from the ongoing discussion is the fact that Allah is He who is in control of all creation, both in the heavens and earth and all that they contain. He is firmly established on the throne of authority, and is the knower and seer of all things that are revealed or hidden, the exalted in power and mercy.

In recent years, man has witnessed a pattern of hurricanes and floods to a magnitude that is unimaginable. Does it imply, therefore, that man's negligence and prevailing ways of life, as briefly explained above, are contributing factors to such natural disasters? Or do we have to change our habits and attitudes toward the aggressive nature in the planet we inhabit?

So far in this chapter we have explained matters related to God's Creation of the heavens and the earth and some of what they contain, and for man to learn how to appreciate and acknowledge the amazing aspects of these creations and their benefits to mankind. To this end, we will now explore further some of the effects of man's inheritance of planet Earth, more from a spiritual context.

For example, God made the atmospheric nature of planet Earth pure and then sent down Adam and Eve to inhabit it and dwell on it with fresh air, rivers and seas, with marine life and precious gems, including oil that is embedded underground—all for the benefit and survival of mankind. Interestingly, God did warn mankind not to make mischief on earth and to maintain a good character. The Quran reminded us of Allah's warning:

> Do no mischief on the earth after it hath been set in order, *but call on Him with fear and longing in your hearts, for the mercy of Allah is always near to those who do good. (Sura al-Araf 7:56)*

But what happened when the children of Adam inherited the earth? Today, there is an epidemic of greed, violence, hatred, corruption, pollution, nuclear weapons of mass destruction, massacre of innocent civilians: men, women, and children, among mankind all over the globe. There is no country on earth that is free from all of these stated mischiefs, of which God warned mankind after He had balanced the earth with purity and set it in order. Because man has failed to take heed of God's warning, we are living in a turbulent world, where the evidence has perpetually indicated man's owns destruction of self and the very planet that God purified and set in order for our own benefit and survival.

Not only is mankind polluting the atmosphere (i.e., the air we breathe) with carbon monoxide but we live in a period where nuclear and toxic waste is being secretly dumped both on land sites and in the sea, poisoning and eroding marine life, especially in underdeveloped countries. The crux of the matter is that some men and/or multinational philanthropic organizations have chosen these unscrupulous and mischievous economic methods of operation as a means to maximize their profits at the peril of planet Earth and mankind at large. In this regard, the Muslim should remain proactive and take a lead in this struggle, and seek moderation when it comes to balancing the duties of religion and duties of worldly life. The Quran addresses matters of this nature when Allah said:

> But seek, with the wealth which Allah has bestowed on thee the home of the hereafter by that which Allah has given you, but do not forget your share of the world but do you good, as Allah has been good to thee, and seek not occasions for mischief in the land, for Allah loves not those who do mischief. (Sura Al-Qasas28:77)

In fact, the temptations of this *dunyah* (world) are bait that may easily lead some men to engage in mischief and/or transgress against the will of Allah. For this reason, it is important for the Muslim to acknowledge the fact that the life of this world is short-lived and are just a counted number of days; whereas, the *akhira* (the hereafter) is everlasting and rewarding for those who fear Allah and do good deeds. Relative to this fact, Al-Ghazali (1995) stated:

> *Who so transgresses and prefers the life of this world, for him hellfire shall be the place of resort, and whoever fears the standing before His Lord and forbids his nafs its "hawa," for him heaven shall be the place of resort.*

He further elaborated that the world (*dunyah*) for which the *nafs* yearns is not a pleasant thing. It is the comfort of illusion and naught but a game and play.

The Muslim should also endeavor to work relentlessly to be among those men of understanding who believe and fear Allah and shy away from the temptations of this world so as to earn the reward of his creator, both in this world and the hereafter. The believer who fears Allah will sacrifice and fight (*jihad*) with his *nafs* to reject the temptations of this life, and will rather use the opportunities that he is blessed with by his creator to worship Him, do good deeds, stay righteous in order to control and discipline his *nafs* away from the lust, desires, and temptations that will corrupt it. As a guideline to protect his *nafs* from corrupt and evil deeds, the Muslim should venture to adhere to the relevant Islamic principles and guidelines that will facilitate a balance in the middle path, such as rigorous discipline and control of self, purification of the *nafs*, restraint of his *hawa* to avoid any form of transgression, and praying for Allah's mercy and guidance.

The reason for the Muslim to adhere to these Islamic principles and guidelines is also to combat the nature of our imperfections as humans, which is due to our weakness to make mistakes, or submission to the dictates of the *nafs*, which may lead us to falter and transgress. However, one approach to fight or prevent the *nafs* from such transgression or committing sinful deeds depends on the individual intension and commitment to combat (or *jihad*) against the lower soul is by virtue of *tawakkul*, meaning reliance upon God. An example of such kind of *tawakkul* is manifested by Prophet Yusuf when Pharaoh's wife tried to seduce him in her house in the palace. The evidence of this statement is revealed in the Quran when it says:

> But she (Pharaoh's wife) in whose house he was, sought to seduce him from his true self. She fastened the doors and said: "Now come, thou dear one! 'He said: 'Allah forbid (Sura Yusuf 12:23)!'"

Another approach to purifying the *nafs* apart from *tawakkul* is the acknowledgment of one's own transgression of wrongful or sinful deeds, which should compel the individual to repent his wrongdoing by performing *tawbah*. The performance of *tawbah* will imply man's turning to God in repentance, with sincerity and fear of Allah, and a commitment not to indulge in the same kind of sinful act. These two approaches are essential ingredients for the Muslim to purify his *nafs*, and also of paramount importance for him to try and maintain a strong faith in Islam. In fact, the more he inclines to his faith, adheres to the fundamentals spiritual and moral principles and guidelines of Islam, the more likely it is for him to do righteous deeds, perform regular prayers, and venture sincerely toward the course of Allah so that he can receive the guidance necessary to purify his soul and to stay on the straight path, which is rewarding. In this regard, as Muslims, we must venture to be among those who strive for our (Allah) sake in order to seek His blessings and guidance to the straight path. The fact of the matter is that he who is guided by Allah will reap the benefits of consistency to do right, and to always refrain from wrongful and evil deeds.

Efforts by the Muslim to try and retain these noble traits will obviously assist him in his life's journey to be righteous and in building a good and noble character. Actually, Islam commands the Muslim to try and nurture all noble moral virtues, and forbids all ill and despicable manners. It also commands righteousness and forbids wrong. This implies that the Muslim should also venture into assisting those who are close to him, such as his immediately family, friends, and loved ones to try and possess such good and noble character. The reason being that as human beings we are each other's mirror, plus the fact that one should always endeavor to promote good moral values and character starting with our homes, schools, communities, and if possible at both national and international levels. Efforts by the Muslim to reach out in such a diverse scope are due to the fact that we are each other's mirror, and to try and ensure that what you wish for yourself you should also wish for your brother. The nature of this unified scope of brotherhood will generate a healthy and cordial atmosphere, foster good human relations and understanding of each other and our communities at large.

Allah said:

> O Mankind! We have created you from a single pair of male and female, and have made you intonations and tribes that you may know each other, not that you may despise each other. The most honored of you in the sight of Allah is he who is the most righteous. . . can understand each other. (Sura al-Hujurat49:13)

In order to throw some light in the understanding of the basic five Islamic concepts and guidelines in nurturing good human relationships with each other, it is vital for the Muslim to be wary of these fundamental moral factors. First is the word *al-ihsaan*, which denotes being patient in performance of the Sunnah of the Prophet Muhammad (saw) in a perfect manner. Second, the degree of kinship from an Islamic perspective gives the first right to your parents, then your offspring, then your brothers and sisters, then your paternal uncles and aunts and aunties (from the mother's side), and then other relatives. Third is *al-fahsaa,* which points to all evil deeds; e.g., illegal sexual intercourse, disobedience to parents, telling lies, stealing, etc. Fourth is *al-munkar,* which relates to all that is prohibited by Islamic Law: polytheism, disbelief, and every kind of evil deed, etc. And fifth is *al-baghy,* which deals with all kinds of oppression.

The bone of contention relating to all of these narratives reminds us of the beauty, moral discipline, and the strengthening of family ties, among other factors. All of these factors mentioned above contradict the views of those critics who slander and tarnish the name and image of

Islam without having or understanding an iota of what the religion is all about. Because Islam is about peace, Muslims, according to the Quran, are advised to try and adhere to a moral discipline of not condemning people of the Book who believe in God. Pertaining to these kinds of issues, the Quran states:

> *And dispute you not with the people of the Book, except with means better than mere disputation, unless it be with those of them who inflict wrong and injury. But say we believe in the revelation which has come down to you; our Allah and your Allah is one; and it is to him we bow in Islam. (Sura al-Ankabut29:46)*

Another beauty associated with Islam is the noncompulsion aspect of the religion and the manner in which it promotes purity, guidance, and understanding of the two ways (right from wrong) to its believers in order that they may stay righteous. For instance, Islam teaches believers how to proclaim the message of God and pray to him for purity and guidance. Moreover, mankind has to take cognizance of the fact that God's revelation carries its own proof and is recognized by men of wisdom.

On the contrary, those who reject faith and fail to acknowledge and adhere to God's revelations to His prophets lose their own chances of profiting by the truth and attaining the paths that lead to God's own gracious presence. The mere fact which remains in triumph is the reality that Islam is not the voice or revelation of any man, but rather it is a revelation from God through Angel Gabriel to Prophet Muhammad (saw) who was not literate. This revelation we have explained earlier in this Book with reference to the Quran when God says, "Proclaim (or read) in the name of your Lord and cherisher, who created man out of a mere cloth of concealed blood."

As Muslims we acknowledge and reaffirm the significant of the first verse of Sura al-AIaq, which is confirmed to be an account of the circumstances in which the first revelation and/or divine commission which directs Prophet Muhammad to read or recite/proclaim aloud

God's message to mankind. This first message came to him while he was in the cave of Hiran searching for God in solitude. In this regard, he was in direct contact with Angel Gabriel.

Another significant factor in this revelation is God's affirmation that he teaches man by the mystic of the pen drawing reference to the fact that God is imparting to man new knowledge at every given moment. In reality, we learn more and more day by day. The ability to learn daily also cuts across families, communities, societies, nations, and humanity in general. However, man's arrogance and egocentric attitudes and tendencies make him think and believe that he is self-sufficient, individually, as a group, society, and/or nations. The crux of the matter is man's inept attitude, ungratefulness to acknowledge the reality that all our knowledge and capabilities come to us as a gift from God. But man, in his inordinate vanity and insolence, tends to mislead himself by mistakenly rejecting God's gift for his own achievements. For instance, this gift maybe beauty, power, strength, knowledge, wealth, talents found in individuals, or structural achievements associated with governments, institutions, nations, or mankind in general. The fact of the matter is that many a time man's insolence leads to either self-destruction through self-misguidance and/or misleading and propagating false example and guidance to others. In this regard, the righteous man, with God's guidance, must therefore test human example or guidance by asking if there is God's guidance behind it. The essence of this kind of check and balance when dealing with your fellow human beings is of paramount importance.

Apart from the Muslim seeking guidance, we have also discussed that repentance could be facilitated by the fear of Allah, acknowledgment of one's wrongdoing, and vowing not to repeat such kind of transgression again. In fact, we have discussed the issue of repentance (*tawbah*) in detail in chapter 5.0 to 5.7 above. If only man will ponder for a while before committing a sin that it is going to be an act that will be recorded by the angels in his book of deeds, which will be read to him in the Day of Judgment, then these factors should serve as a stern reminder to make him desist from doing so. Furthermore, man has to acknowledge the fact that at one time we didn't exist and there will also come a time when we will abruptly disappear from the face of this earth. This reality remains a fact of life, and we have discussed this in chapter 6:2 in which we explained about the wisdom in spiritual inspiration and hidden knowledge, including the period when man was nothing to make mention of.

There is also the reality that men of understanding and knowledge can impart what they learn and know to others, but may lack the requisite wisdom on divine and spiritual matters that are only known to Allah unless He decides to unleash that wisdom to whomsoever He pleases. The reason is based on the fact that "Allah granted wisdom to whom he pleaseth; and to whom wisdom is granted receiveth indeed a benefit overflowing; but none will grasp the message but men of understanding" (Sura al-Baqarah 2:269).

However, we have also explained earlier in our discussion the reality that the world we inhabit today is tempting man more and more toward the affinity toward the desires that man thinks will make him happy, such as the "rat race" for material gains, power, and prestige, with the belief that he will endure. Experience has taught man that his affinity and cravings for the desires of this world don't equate happiness. For instance, we have seen how some people of prestige, fame, and wealth in the Hollywood arena have failed miserably due to their unhappiness, irrespective of their high status as celebrity in modern society. The crux of the matter is to acknowledge the fact that the love of this *dunyah* (world) can lead to a downward spiraling negative effect that is understood by men of understanding who fear God, different from other men who outwardly claim to be a Muslim and constantly engage in sinful and wrongful behavior.

It is one thing to be a Muslim, but quite another to nurture and emulate those moral and ethical guidelines and values as stipulated in the Quran, and to follow the Sunnah of the Prophet (saw). For the Muslim to attain these values and characteristics, it is vital for him to first affirm his believe in Allah and submit to His will. It is like renewing his testimony and/or *sahadah* to Allah, just like he purifies his ablution before the performance of his prayers. This basic ritual will keep him in track of remembering Allah, accompanied by calling His names as a sign of praise to Him. The reason for such kinds of praises to Allah is based on His promise: great blessings and reward for those who remember him often. In fact, Allah said in the Quran, "If you remember me, I will also remember you and reward your good deed."

Notwithstanding, based on discussions we had with friends, it is ironic to notice the fact that among acquaintances those who failed to remember their creator were prone to be forgetful of performing righteous deeds, and moreover be overwhelmed in the engagement of sinful deeds and disobedient to Allah. Contrary to this statement remains the fact that those who are in constant remembrance of Allah were the ones who attained true success in this life. The nature of success, as discussed here, is not based on material gains but rather on the individual spiritual relation with God in which He promises to reward us both in this world and the hereafter. Relative to this fact, the Quran contends:

> And remember Allah much so that you will be successful. (Sura Al-Jumu'ah 62:10)

In view of the foregoing discussion, we have to emphasize the point that it is incumbent upon the Muslim to remember Allah and not to be heedless of His remembrance so that he will not fall into the category of those who forgot Allah and perpetually live in sin and disobedience to Him. The Darussalam Research Division (2001) pointed out the fact that

> from the best behavior of man, and the best thing that his tongue can say, is the abundant remembrance of Allah, glorifying Him, and reciting His Magnificent Book (the Quran).

Apart from men of understanding acknowledgment of Allah's existence, their fear of Him and submitting to His will are among some of the other noble characteristics that they possessed and propagated in accordance with Islamic principles and guidelines. Among these principles and guidelines are the acknowledgment of and belief in Allah's creations of the heavens and the earth and all that they encompass, including the seen and the unseen. It is common for such men to demonstrate a thorough, comprehensive knowledge and understanding of the Book (Quran) for proper guidance. They also serve as an example to other people due to their high level of tolerance, patience, and sympathy that they exercise in their daily encounters with their fellow humans, including other creations of Allah in the animal world. In addition to these noble virtues and characteristics, they are people who adhere to the norms and practices of the five fundamental pillars of Islam, and will venture to speak the truth at all times.

Due to the fact that Islam is the religion of truth and warns its believers (Muslims) not to engage in condemning other faiths who believe in God, such as the Jews and the Christians, for whom God hath sent down earlier revelations and books. In this regard, the Quran reminds us of this fact when it states:

> *Say ye: "We believe in Allah and the revelations given to us and to Abraham, Ismail, Isaac, Jacob, and the Tribes, and that given to all prophets from their Lord. We make no difference between one and another of them, and we bow to Allah in Islam." (Sura al-Baqarah 2: 136)*

In view of all these noble virtues which Islam possesses to aid in building the character of man from his animal state to a moral state, and from a moral state to that of the highest attainment close to Allah, thereby reinforcing his spiritual state of being. We have discussed these three stages of man's development in his journey to attain spiritual affinity with his creator in chapter 5.3, the wisdom of *tawbah* (repentance) to facilitate man in cleaning his conscience. In this subsection issues relating to the *nafsal-ammara bissu, nafsal-lawwama,* and *nafsal-mutmainnah* are briefly explained as a process to uplift man to his highest spiritual state.

As Muslims, when we display characters that are commensurate to either the moral or spiritual state of man based on Islamic values and principles, that could make, lure, or impress people of different faiths to admire our way of life (the straight path), its purity and the peace and tranquility that is in Islam. It is through the display of genuine values and norms of Islam that could also make such people have the affinity to want to know about Islam or embrace it in general.

Today, we are witnessing the increasing numbers of people entering Islam, despite the negative work and propaganda of extremist and terrorist groups who are pursuing their own political agenda and yet still disguising under the name of Islam. Actually, the nurturing and propagation of Islamic values and principles require man to struggle with his *nafs* and eliminate those desires of this world that have the tendencies to corrupt his soul. All of these virtues which have the potential to shape man's moral and spiritual state of mind are possible through God's guidance and by adhering to the teachings of both the Quran and the Prophet Muhammad (saw). In fact, God reminded us in the Quran when he says:

> *And thou dost see the people enter Allah's religion (Islam) in crowds. (Sura an-Nasr 114:2)*

As Muslims, it is one thing to encourage people to embrace Islam at their own desire and accord, but quite another to continuously remind them to fear Allah. For in reality it is through the fear of Allah as a Muslim that you can strengthen your faith in Islam. Islam, therefore, is a religion which continually reminds the Muslim and mankind to fear Allah and to acknowledge the Day of Judgment when the souls are gathered to individually account for their respective deeds. It will be a day where the righteous will go to heaven, and the evildoers to the hellfire. In this regard, the Quran reminds us of these realities concerning this life and the hereafter when it states:

> *and fear a day when no soul will suffice for another soul at all and no compensation will be accepted from it, nor will any intercession benefit it, nor will they be added. (Sura al-Baqarah 2:123)*

Islam, therefore, is not established to purify its religion, but rather to purify the souls and characters of men. Let us, for a second ponder, and imagine if all of mankind was to spiritually and morally purify their souls and character irrespective of their religious beliefs and strive for the sake and fear of God in order not to transgress upon their fellow human beings and other creations, then there will prevail an everlasting understanding, peace, and brotherhood among all of mankind.

In this kind of environment, there wouldn't be the need to have nuclear weapons which will eventually lead to man's own self-destruction. Also, mankind then will not have the need to waste a huge amount of financial resources that governments invest in jet fighters, armies, and other weapons that are currently used by nations to systematically annihilate each other's civilians, human as well as material and infrastructural damages for no justified reasons apart from power, economic and political dominance, among other related factors.

In fact, all of these are done out of greed without a moral reason and/or justification. We have earlier explained in chapter 7.0 the wisdom in disciplining the soul and the body or how man's lust and evil desires of this world have led him to crave for the abovementioned factors with which he yearns to satisfy his egocentric tendencies. We gave examples of leaders like Pharaoh, Thamud, and their like, who oppressed their people and transgressed beyond bounds and perished because they were unjust.

Islam, therefore, is a religion and a way of life to help reshape man's immoral way of living to one which aids to fine-tune his moral and spiritual character to a pinnacle of human existence guided by God's wisdom. The essence of this spiritual guidance is to assist man to be just, fair, noble, humble, and righteous in his unpredictable life journey, and above all, fear Allah so as not to transgress against his fellow human beings.

Man's vulnerability to transgression against Allah's warnings as well as his fellow human beings remains and issues of great concern both in this world and the hereafter. The nature of such concerns is linked to the severe consequences and/or punishments that are prescribed for sinners and evildoers, both in this world and the hereafter. However, man can avoid being a sinner or an evildoer if he is willing to turn to the straight path that will offer him the necessary spiritual guidance revealed by God in the Quran to Prophet Muhammad over 1,400 years ago, long before modern science came into existence beginning in the nineteenth century. God has reminded us of these facts in the Quran when He says:

> *We send down the Quran in truth, and in truth has it descended;*
> *and we sent thee but to give glad tidings and to warn sinners.*
> *It is a Quran which we have divided into parts from time to*
> *time in order that thou mightiest recite it to men at intervals,*
> *we have revealed it by stages. (Sura Bani Israil 17: 105-106)*

The abovementioned verses in Bani Israil reaffirm the fact that the Quran was sent down by God in truth. The part Angel Gabriel played in its revelation was of messenger responsible for delivering it to Prophet Muhammad. Likewise, the spiritual role which Prophet Muhammad played was as messenger and warner to all of mankind. He fulfilled his mission in promulgating and explaining it and leaving it as a legacy to all of mankind. Irrespective of the fact that such revelations were intermittent, the marvel is that these parts were revealed at differing times and/or periods and in different circumstances. Nonetheless, it is amazing how the suras of the Quran fit so closely and consistently as they do, and above all is fitting for past, present, and future generations.

All of these facts, together with many more, are some of the amazing miracles of the Quran. In this regard, we will proceed and give a few examples of the miracles of the Quran. Among these examples is this consistency found in the Quran. Another miracle of the Quran is the manner in which it has made the Islamic faith unique among the two other Abrahamic faiths (Judaism and Christianity). Another miracle of the Quran is associated with the fact that it was revealed to a prophet who was unlettered and was unable to read and write in Arabic, in which the Quran itself was revealed. Among the recent miracles of the Quran is how it stood out in addressing scientific matters which modern science came to agree upon. We have discussed some of these factors relating to the Quran and its conformity with modern science in certain areas of disciplines in chapter 7, "Wisdom in Discipling the

Soul and the Body." Actually, all of these issues mentioned regarding some of the miracles of the Quran are testimony of the fact that Allah, with His infinite mercy and wisdom, is capable of doing as He wishes, and He knows best.

In view of the foregoing discussion, it is obvious to discern the fact that believing Muslims who adhere to the revelations of the Quran, coupled with the Sunnah (practice of the teachings of the Holy Prophet), are ways by which man can purify and reinforce the natural impulses of the soul. We have, in chapter 7, discussed about the purification of the soul in detail. However, it is imperative to state as a reminder that this purification is the vehicle of enabling man to combine both the teachings of the Quran and the emulation of the practices of the Sunnah into an equilibrium which will allow the mystic to approach God without distraction. The nature of this mystical approach to God will facilitate man to understand and appreciate the reality that this material world and all that it contains is short-lived and temporal. It will also make man shift away from the teachings of modern civilization of being individualistic and egoist, which propagates the notion of being self-assertive, thereby fostering the individual self-expression and self-realization often associated with man's claim for freedom.

The crux of the matter is freedom for whom, the individual or for society in general? As regards the former, God has inculcated that freewill (the freedom to choose) in His creation of man. Therefore, man's claim for his freedom is a misleading phenomenon. Moreover, even the land that God gave for mankind to dwell on was pure and perfect, without boundaries. In fact, it is due to man's greed, arrogance, and attempts to dominate one another for their egocentric economic and power dominance that they created the prevailing artificial boundaries of the world. The restriction of man's freedom is therefore instituted and perpetuated by man himself. Furthermore, such restrictions of freedom are prevalent usually among various facets of society, such as in families, institutions, and larger society by imposed laws, rules, regulations, standards, procedures as a norm to meet their respective needs of daily survival, which then translates into anticipated expectational values as a form of social and/or economic means to control man or society. It is through such regulations which are translated into accepted norms and values of society based on their prevailing culture and traditions. Very often, it is these accepted norms and values of society which often shape the anticipated character of the individual, which are manifested as actions such as being just, fair, impartial, God-fearing, honest, sincere, as good virtues that are commendable and appreciated by those who are considered to be among the truthful and righteous citizens.

On the contrary, among those citizens who choose to operate against some of these norms and values and propagate evil and wrongdoings are normally considered as violators of the norms and values of society and are often punished by law or other prevailing traditional options which are informal (such as in some African societies, where chieftains may have the power and authority to punish culprits in their villages).

However, from an Islamic perspective, the Muslim must endeavor to desist from engaging himself from all forms of evil and wrongful deeds, and venture to lead a life that will enable him to attain the best of character both spiritually and morally. The reason for the Muslim to try and attain this high spiritual and moral kind of behavior is to follow the teachings of the Quran to be righteous, perform good deeds, and adhere to the teachings of the Sunnah of Prophet Muhammad (saw).

Actually, what made Prophet Muhammad a unique example and mercy to all mankind is solely based on his noble traits of character and not his divine knowledge or wisdom. This fact about the Prophet is better stated by Al-Ghazali (1995) when he explicitly states:

> *Visitors to the Prophet's tomb in Medina are sometimes beguiled from their prayers by a large calligraphic device fixed directly above the entrance. Those who have time to decipher it find a line of verse which announces the presence of "A great Prophet, whose created nature was the character which the Merciful has magnified in the master of books." This is the epitaph which Islam has chosen for its founder: A celebration not of his conquests, his divine knowledge, or his eschatological glory,* but his aklaq, his noble traits of character.

However, within the context of the subject matter of this book the term *aklaq* is an Arabic word depicting the practice of virtue, morality, and manners that are associated with Islamic theology. Generally, its meaning is mostly translated in English dictionaries as disposition, nature, temper, ethics, morals, or manners associated with a person.

The vital lesson to be learned from the epitaph designated to the calligraphy fixed on the entrance of the Prophet's tomb as described above complements the fact that in life usually it is the character traits of a man that counts and not the material and knowledge gains we highly cherish in today's world. For instance, a man may be endowed with both knowledge and wealth, but if he lacks good character then his legacy could be one that will be tarnished by bad deeds and memories. On the contrary, apart from the unique and noble character traits of the Prophet (saw) whom God has praised not because of his knowledge but due to his exemplary and noble character which surpasses that of all mankind.

We can also relate to another example in which mankind can also draw a similar lesson as proclaimed by the late Martin Luther King Jr. in his "I Have a Dream Speech," when he said:

> *I have a dream that my four little children will one day live in a nation where they will not be judged by the color of their skin,* but by the content of their character. *(CBS News, January 20, 2013)*

We can discern from the epitaph which Islam has chosen for its leader (Prophet Muhammad) that it laid the most emphasis on his *aklaq*, his noble traits of character. In the same vein, the late Martin Luther King Jr. also laid his emphasis on the content of the character of a man and not by the color of his skin.

On a similar note Sheikh Yassir Fazaga author of the 6C's of character pointed out that

> *we are the author of our character, and nobody can shape it for us except ourselves.*

He further contends that it is our character that shapes our destiny. He explained that people could tarnish your personality, which you have no control of what they say about you. *In reality, what you can control is your character, which is of paramount importance in building a man's legacy.*

We have also explained in the preceding statements that Islam is based on practicing the contents of the Quran and the Sunnah of the Prophet Muhammad (saw), *all of which is to purify the soul and character traits of man.* The confirmation of this statement is also reflected in the final sermon of Prophet Muhammad during his last pilgrimage to perform *Hajj* in Mecca. A significant part of his sermon states:

> *O people, no prophet or apostle will come after me, and no new faith will be born. Reason well, therefore, O people, and understand words which I convey to you.* I leave behind me two things, the Quran and my example, the Sunnah, and if you follow these, you will never go astray.

The crux of the matter is for the Muslim to acknowledge the importance of these two things that the Prophet left behind for Muslims to follow vigorously so that they will be successful and will never go astray. The significance of these two things is insurmountable, and their significance surpasses man's imagination and explanation. Notwithstanding, the former (the Quran) has the tenacity to remove man from darkness to light. This fact is revealed in the Quran when it states:

> *ALA. a Book which we have revealed unto thee in order that thou mightiest lead mankind out of the depths of darkness into light, by the leave of their Lord, to the way of Him, exalted in power, worthy of all praise. (Sura Ibrahim 14:1)*

As regards the latter to follow the example of the Prophet (his Sunnah) simply meant to emulate his character, both morally and spiritually, as much as possible based on the principles and guidelines that are established for Muslims.

In order to conclude on our discussions of this Book, we will finally refer to our beloved Prophet Muhammad (saw) when he completed his final sermon and upon it, near the summit of Arafat, the revelation came down:

> *This day have I perfected your religion for you, completed my grace upon you, and have chosen Islam for you as your religion. (Sura Al-Maidah 5:3)*

It is this above stipulated revelation that established Islam as a religion of truth, wisdom, and of the straight path. On this note, we wish to close the discussion of this book by thanking God for His infinite guidance and wisdom which facilitated the work and completion of this book. Praise be to God, the cherisher and sustainer of the worlds. *Alhamdu lilaahi rabbilalameen.*

Made in the USA
Lexington, KY
23 April 2018